CRE▲TIVE
HOMEOWNER®

BIG BOOK OF
SMALL HOME PLANS
2ND EDITION

COPYRIGHT © 2021, 2022

CRE/\TIVE
H O M E O W N E R®

Book content provided by Design America, Inc., St. Louis, MO.

Current Printing (last digit)
10 9 8 7 6 5 4 3 2

Printed in China

Big Book of Small Home Plans, 2nd Edition
ISBN-13: 978-1-58011-869-9

Library of Congress Control Number: 2021931901

CREATIVE HOMEOWNER®
www.creativehomeowner.com

Creative Homeowner®, www.creativehomeowner.com, is an imprint of New Design
Originals Corporation and distributed exclusively in North America by Fox Chapel
Publishing Company, Inc., 800-457-9112, 903 Square Street, Mount Joy, PA 17552,
and in the United Kingdom by Grantham Book Services, Trent Road, Grantham,
Lincolnshire, NG31 7XQ.

The homes on the cover are: Top, Plan #F07-032D-0730 on page 27; Bottom, left to
right: Plan #F07-032D-0872 on page 68; Plan #F07-011D-0612 on page 261;
Plan #F07-011D-0676 on page 37. Unless noted, all images copyrighted by the
designer/architect.

Page 3, Top to bottom: Plan #F07-080D-0004 on page 22; Plan #F07-032D-0358 on
page 51; Plan #F07-111D-0032, on page 13; Plan #F07-101D-0155 on page 11;
Plan #F07-084D-0052 on page 44; Plan #F07-071D-0013 on page 33.

CONTENTS

What's The Right Plan For You?	4
10 Steps To Building Your Dream Home	5-6
Small Homes Introduction	7
Small Home Plans	8-51
Dream Big, While Living Small	52-59
Small Home Plans	60-132
Design America 3D: See Your Home On Your Lot Before It's Built	133-147
Small Home Plans	148-151
No Excuses...It's Time To Get Organized	152-155
Bathroom Storage Solved	156
Banish Kitchen Clutter Forever	157
20 Kitchen Organizing Tips	158
Pantry Organization 101	159
Small Home Plans	160-181
What Home Buyers Want: Wide Open Spaces	182-186
Making Your Tiny Kitchen Feel Spacious	187-189
Small Home Plans	190-233
Economize Your Home And Save More Money By Building Green	234-236
The Big Advantages Of Living In A Small Home	237
Saving Money For Your Home And Life	238
Tips For Saving Money	239
Small Home Plans	240-275
Home Plans Index	276-279
Why Buy Stock Plans?	280-281
How Can I Find Out If I Can Afford To Build A Home?	282
What Kind Of Plan Package Do I Need?	283
Our Plan Packages Include...	284
Do You Want To Make Changes To Your Plan?	285
Helpful Building Aids	286
Before You Order	287
Home Plan Order Form	288

what's the right
PLAN for you?

Choosing a house design is exciting, but can be a difficult task. Many factors play a role in what home plan is best for you and your family. To help you get started, we have pinpointed some of the major factors to consider when searching for your dream home. Take the time to evaluate your family's needs and you will have an easier time sorting through all of the house designs offered in this book.

BUDGET is the first thing to consider. Many items take part in the budget, from ordering the blueprints to the last doorknob purchased. When you find the perfect house plan, visit houseplansandmore.com and get a cost-to-build estimate to ensure that the finished home will be within your cost range. A cost-to-build report is a detailed summary that gives you the total cost to build a specific home in the zip code where you're wanting to build. It is interactive allowing you to adjust labor and material costs, and it's created on demand when ordered so all pricing is up-to-date. This valuable tool will help you know how much your dream home will cost before you buy plans (see page 282 for more information).

Make a list!
Experts in the field suggest listing everything you like or dislike about your current home to begin your home plan search.

FAMILY LIFESTYLE After your budget is deciphered, you need to assess you and your family's lifestyle needs. Think about the stage of life you are in now, and what stages you will be going through in the future. Ask yourself questions to figure out how much room you need now and if you will need room for expansion. Are you married? Do you have children? How many children do you plan on having? Are you an empty-nester? How long do you plan to live in this home?

Incorporate into your planning any frequent guests you may have, including elderly parents, grandchildren or adult children who may live with you.

Does your family entertain a lot? If so, think about the rooms you will need to do so. Will you need both formal and informal spaces? Do you need a gourmet kitchen? Do you need a game room and/or a wet bar?

FLOOR PLAN LAYOUTS When looking through these home plans, imagine yourself walking through the house. Consider the flow from the entry to the living, sleeping and gathering areas. Does the layout ensure privacy for the master bedroom? Does the garage enter near the kitchen for easy unloading? Does the placement of the windows provide enough privacy from any neighboring properties? Do you plan on using furniture you already have? Will this furniture fit in the appropriate rooms? When you find a plan you want to purchase, be sure to picture yourself actually living in it.

EXTERIOR SPACES With many different home styles throughout ranging from Traditional to Contemporary, flip through these pages and find which style appeals to you the most and think about the neighborhood in which you plan to build. Also, think about how the house will fit on your site. Picture the landscaping you want to add to the lot. Using your imagination is key when choosing a home plan.

Choosing a house design can be an intimidating experience. Asking yourself these questions before you get started on the search will help you through the process. With our large selection of sizes and styles, we are certain you will find your dream home in this book.

10 steps to BUILDING your dream home

1 talk to a lender

If you plan to obtain a loan in order to build your new home, then it's best to find out first how much you can get approved for before selecting a home design. Knowing the financial information before you start looking for land, or a home, will keep you from selecting something out of your budget and turning a great experience into a major disappointment. Financing the home you plan to build is somewhat different than financing the purchase of an existing house. You're going to need thousands of dollars for land, labor, and materials. Chances are, you're going to have to borrow most of it. Therefore, you will probably need to obtain a construction loan. This is a short-term loan to pay for building your house. When the house is completed, the loan is paid off in full, usually out of the proceeds from your long-term mortgage loan.

2 determine needs

Selecting the right home plan for your needs and lifestyle requires a lot of thought. Your new home is an investment, so you should consider not only your current needs, but also your future requirements. Versatility and the potential for converting certain areas to other uses could be an important factor later on. So, a home office may seem unnecessary now, but in years to come, the idea may seem ideal. Home plans that include flex spaces, or bonus rooms can really adapt to your needs in the future.

3 choose a home site

The site for your new home will have a definite impact on the design you select. It's a good idea to select a home that will complement your site. This will save you time and money when building. Or, you can then modify a design to specifically accommodate your site. However, it will most likely make your home construction more costly than selecting a home plan suited for your lot right from the start. For example, if your land slopes, a walk-out basement works perfectly. If it's wooded, or has a lake in the back, an atrium ranch home is a perfect style to take advantage of surrounding backyard views.

SOME IMPORTANT CRITERIA TO CONSIDER WHEN SELECTING A SITE:

- Improvements will have to be made including utilities, walks and driveways
- Convenience of the lot to work, school, shops, etc.
- Zoning requirements and property tax amounts
- Soil conditions at your future site
- Make sure the person or firm that sells you the land owns it free and clear

4 select a home design

We've chosen the "best of the best" small home plans from our website, houseplansandmore.com to be featured in this book. With over 18,000 home plans from the best architects and designers across the country in our collection, this book includes a variety of architectural styles all 1,200 square feet and under that will suit the needs and tastes of a broad spectrum of today's homeowners.

5 get the cost to build

If you feel you have found "the" home, then before taking the step of purchasing house plans, order an estimated cost-to-build report for the exact zip code where you plan to build. Requesting this custom cost report created specifically for you will help educate you on all costs associated with building your new home. Simply order this report and gain knowledge of the material and labor cost associated with the home you love. Not only does the report allow you to choose the quality of the materials, you can also select options in every aspect of the project from lot condition to contractor fees. This report will allow you to successfully manage your construction budget in all areas, clearly see where the majority of the costs lie, and save you money from start to finish.

A COST-TO-BUILD REPORT WILL HELP YOU DETERMINE THE OVERALL COST OF YOUR NEW HOME INCLUDING THESE 5 MAJOR EXPENSE CATEGORIES:

- Land
- Foundation
- Materials
- General Contractor's fee - Some rules-of-thumb that you may find useful are: (a) the total labor cost will generally run a little higher than your total material cost, but it's not unusual for a builder or general contractor to charge 15-20% of the combined cost for managing the overall project.
- Site improvements - Don't forget to add in the cost of your site improvements such as utilities, driveway pavement, sidewalks, landscaping, etc.

6 hire a contractor

If you're inexperienced in construction, you'll probably want to hire a general contractor to manage the project. If you do not know a reputable general contractor, begin your search by contacting your local Home Builders Association to get references. Many states require building contractors to be licensed. If this is the case in your state, its licensing board is another referral source. Finding a reputable, quality-minded contractor is a key factor in ensuring that your new home is well constructed and is finished on time and within budget. It can be a smart decision to discuss the plan you like with your builder prior to ordering plans. They can guide you into choosing the right type of plan package option especially if you intend on doing some customizing to the design.

7 customizing

Sometimes your general contractor may want to be the one who makes the modifications you want to the home you've selected. But, sometimes they

want to receive the plans ready to build. That is why we offer home plan modification services. Please see page 285 for specific information on the customizing process and how to get a free quote on the changes you want to make to a home before you buy the plans.

8 order plans

If you've found the home and are ready to order blueprints, we recommend ordering the PDF file format, which offers the most flexibility. A PDF file format will be emailed to you when you order, and it includes a copyright release from the designer, meaning you have the legal right to make changes to the plan if necessary, as well as print out as many copies of the plan as you need for building the home one-time. You will be happy

to have your blueprints saved electronically so they can easily be shared with your contractor, subcontractors, lender and local building officials. We do, however, offer several different types of plan packages depending on your needs, so please refer to page 283 for all plan package options available and choose the best one for your particular situation.

Another helpful component in the building process that is available for many of the house plans in this book is a material list. A material list includes not only a detailed list of materials, but it also indicates where various cuts of lumber and other building components are to be used. This will save your general contractor significant time and money since they won't have to create this list before building begins. If a material list is available for a home, it is indicated on the index on pages 276-279 in this book.

9 order materials

You can order materials yourself, or have your contractor do it. Nevertheless, in order to thoroughly enjoy your new home you will want to personally select many of the materials that go into its construction. Today, home improvement stores offer a wide variety of quality building products. Only you can decide what specific types of windows, cabinets, bath fixtures, etc. will make your new home yours. Spend time early on in the construction process looking at the endless materials and products available.

10 move in

With careful planning and organization, your new home will be built on schedule and ready for your move-in date. Be sure to have all of your important documents in place for the closing of your new home and then you'll be ready to move in and start living your dream.

Browse the pages of the Big Book of Small Home Plans and discover over 360 best-selling small home designs all 1,200 square feet and under in a variety of today's most popular styles. From Craftsman and Country, to Contemporary and Traditional, there is a small home design here for everyone with all of the amenities and features homeowners are looking for in a new home today. Start your search right now for the perfect small home!

Top, left: Plan #F07-032D-0358 on page 51; top, right: Plan #F07-084D-0052 on page 44;
Bottom, left: Plan #F07-071D-0013 on page 33; bottom, right: Plan #F07-111D-0033, on page 15.

Plan #F07-011D-0313

Dimensions:	24' W x 44' D
Heated Sq. Ft.:	782
Bedrooms: 2	**Bathrooms:** 1
Exterior Walls:	2" x 6"

Foundation: Crawl space or slab standard; basement available for an additional fee

See index for more information

© Copyright by designer/architect

Features

- Live life like a fairytale in this European inspired quaint cottage
- With attention to detail at every turn, cottage life is definitely not primitive in this luxurious cottage that boasts an amenity-packed kitchen with nearby walk-in closet that doubles as a pantry
- The vaulted living area has a cozy corner fireplace
- The vaulted master suite has a corner built-in for interest and plenty of windows for added sunlight
- Bedroom 2 is also vaulted and features built-in and ample closetspace

Images provided by designer/architect

Plan #F07-011D-0431

Dimensions:	17'6" W x 23' D
Heated Sq. Ft.:	300
Bedrooms: 1	**Bathrooms: 1**
Exterior Walls:	2" x 6"
Foundation:	Slab

See index for more information

Features

- Imagine how thrilled your guests will be when they discover you have this adorable cottage ready for their visit
- The covered porch leads into the vaulted guest room with a cozy corner fireplace
- The full bath includes a walk-in oversized shower for extra ease
- There is also a galley-style kitchen that includes a small stove, a microwave oven, and a sink
- Near the front entry is a large walk-in closet, perfect for storage
- This cottage would also make the perfect private in-law quarters

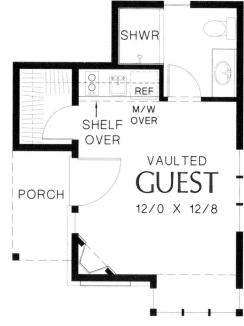

Plan #F07-101D-0155

Dimensions:	34' W x 28' D
Heated Sq. Ft.:	952
Bedrooms: 1	Bathrooms: 1
Exterior Walls:	2" x 6"
Foundation:	Slab

See index for more information

Features

- Whether lakeside or near the shore, cabin living will not disappoint thanks to the open sun-filled floor plan with a fireplace in the living room
- Retreat outdoors onto a pleasing open deck off the kitchen for mealtimes, or to enjoy some quiet time before you get the day started
- A cozy bedroom provides a restful spot for a good night's sleep, and it's handy to a centered bathroom
- If you need to do a load of laundry, then the closet for a stackable washer and dryer is not hard to reach right near the bathroom door
- A quiet office is tucked away from the main gathering spaces for privacy

OFFICE
9-6x8-0

BEDROOM
13-7x9-11

COV'D DECK

DINING
14-6x7-6

LIVING
14-6x13-11

DECK

© Copyright by designer/architect

Images provided by designer/architect

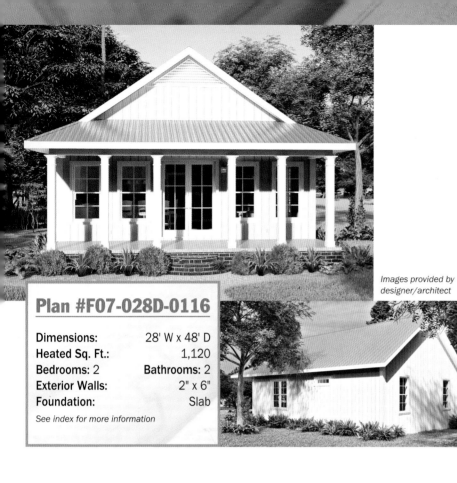

Images provided by designer/architect

Plan #F07-028D-0116

Dimensions:	28' W x 48' D
Heated Sq. Ft.:	1,120
Bedrooms: 2	Bathrooms: 2
Exterior Walls:	2" x 6"
Foundation:	Slab

See index for more information

BEDROOM 1 11-8 x 12-0

BEDROOM 2 11-8 x 12-0

BATH 1 **HALL** **BATH 2**

LAUNDRY 11-8 x 6-8

GREAT ROOM/ DINING AREA 16-4 x 22-0

STOVE WITH VENT HOOD COMBO ABOVE

KITCHEN 11-8 X 15-6

© Copyright by designer/architect

8 FT. DEEP PORCH

Plan #F07-163D-0004

Images provided by designer/architect

Dimensions:	40' W x 22' D
Heated Sq. Ft.:	681
Bedrooms: 2	Bathrooms: 2
Exterior Walls:	2" x 6"
Foundation: Crawl space or slab, please specify when ordering	

See index for more information

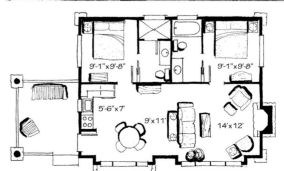

9'-1"x9'-8"

9'-1"x9'-8"

5'-6"x7'

9'x11'

14'x12'

© Copyright by designer/architect

Images provided by designer/architect

© Copyright by designer/architect

Plan #F07-032D-0905

Dimensions:	40' W x 30' D
Heated Sq. Ft.:	1,146
Bedrooms: 2	Bathrooms: 1
Exterior Walls:	2" x 6"

Foundation: Basement standard; crawl space, floating slab or monolithic slab available for an additional fee

See index for more information

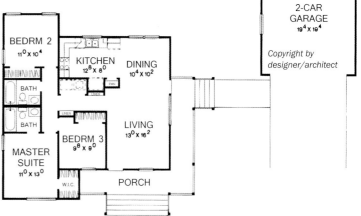

Images provided by designer/architect

Plan #F07-111D-0032

Dimensions:	40' W x 37'6" D
Heated Sq. Ft.:	1,094
Bedrooms: 3	Bathrooms: 2

Foundation: Slab standard; crawl space or basement available for an additional fee

See index for more information

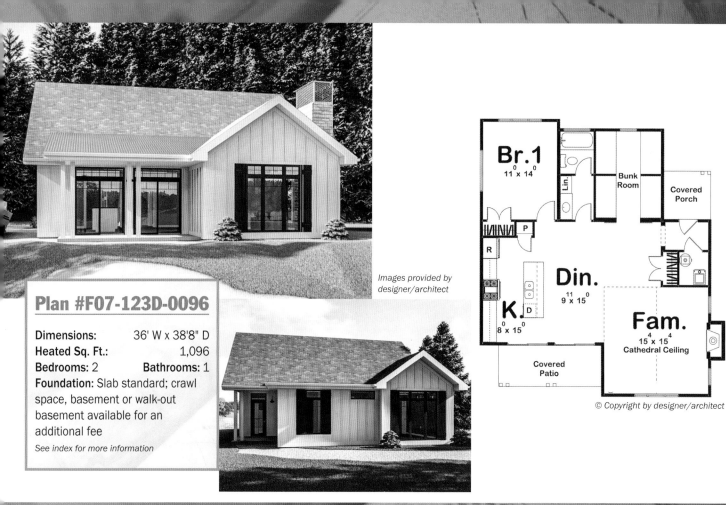

Images provided by designer/architect

© Copyright by designer/architect

Plan #F07-123D-0096

Dimensions: 36' W x 38'8" D
Heated Sq. Ft.: 1,096
Bedrooms: 2   **Bathrooms:** 1
Foundation: Slab standard; crawl space, basement or walk-out basement available for an additional fee

See index for more information

Images provided by designer/architect

Plan #F07-172D-0002

Dimensions: 56' W x 28' D
Heated Sq. Ft.: 1,190
Bedrooms: 2   **Bathrooms:** 1
Exterior Walls: 2" x 6"
Foundation: Crawl space standard; monolithic slab, stem wall slab, basement, daylight basement or walk-out basement available for an additional fee

See index for more information

Second Floor
338 sq. ft.

BDRM 3
8⁸ X 10⁰

BA 2

BDRM 2
9¹⁰ X 10⁰

HALL

SHELF

SHELF

SHELF

COVERED PATIO

© Copyright by designer/architect

WIC

BA 1

DINING
8² X 9⁴

KITCHEN
9⁰ X 9⁴

MASTER BEDROOM
11⁰ X 12⁸

LIVING
17⁶ X 13⁸

WIC

First Floor
819 sq. ft.

COVERED PORCH

Plan #F07-111D-0033

Images provided by designer/architect

Dimensions:	36' W x 38' D
Heated Sq. Ft.:	1,157
Bedrooms: 3	Bathrooms: 2

Foundation: Slab standard; basement or crawl space available for an additional fee

See index for more information

© Copyright by designer/architect

12'-0" X 10'-4"

10'-4" X 10'-0"

16'-4" X 11'-8"

Optional Lower Level
1,024 sq. ft.

16'-0" X 8'-0"

9'-2" X 11'-6"

15'-8" X 11'-8"

9'-2" X 11'-6"

16'-8" X 11'-0"

12'-0" X 11'-0"

9'-0" X 4'-0"

First Floor
1,024 sq. ft.

Plan #F07-032D-0965

Images provided by designer/architect

Dimensions:	36' W x 32' D
Heated Sq. Ft.:	1,024
Bonus Sq. Ft.:	1,024
Bedrooms: 3	Bathrooms: 1
Exterior Walls:	2" x 6"

Foundation: Basement standard; crawl space, floating slab or monolithic slab available for an additional fee

See index for more information

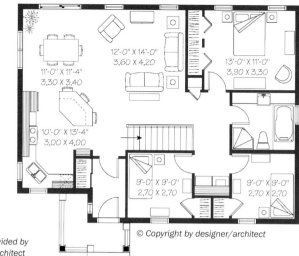

Images provided by designer/architect

Plan #F07-032D-0732

Dimensions:	40' W x 30' D
Heated Sq. Ft.:	1,160
Bedrooms: 3	Bathrooms: 1
Exterior Walls:	2" x 6"

Foundation: Basement standard; crawl space, floating slab or monolithic slab available for an additional fee

See index for more information

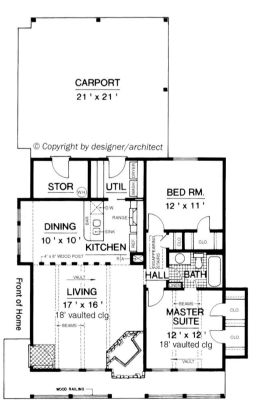

Images provided by designer/architect

Plan #F07-020D-0056

Dimensions:	37'6" W x 57' D
Heated Sq. Ft.:	963
Bedrooms: 2	Bathrooms: 1

Foundation: Slab standard; crawl space available for an additional fee

See index for more information

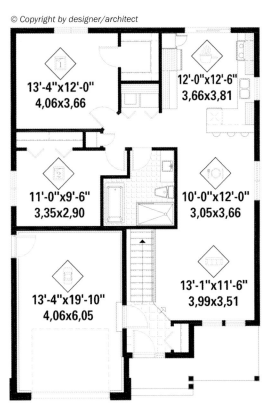

© Copyright by designer/architect

13'-4"x12'-0"
4,06x3,66

12'-0"x12'-6"
3,66x3,81

11'-0"x9'-6"
3,35x2,90

10'-0"x12'-0"
3,05x3,66

13'-4"x19'-10"
4,06x6,05

13'-1"x11'-6"
3,99x3,51

Plan #F07-126D-1354

Images provided by designer/architect

Dimensions:	32'5" W x 46'5" D
Heated Sq. Ft.:	1,051
Bedrooms: 2	Bathrooms: 1
Exterior Walls:	2" x 6"
Foundation:	Basement

See index for more information

DN.

ATTIC

LOFT
13 x 12

Second Floor
148 sq. ft.

VAULTED CLG.
@ PORCH
BELOW

© Copyright by designer/architect

CLO.
4 x 3

BEDROOM
10 x 10

LAUNDRY

BATH
5 x 10

HALL

KITCHEN
8 x 15

UP

LIVING AREA
16 x 11

PAN.

"VAULTED"
PORCH
21 x 5

First Floor
592 sq. ft.

Images provided by designer/architect

Plan #F07-087D-1682

Dimensions:	25' W x 32' D
Heated Sq. Ft.:	740
Bedrooms: 1	Bathrooms: 1
Foundation:	Slab

See index for more information

Plan #F07-020D-0394

Dimensions:	36' W x 44' D
Heated Sq. Ft.:	902
Bedrooms: 1	**Bathrooms:** 1½
Exterior Walls:	2" x 6"

Foundation: Crawl space standard; slab available for an additional fee

See index for more information

Images provided by designer/architect

Features

- Unbelievable charm and style combine to create this one-of-a-kind small home filled with luxury
- A deep covered front porch and rear wrap-around covered porch add a tremendous amount of outdoor living space, perfect when entertaining
- The kitchen/dining area has an open feel to the nearby living area
- The kitchen includes a handy island with snack bar seating
- The utility room is conveniently located near the kitchen
- The master bedroom is to the right upon entering the home and features its own private bath and walk-in closet

© Copyright by designer/architect

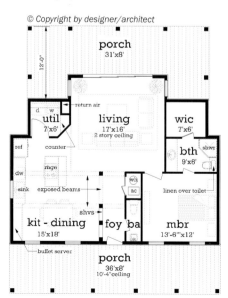

Plan #F07-028D-0115

Dimensions:	44' W x 36'6" D
Heated Sq. Ft.:	1,035
Bedrooms: 3	Bathrooms: 2
Exterior Walls:	2" x 6"
Foundation:	Slab

See index for more information

Features

- This terrific cottage is everything today's homeowner is looking for with its modern farmhouse style and compact, yet open split bedroom floor plan

- Enter the great room from the covered front porch and discover a living space that blends seamlessly with the kitchen/dining area

- The master bedroom has a walk-in closet and a private bath with a double-bowl vanity, and an oversized walk-in shower

- The two secondary bedrooms share the full bath between them

- Near the laundry room is access to the rear covered porch with plenty of space for outdoor living and entertaining

© Copyright by designer/architect

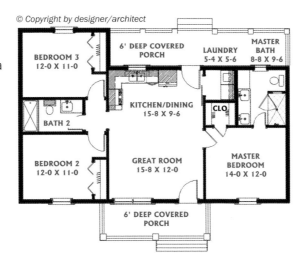

Images provided by designer/architect

9'-0" x 10'-4"
2,70 x 3,10

12'-4" x 10'-0"
3,70 x 3,00

11'-0" x 12'-8"
3,30 x 3,80

12'-4" x 14'-0"
3,70 x 4,20

10'-0" x 8'-8"
3'00 x 2,60

Images provided by designer/architect

© Copyright by designer/architect

Plan #F07-032D-0904

Dimensions: 37' W x 28' D
Heated Sq. Ft.: 975
Bedrooms: 2   **Bathrooms:** 1
Exterior Walls: 2" x 6"
Foundation: Basement standard; crawl space, floating slab or monolithic slab available for an additional fee

See index for more information

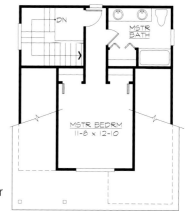

MSTR BATH

MSTR BEDRM
11-8 x 12-10

Second Floor
350 sq. ft.

© Copyright by designer/architect

Images provided by designer/architect

Plan #F07-071D-0014

Dimensions: 24' W x 30' D
Heated Sq. Ft.: 1,000
Bedrooms: 2   **Bathrooms:** 2
Exterior Walls: 2" x 6"
Foundation: Crawl space

See index for more information

BA 2

BEDRM 2
8-10 x 9-4

LIVING
13-8 x 15-2

KITCHEN
7-6 x 9-4

COV'D PORCH

DINING
9-4 x 9-4

First Floor
650 sq. ft.

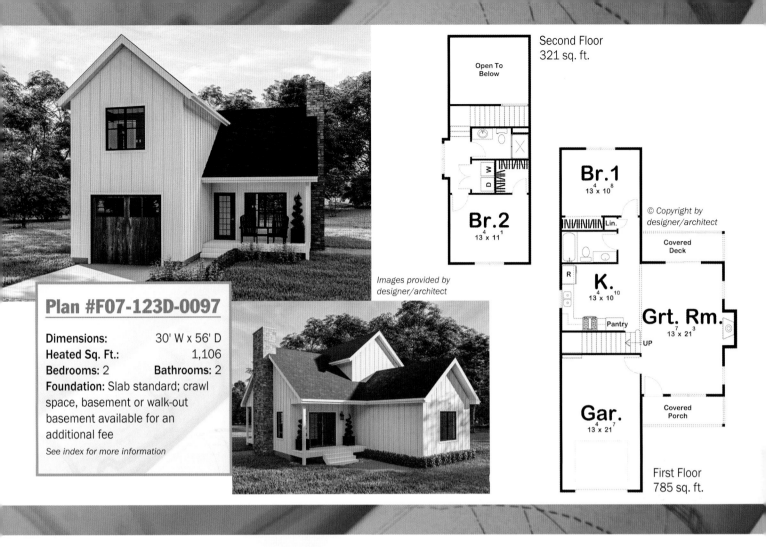

Second Floor
321 sq. ft.

Open To
Below

Br.2
13 x 11

Images provided by
designer/architect

Br.1
13 x 10⁸

Lin.

K.
13 x 10¹⁰

Pantry

Gar.
13 x 21⁷

© Copyright by
designer/architect

Covered
Deck

Grt. Rm.
13⁷ x 21³

UP

Covered
Porch

First Floor
785 sq. ft.

Plan #F07-123D-0097

Dimensions: 30' W x 56' D
Heated Sq. Ft.:   1,106
Bedrooms: 2   Bathrooms: 2
Foundation: Slab standard; crawl space, basement or walk-out basement available for an additional fee

See index for more information

Images provided by
designer/architect

© Copyright by
designer/architect

8'-8" X 10'-4"
2,60 X 3,10

11'-4" X 10'-0"
3,40 X 3,00

10'-0" X 10'-0"
3,00 X 3,00

9'-4" X 9'-0"
2,80 X 2,70

12'-4" X 16'-4"
3,70 X 4,90

Plan #F07-032D-0903

Dimensions: 34' W x 28' D
Heated Sq. Ft.:   880
Bedrooms: 2   Bathrooms: 1
Exterior Walls: 2" x 6"
Foundation: Basement standard; crawl space, floating slab or monolithic slab available for an additional fee

See index for more information

Images provided by designer/architect

Plan #F07-080D-0004

Dimensions:	36' W x 42'6" D
Heated Sq. Ft.:	1,154
Bedrooms: 2	**Bathrooms:** 2
Exterior Walls:	2" x 6"
Foundation:	Crawl space

See index for more information

Features

- The multi-purpose vaulted living/dining area is up to the challenges of evolving cottage activities

- Designed for relaxed living, this home enjoys access front and back onto the large deck

- A wrap-around window seat in the living/dining area is a cozy place to curl up with a book, or add a table for built-in dining space

- The second floor studio would make a perfect artist's retreat, a home office, or private escape ideal for taking in views on the balcony

© Copyright by designer/architect

First Floor
672 sq. ft.

Second Floor
482 sq. ft.

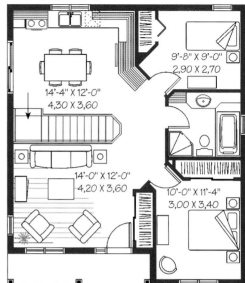

© Copyright by designer/architect

9'-8" X 9'-0"
2,90 X 2,70

14'-4" 12'-0"
4,30 X 3,60

14'-0" X 12'-0"
4,20 X 3,60

10'-0" X 11'-4"
3,00 X 3,40

Images provided by designer/architect

Plan #F07-032D-0902

Dimensions: 28' W x 32' D
Heated Sq. Ft.: 835
Bedrooms: 2   **Bathrooms:** 1
Exterior Walls: 2" x 6"
Foundation: Basement standard; crawl space, floating slab or monolithic slab available for an additional fee

See index for more information

9'-8" X 13'-2"
2,90 X 3,95

11'-2" X 13'-4"
3,35 X 4,00

11'-2" X 13'-2"
3,35 X 3,95

12'-10" X 17'-0"
3,85 X 5,10

10'-0" X 11'-2"
3,00 X 3,35

© Copyright by designer/architect

Images provided by designer/architect

Plan #F07-032D-0656

Dimensions: 36' W x 40' D
Heated Sq. Ft.: 1,184
Bedrooms: 2   **Bathrooms:** 1
Exterior Walls: 2" x 6"
Foundation: Basement standard; crawl space, floating slab or monolithic slab available for an additional fee

See index for more information

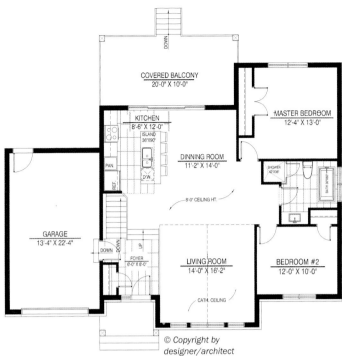

© Copyright by designer/architect

Images provided by designer/architect

Plan #F07-148D-0405

Dimensions:	50' W x 38' D
Heated Sq. Ft.:	1,168
Bedrooms: 2	Bathrooms: 1
Exterior Walls:	2" x 6"
Foundation:	Basement

See index for more information

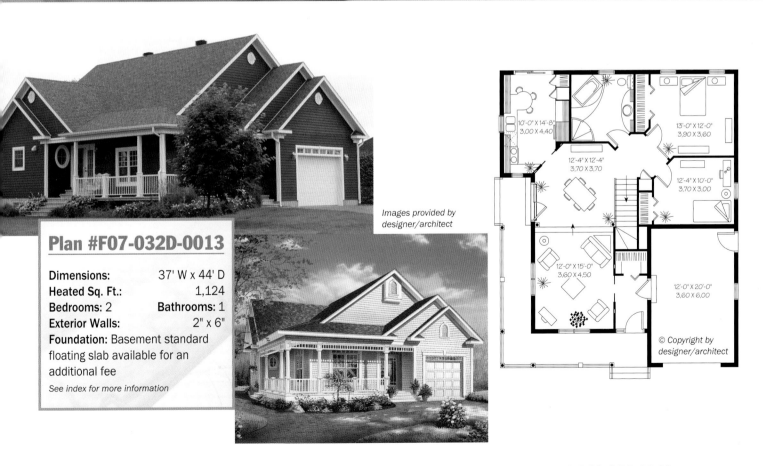

Images provided by designer/architect

© Copyright by designer/architect

Plan #F07-032D-0013

Dimensions:	37' W x 44' D
Heated Sq. Ft.:	1,124
Bedrooms: 2	Bathrooms: 1

Exterior Walls: 2" x 6"

Foundation: Basement standard floating slab available for an additional fee

See index for more information

18'-0" X 12'-0"
5,40 X 3,60

10'-4" X 9'-6"
3,10 X 2,85

13'-0" X 15'-0"
3,90 X 4,50

13'-0" X 11'-0"
3,90 X 3,30

Images provided by
designer/architect

Plan #F07-032D-0116

Dimensions: 30' W x 35' D
Heated Sq. Ft.: 946
Bedrooms: 2   **Bathrooms:** 1
Exterior Walls: 2" x 6"
Foundation: Basement standard;
crawl space, floating slab or
monolithic slab available for an
additional fee

See index for more information

BEDROOM 2
13'-4"X13'-2"

VAULTED
CEILING

VAULTED
CEILING

DRAWER CAB.

DRAWER CAB.

BEDROOM 1
11'-8"X15'-4"

BATH
9'-0"X
7'-0"

PORCH
12'-0"X8'-0"

STACKED
W/D

HVAC   WH

STOR.

DEN / KIT
13'-4"X
10'-8"

VAULTED
CEILING

REF.

RG

Images provided by
designer/architect

ENTRY PORCH
14'-0"X8'-0"

Plan #F07-155D-0220

Dimensions: 26' W x 44' D
Heated Sq. Ft.: 696
Bedrooms: 2   **Bathrooms:** 1
Foundation: Crawl space or slab,
please specify when ordering

See index for more information

Plan #F07-026D-1833

Dimensions:	40' W x 48'8" D
Heated Sq. Ft.:	1,195
Bedrooms: 3	**Bathrooms:** 2

Foundation: Basement standard; crawl space, slab or walk-out basement available for an additional fee

See index for more information

Images provided by designer/architect

Plan #F07-032D-0730

Dimensions:	30' W x 36' D
Heated Sq. Ft.:	1,017
Bedrooms: 2	**Bathrooms:** 1
Exterior Walls:	2" x 6"

Foundation: Basement standard; crawl space, floating slab or monolithic slab available for an additional fee

See index for more information

Images provided by designer/architect

Plan #F07-137D-0271

Dimensions:	41' W x 40' D
Heated Sq. Ft.:	1,094
Bedrooms: 3	Bathrooms: 2
Foundation:	Slab

See index for more information

Images provided by designer/architect

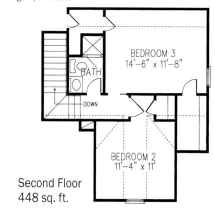

BEDROOM 3
14'-6" x 11'-8"

BATH

DOWN

BEDROOM 2
11'-4" x 11'

Second Floor
448 sq. ft.

Features

- This rustic beauty provides plenty of space in a small amount of square footage

- Step into the living/dining space and notice the large amount of windows on one wall adding a tremendous amount of sunlight

- A small, yet efficient kitchen offers all of the essentials for cooking daily meals

- One bedroom is found on the first floor near a full bath, and two other bedrooms and a full bath reside on the second floor for extra privacy

- Two additional spaces for storage make this small home easy to downsize

- 2-car front entry garage

STORAGE
8' x 6'

LINEN

BATH

STORAGE
13'-8" x 9'

BEDROOM 1
11'-8" x 11'-4"

HVAC

UP

LIVING ROOM
15'-4" x 12'-2"

2 – CAR GARAGE
19'-4" x 22'-4"

STORAGE

PORCH

DINING

KITCHEN
8' x 8'

© Copyright by designer/architect

First Floor
646 sq. ft.

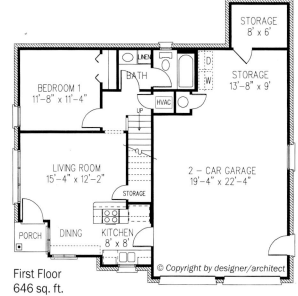

houseplansandmore.com

Plan #F07-028D-0109

Dimensions:	33' W x 40' D
Heated Sq. Ft.:	890
Bedrooms: 2	Bathrooms: 1
Exterior Walls:	2" x 6"

Foundation: Crawl space or slab, please specify when ordering

See index for more information

Images provided by designer/architect

Features

- A perfect smaller dwelling for a vacation home, retirement home or a starter home
- The great room has a fireplace flanked by cabinets
- The laundry room is close to the kitchen and rear entry for convenience
- There's plenty of storage throughout, starting in the kitchen
- Two 8' deep covered porches provide a tremendous amount of extra living space, perfect for entertaining

© Copyright by designer/architect

PORCH
8'-0" DEEP

LAUNDRY
7-3 X 6-6

BEDROOM 2
14-0 X 10-0

BATH
7-0 X 10-0

KITCHEN
12-0 X 11-6

BEDROOM 1
13-0 X 10-0

GREAT ROOM
20-0 X 14-0

PORCH
8'-0" DEEP

© Copyright by designer/architect

Images provided by designer/architect

Plan #F07-032D-0928

Dimensions: 44' W x 36'4" D
Heated Sq. Ft.: 1,028
Bedrooms: 2   **Bathrooms:** 1
Exterior Walls: 2" x 6"
Foundation: Basement standard; crawl space, monolithic slab or floating slab available for an additional fee

See index for more information

Mbr.
11⁸ x 11⁰

Grt.
Rm.
11⁸ x 15⁹

K.
11 x 12

Cathedral Ceiling

R

Covered
Porch

© Copyright by designer/architect

Images provided by designer/architect

Plan #F07-123D-0068

Dimensions: 32' W x 32' D
Heated Sq. Ft.: 576
Bedrooms: 1   **Bathrooms:** 1
Foundation: Crawl space

See index for more information

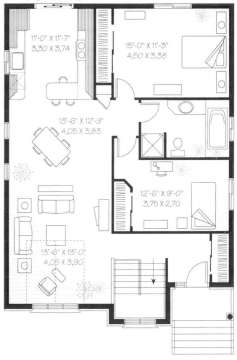

11'-0" X 11'-7"
3,30 X 3,74

15'-0" X 11'-3"
4,50 X 3,38

13'-6" X 12'-9"
4,05 X 3,83

12'-6" X 9'-0"
3,75 X 2,70

13'-6" X 13'-0"
4,05 X 3,90

Images provided by designer/architect

Plan #F07-032D-0414

Dimensions:	30' W x 41' D
Heated Sq. Ft.:	1,163
Bedrooms: 2	**Bathrooms:** 1
Exterior Walls:	2" x 6"

Foundation: Basement standard; crawl space, floating slab or monolithic slab available for an additional fee

See index for more information

LAUNDRY
12' X 6'

BEDROOM 2
13' X 10'

KITCHEN
12' X 10'

BEDROOM 1
13' X 10'

GREAT ROOM
20' X 14'

Images provided by designer/architect

PORCH - 6' DEEP

Plan #F07-028D-0001

Dimensions:	33' W x 36' D
Heated Sq. Ft.:	864
Bedrooms: 2	**Bathrooms:** 1

Foundation: Crawl space or slab, please specify when ordering

See index for more information

Plan #F07-032D-0709

Dimensions:	24' W x 20' D
Heated Sq. Ft.:	480
Bedrooms: 2	Bathrooms: 1
Exterior Walls:	2" x 6"

Foundation: Screw pile standard; crawl space, monolithic slab or floating slab available for an additional fee

See index for more information

Images provided by designer/architect

Features

- This terrific cottage features plenty of windows and a covered front porch adding great curb appeal
- One main room combines the living and dining area together with the kitchen nearby
- The bedroom is large enough for several beds making it ideal for a vacation getaway
- In order to respect the building code and also meet the multiple needs of customers, when this plan is ordered you will have two versions of the cottage design included
- The first version includes an uninsulated and unheated version for seasonal use only (3 seasons) with 2" x 4" walls, 2" x 8" floor joists and 2" x 8" rafters
- The second version is an insulated and heated version for permanent occupation (4 seasons) with 2" x 6" walls, 2" x 10" floor joists and roof trusses
- Both versions are provided on screw piles to ensure stability

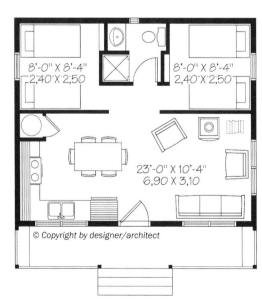

8'-0" X 8'-4"
2,40 X 2,50

8'-0" X 8'-4"
2,40 X 2,50

23'-0" X 10'-4"
6,90 X 3,10

© Copyright by designer/architect

Plan #F07-071D-0013

Dimensions:	24' W x 30' D
Heated Sq. Ft.:	1,000
Bedrooms: 2	**Bathrooms:** 2
Exterior Walls:	2" x 6"
Foundation:	Crawl space

See index for more information

Images provided by designer/architect

Features

- The lovely U-shaped kitchen is highly functional and can overlook into the living area
- The romantic master bedroom is privately located on the second floor and features a large window
- Simple, yet beautiful window accents bring interest to the exterior of this home
- An intimate dining area offers a lovely place for casual and formal meals
- Bedroom 2 and a full bath are located on the first floor

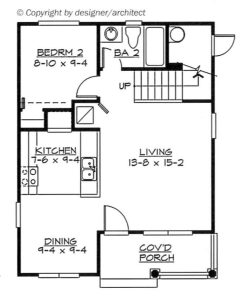

© Copyright by designer/architect

BEDRM 2
8-10 x 9-4

BA 2

UP

KITCHEN
7-6 x 9-4

LIVING
13-8 x 15-2

DINING
9-4 x 9-4

COV'D
PORCH

First Floor
650 sq. ft.

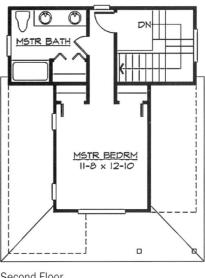

MSTR BATH

DN

MSTR BEDRM
11-8 x 12-10

Second Floor
350 sq. ft.

Plan #F07-155D-0217

Dimensions: 40' W x 47' D
Heated Sq. Ft.: 1,025
Bedrooms: 3 **Bathrooms:** 2
Foundation: Crawl space or slab, please specify when ordering

See index for more information

Images provided by designer/architect

© Copyright by designer/architect

© Copyright by designer/architect

Images provided by designer/architect

Plan #F07-032D-0091

Dimensions: 32'8" W x 37' D
Heated Sq. Ft.: 1,102
Bedrooms: 2 **Bathrooms:** 1
Exterior Walls: 2" x 6"
Foundation: Basement standard; crawl space, monolithic slab or floating slab available for an additional fee

See index for more information

First Floor
1,192 sq. ft.

Din.
13 x 9
10'-0" Ceiling

Fam.
12 x 16
10'-0" Ceiling

Mbr.
12 x 12
10'-0" Ceiling

K.
13 x 11
10'-0" Ceiling

Pantry

Mud Room

DN

Catch-All

Br.2
13 x 10

Gar.
19 x 22

Covered Stoop

Images provided by designer/architect

Br.3
11 x 12

Wet Bar

Fam.
17 x 15

Built-In

UP

Stor.

Br.4
11 x 13

Optional Lower Level
928 sq. ft.

Plan #F07-123D-0172

Dimensions: 39' W x 48'8" D
Heated Sq. Ft.: 1,192
Bonus Sq. Ft.: 928
Bedrooms: 2   Bathrooms: 2
Foundation: Basement standard; slab, crawl space or walk-out basement available for an additional fee

See index for more information

Images provided by designer/architect

9'-8" X 13'-0"
2,90 X 3,90

10'-0" X 10'-0"
3,00 X 3,00

8'-4" X 11'-4"
2,50 X 3,40

12'-0" X 15'-0"
3,60 X 4,50

11'-0" X 13'-0"
3,30 X 3,90

Plan #F07-032D-0108

Dimensions: 32'8" W x 42' D
Heated Sq. Ft.: 1,094
Bedrooms: 2   Bathrooms: 1
Exterior Walls: 2" x 6"
Foundation: Basement standard; crawl space, monolithic slab or floating slab available for an additional fee

See index for more information

Images provided by designer/architect

© Copyright by designer/architect

Plan #F07-026D-0219

Dimensions: 40' W x 48'8" D
Heated Sq. Ft.: 1,195
Bedrooms: 3 **Bathrooms:** 2
Foundation: Basement standard; slab, crawl space or walk-out basement available for an additional fee

See index for more information

Images provided by designer/architect

First Floor
536 sq. ft.

© Copyright by designer/architect

Lower Level
536 sq. ft.

Front Elevation

Plan #F07-148D-0008

Dimensions: 24' W x 24' D
Heated Sq. Ft.: 1,072
Bedrooms: 3 **Bathrooms:** 1½
Exterior Walls: 2" x 6"
Foundation: Walk-out basement

See index for more information

Plan #F07-141D-0327

Dimensions: 30' W x 41' D
Heated Sq. Ft.: 1,050
Bedrooms: 2   **Bathrooms:** 2
Exterior Walls: 2" x 6"

Foundation: Crawl space or slab standard; basement or walk-out basement available for an additional fee

See index for more information

Images provided by designer/architect

© Copyright by designer/architect

Plan #F07-011D-0676

Dimensions: 40' W x 55'6" D
Heated Sq. Ft.: 1,196
Bedrooms: 3   **Bathrooms:** 2
Exterior Walls: 2" x 6"

Foundation: Crawl space or slab standard; basement available for an additional fee

See index for more information

Images provided by designer/architect

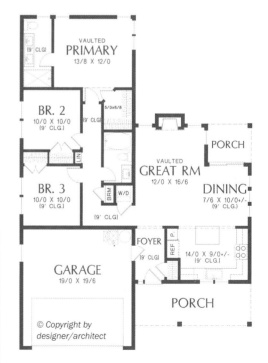

© Copyright by designer/architect

Plan #F07-101D-0161

Dimensions:	35'6" W x 45' D
Heated Sq. Ft.:	744
Bedrooms: 1	**Bathrooms:** 1
Exterior Walls:	2" x 6"
Foundation:	Crawl space

See index for more information

Images provided by designer/architect

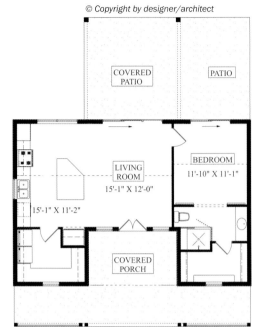

© Copyright by designer/architect

COVERED PATIO

PATIO

LIVING ROOM
15'-1" X 12'-0"

BEDROOM
11'-10" X 11'-1"

15'-1" X 11'-2"

COVERED PORCH

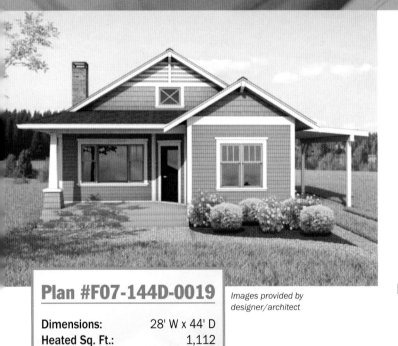

Plan #F07-144D-0019

Dimensions:	28' W x 44' D
Heated Sq. Ft.:	1,112
Bedrooms: 2	**Bathrooms:** 1
Exterior Walls:	2" x 6"
Foundation:	Crawl space

See index for more information

Images provided by designer/architect

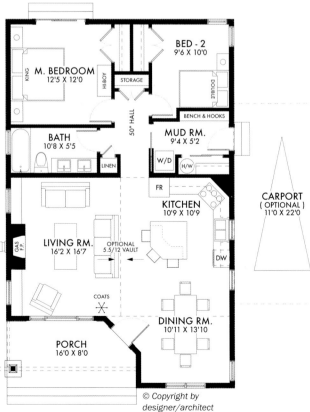

M. BEDROOM
12'5 X 12'0

BED - 2
9'6 X 10'0

STORAGE

BATH
10'8 X 5'5

LINEN

MUD RM.
9'4 X 5'2

BENCH & HOOKS

W/D   H/W

FR

KITCHEN
10'9 X 10'9

CARPORT
(OPTIONAL)
11'0 X 22'0

DW

LIVING RM.
16'2 X 16'7

OPTIONAL
5.5/12 VAULT

COATS

DINING RM.
10'11 X 13'10

PORCH
16'0 X 8'0

© Copyright by designer/architect

Plan #F07-055D-0941

Dimensions: 24' W x 39' D
Heated Sq. Ft.: 691
Bedrooms: 2   Bathrooms: 1
Foundation: Crawl space or slab, please specify when ordering

See index for more information

Images provided by designer/architect

BATH
5'-8"X
12'-0"

KIT

BEDROOM 2
9'-2" X 11'-0"

DINING
9'-0" X 8'-0"

BEDROOM 1
9'-2" X 10'-5"

LIVING
13'-8" X 12'-0"

COVERED ENTRY
PORCH
15'-0" X 8'-0"

Plan #F07-139D-0001

Dimensions: 39'7" W x 51'9" D
Heated Sq. Ft.: 1,068
Bedrooms: 2   Bathrooms: 1
Exterior Walls: 2" x 6"
Foundation: Crawl space standard; slab, basement, daylight basement or walk-out basement available for an additional fee

See index for more information

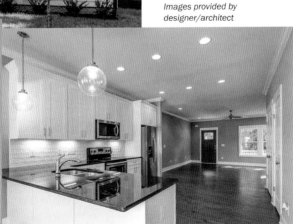

Images provided by designer/architect

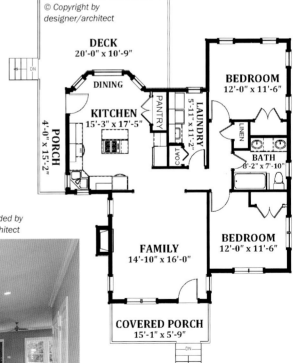

DECK
20'-0" x 10'-9"

DINING

KITCHEN
15'-3" x 17'-5"

PANTRY

LAUNDRY
5'-11" x 11'-2"

PORCH
4'-0" x 15'-2"

BEDROOM
12'-0" x 11'-6"

LINEN

BATH
8'-2" x 7'-10"

FAMILY
14'-10" x 16'-0"

BEDROOM
12'-0" x 11'-6"

COVERED PORCH
15'-1" x 5'-9"

Plan #F07-144D-0023

Dimensions:	58' W x 32' D
Heated Sq. Ft.:	928
Bedrooms: 2	Bathrooms: 2
Exterior Walls:	2" x 6"

Foundation: Slab or crawl space standard; basement, daylight basement or walk-out basement for an additional fee

See index for more information

Images provided by designer/architect

Features

- Stylish and charming, this small Craftsman Modern Farmhouse home has an inviting entry with space for outdoor relaxation

- Enter the home and discover an open living room with a kitchen behind it

- The kitchen features a large breakfast bar with space for up to four people

- To the left of the entry is an office/ guest room with direct access to a full bath and beyond into a mud room

- To the right of the entry is the master bedroom with a large bath and walk-in closet

- 2-car front entry garage

Plan #F07-126D-1076

Dimensions:	40' W x 33' D
Heated Sq. Ft.:	896
Bedrooms: 2	Bathrooms: 1
Exterior Walls:	2" x 6"
Foundation:	Basement

See index for more information

Images provided by designer/architect

10'-8"x10'-6"
3,25x3,20

11'-6"x23'-0"
3,51x7,01

11'-4"x11'-2"
3,45x3,40

12'-4"x13'-8"
3,76x4,17

12'-0"x11'-2"
3,66x3,40

Plan #F07-026D-1861

Images provided by designer/architect

Dimensions:	36' W x 48' D
Heated Sq. Ft.:	1,136
Bedrooms: 1	Bathrooms: 2

Foundation: Slab standard; basement, crawl space or walk-out basement available for an additional fee

See index for more information

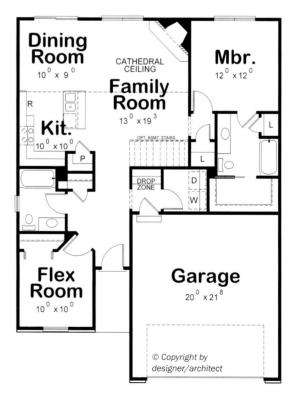

Dining Room
10^0 x 9^0

CATHEDRAL CEILING

Mbr.
12^0 x 12^0

Family Room
13^0 x 19^3

Kit.
10^0 x 10^0

OPT. BSMT STAIRS

R

P

DROP ZONE

D

W

L

L

L

Flex Room
10^0 x 10^0

Garage
20^0 x 21^8

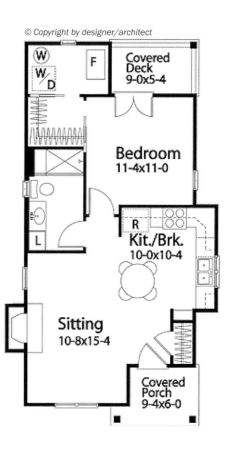

Plan #F07-058D-0213

Images provided by designer/architect

Dimensions:	22'8" W x 39'4" D
Heated Sq. Ft.:	644
Bedrooms: 1	Bathrooms: 1
Foundation:	Crawl space

See index for more information

Plan #F07-141D-0207

Images provided by designer/architect

Dimensions:	40' W x 25' D
Heated Sq. Ft.:	1,000
Bedrooms: 2	Bathrooms: 1

Foundation: Slab standard; crawl space, basement or walk-out basement available for an additional fee

See index for more information

Plan #F07-084D-0052

Images provided by designer/architect

Dimensions: 38'6" W x 48'6" D
Heated Sq. Ft.: 1,170
Bedrooms: 2 **Bathrooms:** 2
Foundation: Slab standard; crawl space or basement available for an additional fee

See index for more information

Features

- Undeniable charm in this stylish European 1-story home with tons of curb appeal
- Step inside and find a pleasing open floor plan in the living room that enjoys a 12' ceiling for added spaciousness
- Continue to the dining area that is topped with a 10' ceiling and has access to the covered porch and outdoor trellis patio
- The kitchen has an angled snack bar and ample cabinet space
- The master bedroom enjoys a large walk-in closet and a private bath, while the second bedroom is just steps from another full bath
- 1-car front entry garage

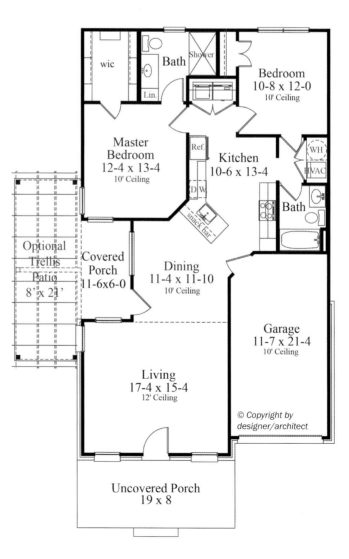

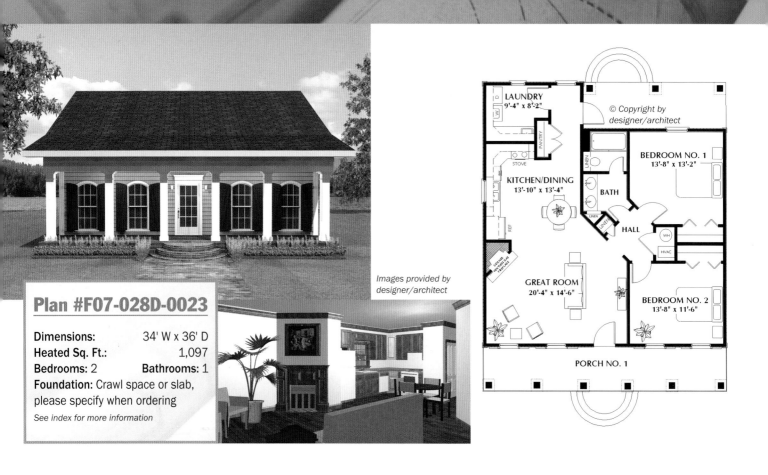

Plan #F07-028D-0023

Dimensions: 34' W x 36' D
Heated Sq. Ft.: 1,097
Bedrooms: 2 **Bathrooms:** 1
Foundation: Crawl space or slab, please specify when ordering

See index for more information

Images provided by designer/architect

© Copyright by designer/architect

LAUNDRY
9'-4" x 8'-2"

PANTRY

STOVE

KITCHEN/DINING
13'-10" x 13'-4"

REF

LINEN

BATH

LINEN

HALL

WH

HVAC

BEDROOM NO. 1
13'-8" x 13'-2"

GREAT ROOM
20'-4" x 14'-6"

BEDROOM NO. 2
13'-8" x 11'-6"

PORCH NO. 1

Plan #F07-111D-0042

Dimensions: 29' W x 30' D
Heated Sq. Ft.: 1,074
Bedrooms: 3 **Bathrooms:** 2½
Foundation: Slab standard; crawl space available for an additional fee

See index for more information

Images provided by designer/architect

MASTER BEDROOM
10⁴ x 12¹⁰

W&D

MSTR. BATH

BEDROOM 3
9⁸ x 10⁸

BEDROOM 2
10⁰ x 11⁰

BATH 2

Second Floor
605 sq. ft.

© Copyright by designer/architect

PATIO

KITCHEN
9⁰ x 10⁰

PWDR

DINING & LIVING
14⁰ x 19⁰

GARAGE
10⁰ x 19⁸

PORCH

First Floor
469 sq. ft.

Br.2
12 x 10⁰

Second Floor
508 sq. ft.

Mbr.
12 x 13¹
9'-0" Ceiling

Images provided by
designer/architect

© Copyright by
designer/architect

K.
11 x 9¹⁰

Gar.
12 x 24⁴⁰

Fam.
12 x 15¹

UP

Covered
Porch

First Floor
424 sq. ft.

Plan #F07-123D-0119

Dimensions: 29'4" W x 28'8" D
Heated Sq. Ft.:   932
Bedrooms: 2   Bathrooms: 1½
Foundation: Basement standard;
slab, crawl space or walk-out base-
ment available for an additional fee

See index for more information

8'-6"x9'-6"
2,59x2,90

10'-0"x9'-6"
3,05x2,90

10'-0"x9'-6"
3,05x2,90

9'-10"x13'-0"
3,00x3,96

13'-6" (17'-6")x20'-8"
4,12 (5,33)x6,30

12'-0"x11'-10"
3,66x3,61

11'-6"x15'-2"
3,51x4,62

© Copyright by
designer/architect

Plan #F07-126D-0545

*Images provided by
designer/architect*

Dimensions: 54' W x 26' D
Heated Sq. Ft.:   992
Bedrooms: 3   Bathrooms: 1
Exterior Walls: 2" x 6"
Foundation: Basement

See index for more information

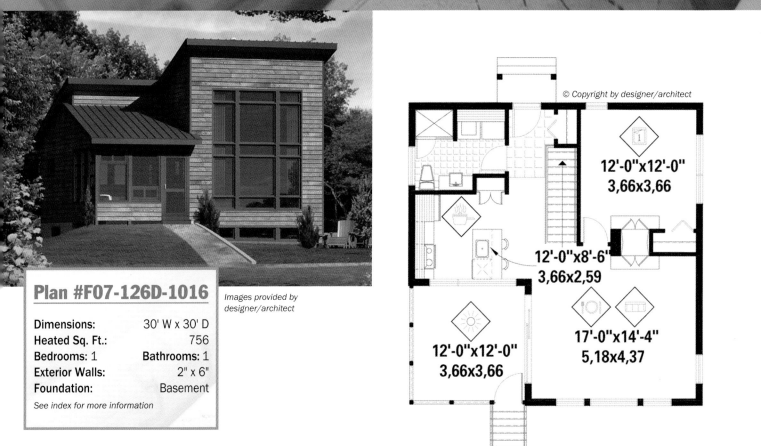

© Copyright by designer/architect

12'-0"x12'-0"
3,66x3,66

12'-0"x8'-6"
3,66x2,59

17'-0"x14'-4"
5,18x4,37

12'-0"x12'-0"
3,66x3,66

Plan #F07-126D-1016

Images provided by designer/architect

Dimensions:	30' W x 30' D
Heated Sq. Ft.:	756
Bedrooms: 1	Bathrooms: 1
Exterior Walls:	2" x 6"
Foundation:	Basement

See index for more information

SLOPE   SLOPE

Master Bedroom
13'-9" x 12'-6"

© Copyright by designer/architect

Bath

Closet

Kitchen
12'-10" x 11'-6"

Walk In Closet

Linen

DOWN

Dining
13' x 9'-3"
9' CLG HGT

Bath

Closet

Bedroom
10' x 11'-11"
9' CLG HGT

Built In Cabinets

Great Room
14' x 16'-11"

Closet

SLOPE   SLOPE

9' CLG HGT

Porch

Plan #F07-065D-0397

Images provided by designer/architect

Dimensions: 25' W x 61'4" D
Heated Sq. Ft.:   1,136
Bedrooms: 2   Bathrooms: 2
Foundation: Basement standard; crawl space available for an additional fee

See index for more information

Patio

Br 2
13-7x11-7

MBr
15-0x11-7

Hall
Dn

Kit
9-7x
8-0

Living Rm.
13-0x14-0

Garage
11-8x22-0

Brk'ft
9-4x8-0

Entry

Porch

© Copyright by
designer/architect

*Images provided by
designer/architect*

Plan #F07-007D-0109

Dimensions: 35' W x 38' D
Heated Sq. Ft.: 888
Bedrooms: 2   **Bathrooms:** 1
Foundation: Basement standard;
crawl space or slab available for an
additional fee

See index for more information

Covered Or
Screened Porch
10 x 6

Rear Porch
20 x 6

Tub/Shwr.

Kitchen
12-6 x 9-2

RANGE

Bath
5-6 x 9

RAISED BAR

Ref.

Bedroom
12 x 12-6

Living Room
18 X 11

FIREPLACE

Bonus Room
12 x 7-4

Front Porch
30 x 6

© Copyright by
designer/architect

*Images provided by
designer/architect*

Plan #F07-077D-0008

Dimensions: 31'8" W x 26' D
Heated Sq. Ft.: 600
Bedrooms: 1   **Bathrooms:** 1
Foundation: Basement, crawl
space or slab, please specify when
ordering

See index for more information

Plan #F07-032D-0887

Dimensions:	42' W x 40' D
Heated Sq. Ft.:	1,212
Bonus Sq. Ft.:	1,212
Bedrooms: 2	Bathrooms: 1
Exterior Walls:	2" x 6"

Foundation: Basement standard; crawl space, floating slab or mono-lithic slab available for an additional fee

See index for more information

Images provided by designer/architect

Features

- This highly efficient home offers an open floor plan with beamed ceilings above adding a tremendous amount of architectural interest to the interior

- A fireplace acts like a partition between the bedrooms and the gathering spaces

- The large covered porch is a wonderful extension of the interior living spaces

- The island in the kitchen includes casual dining space and a double basin sink and dishwasher

- The optional lower level has an additional 1,212 square feet of living area

First Floor
1,212 sq. ft.

© Copyright by designer/architect

Optional
Lower Level
1,212 sq. ft.

Plan #F07-032D-0358

Dimensions: 28' W x 26' D
Heated Sq. Ft.: 1,148
Bedrooms: 1   **Bathrooms:** 1½
Exterior Walls: 2" x 6"
Foundation: Basement standard; crawl space, floating slab or monolithic slab available for an additional fee

See index for more information

Features

- The first floor is completely open for a bright atmosphere
- The kitchen includes a unique island with seating for quick meals or space to serve buffet-style dinners
- The living/dining area features a huge fireplace centered between two sets of sliding glass doors that lead to a large outdoor deck
- French doors lead into the majestic second floor master bedroom which enjoys a walk-in closet and a private bath

Images provided by designer/architect

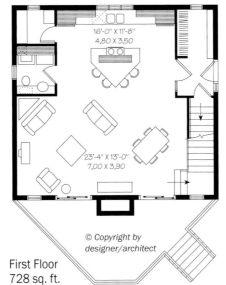

16'-0" X 11'-8"
4,80 x 3,50

23'-4" X 13'-0"
7,00 x 3,90

© Copyright by designer/architect

First Floor
728 sq. ft.

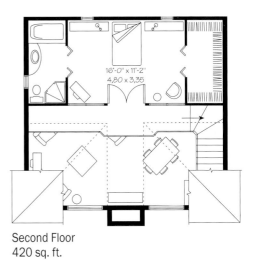

16'-0" X 11'-2"
4,80 x 3,35

Second Floor
420 sq. ft.

dream
BIG
while living small

"RIGHT" SIZE YOUR HOME & LIFE

When you call out to another family member does your home seem to echo? Are there more spaces that aren't being used in your home than are? Like many home buyers who once thought, "bigger is better," you have now changed your tune. Many are learning that downsizing is the way of the future. We have learned that it is possible to have simplicity in our lives, spend less money, and live an even fuller life by living in a smaller home.

Once considered standard practice for empty-nesters and retirees only, downsizing is now reaching all ages and incomes and it is for a multitude of reasons. Many homeowners have chosen to downsize their home because they want a simpler lifestyle with less home maintenance. People who love to travel, or who are involved with many hobbies outside their home also want less maintenance. Downsizing has also come to the forefront of society because of those who faced financial difficulties in the past, or saw their parents or families do so. Younger adults have realized from the start the importance of re-purposing existing materials, reinventing items that were once old or seemed unusable, and they've discovered they need far less space than generations before them. People now realize obtaining countless material things doesn't equate to happiness, or feeling accomplished in the world today. It simply adds more static and unnecessary clutter to their already complicated lives that seem to be filled with never-ending "noise" and distractions.

CLUTTER BE GONE

With so many benefits, it's no wonder that many families are making the switch to more modestly sized abodes. However, it's important to remember the cost: less space! This means you must maintain optimal use of your available space, clear out the clutter, and plan everything. No more impulse buys because they simply won't fit in a smaller home. You will soon realize that your charming tiny house is a little short on true square footage, but don't let it discourage you. It just means every single thing in your home must have a purpose. In fact, let it challenge you into finding ways to "size up" the small spaces and make guests never even notice the true deficit of space that surrounds them.

EVERYTHING OLD IS NEW AGAIN

Interestingly enough, the floor plan of today's smaller style homes is very similar to the common English style cottage from the 17th and 18th centuries. This style of house was two rooms deep with two large fireplaces back-to-back. The household spent most of its time in the larger keeping room where food was prepared and the smaller living space often referred to as a "parlor" sometimes doubled as the master bedroom. Two bedrooms could be found on the second floor. Today's version would be bigger than its English counterpart, but this style of home certainly fits the look and feel of today's neighborhoods and their long and narrow lots and the open floor plans now so popular today.

NEW HEIGHTS

For the smaller home, an open floor plan with few interior walls opens up your available space and creates the illusion of even more space since pesky walls aren't obstructing views. High ceilings also open your home for a relatively low cost and they help reduce the feeling of claustrophobia and restriction. If you're building a smaller home, consider the visual advantage of increasing the ceiling height perhaps from 8' to 9', or even better to 10', or add a vaulted ceiling. These are features that can't be added later and will tremendously increase the appearance of the home's size.

Be Creative!

Think of unexpected ways to get all of the amenities you want in your new home within a smaller amount of space.

Additionally, certain rooms such as formal dining and living rooms have outlived their usefulness today. Only utilized a handful of times a year, converting these outdated rooms into multipurpose spaces or offices is a more viable option.

Some home design ideas for conserving space you may want to consider when looking at small home floor plans include combining a laundry space with a bath, or even the kitchen. Or, maybe the home you like includes a laundry room, but you have no problem putting the washer and dryer in the garage or basement in order to have more storage for a walk-in pantry near the kitchen. Also, try running cabinets up to the ceiling for added space, or tuck the powder room under the stairs.

Door selection is another thing to consider for your smaller home. With the limited supply of space, every little bit counts and installing pocket doors, bracket doors, or popular barn style doors instead of hinge doors can free up an average of 10 square feet. That's a lot of space that can be put to good use!

Large windows, skylights, and small tubular skylights are other ways to create the impression of space by using glass and added light.

Bonus Points Skylights can often result in tax deductions. They filter in additional natural light, which brightens the interior reinforcing a feeling of spaciousness, while also, providing extra warmth naturally.

55

Another way to broaden the appearance of interior space is to keep the flooring uniform. So, if you want carpet, make sure it is "wall to wall." And, if wood flooring is your thing, try to stay away from an area rug so the flooring runs the entire length of the room.

Whether you're painting your small house yourself, or the builder is doing it for you, remember that dark colors create a more intimate, enclosed feeling whereas a lighter hue opens up the space. So, depending upon how you want your home to feel, consider your color choices wisely. You may want a cozy home, or you may want an open and airy feeling in your home. You may even want a mix of dark and light rooms. In creating an effective light color scheme, it is especially important to choose pale paint colors for your walls and then use your furniture to create the colored accents.

When it's time to decorate your home, don't waste space on flashy, useless decorations. Instead, you should keep accessories to a minimum to reduce visual clutter and give a more open, airy feel. Without all of the odds and ends closing in on your visual field, you're free to appreciate the few well selected, thoughtful pieces that are on display without feeling crowded out of your own home. Also, hanging mirrors on your walls will give the illusion of more space and provide an attractive and timeless wall embellishment.

Other ways to eliminate visual clutter include keeping extras from being in the way. Pop-up outlets in the kitchen, or in a home office offer a simple streamline solution when multiple outlets are necessary. So, take all of the appliances off your countertops and pull them out only when needed.

One way to take eyes off the obvious space shortage is to use a "more is more" attitude. Find ways to layer the rooms in your home whether with different colors, textures or patterns by choosing the right furniture.

Furnishing your small space can be both exciting and frustrating. Not everything that you see will fit well, so remember to plan your furniture layout. Instead of choosing a myriad of smaller furnishings, pick out a few key pieces to create a focal point in the room and avoid the muddled, chaotic feel of too much furniture. Also, consider the multipurpose potential of your furniture. Ottomans and chests can double as storage or coffee tables. Try using stacking tables that nest under each other. Slip ottomans partially under coffee tables, or use an ottoman as an actual coffee table with a tray on top of it. The ottoman becomes multi-functional by acting as extra seating, or as a table depending on your need at the time. As you can see, layering not only adds visual interest, but it's multi-functional. Let your creativity reign and give your house a unique, yet functional décor that is perfect for living large in your tiny home.

Take note, larger pieces of furniture should remain a solid neutral color, or upholstered in subtle fabric so that the object doesn't overcome a small space. Solid colors and unpatterned choices will create a serene backdrop to the playful accessories that can liven up the surroundings.

VERTICALLY CHALLENGED NO MORE

Another cool way to make a room seem bigger is to visually find ways to make the room seem taller. If you have a couple of standard sized windows on one wall, why not have the drapery pole mounted where the wall and ceiling meet? Taking the draperies from the ceiling to the floor make the windows seem larger than life instead of average size. This trick also works well in a bathroom with the shower curtain. Mount the pole right at ceiling height for added drama and heightened style.

Trick: Buy vintage furniture because it tends to be smaller in scale. Sofas of yesteryear were often only 2' deep instead of the standard 3' deep size of today.

Let it Shine!

Showcase special books, mixed perfume and other items you use frequently. Arrange sparingly so it appears artistic, not functional.

RAISE THE ROOF

Artwork when hung in the right way can also draw the eye upward just like draperies. Stack artwork on top of one another and take it higher than you normally would and suddenly guests' eyes will take in much more of the room.

If your small home contains several nooks and crannies that seem basically useless, try painting the space a dramatic color, mount a shelf and display a contrasting vase, or hang a painting that will stand out against the interesting wall color choice. Turn it into a stunning focal point that normally would be ignored. This tiny space now has become a big decorating moment.

BE OCD WITH YOUR BOOKCASE

Also, if you need bookcases and shelves for storage in your small home and you need them to house books and items rather than remain half-empty and used for decorating purposes only, why not arrange the items in a way that makes it more artistic and less cluttered looking? For example, if you have a large book collection, then organize the books by color, so suddenly the colors of the books come alive and add a colorful and playful design element to the space. Try this and you will instantly see that a grouping of red spine books will make a bolder statement when placed all together as opposed to scattered about in a more reckless fashion.

If a bedroom is very small or doesn't include much storage, then find a beautiful tray and arrange items such as pins, jewelry or perfumes perhaps so that they become a decorating element. Remember however, this is meant to be a display of collectibles rather than a drop zone for items you don't know where to store. So, choose the displayed items sparingly and make them become a work of art. Plus, by having these possibly overlooked items from your wardrobe more visible, chances are, you will use them more often.

ALWAYS SKIPPING BREAKFAST?

Another great idea is to look around and see if a room offers an unconventional, but possibly a better use for you. Maybe you aren't a breakfast person, let alone someone who cooks very often. If this is the case, forgo the predictable breakfast table steps from the kitchen for a high function home office or computer niche that would suit your needs better. Just because something is supposed to be in a space doesn't mean it has to be.

Using some of these hints inside your quaint and charming abode not only adds great function and style, but it will create an element of surprise that is bound to be loaded with your own personality. Mixing function and small spaces doesn't have to be boring, so try these ideas and create a small home packed with big time style.

STUFF BE GONE!

Once you have the floor plan and furniture layout figured out, it's time to think about storage. Over our lifetimes, we just accumulate stuff; whether it's useful, or full of memories, we need places to put it and with less space in a smaller home, organization and creativity play key roles. The next most crucial step in small home living is to start getting rid of the things you do not need. This sounds easier than it is. Whether you're a young couple with a baby, or a retired couple with 35+ years of family treasures and memories, it is hard for anyone to part with things that mean something to them.

OVER ANALYZE

Instead of a dusty treadmill taking up the entire guest bedroom, why not trade it in for a new pair of sneakers and enjoy outdoor walks? To truly rid yourself of the things you do not need; you need to be honest with yourself. This holds true in almost every area of your home. If you still haven't used your fondue pot, ice cream maker, or food processor, after many years of owning them, it is safe to say you never will. Appliances take up crucial cabinet space and could be thoroughly enjoyed by someone who enjoys cooking. Take this same honesty into your bedroom closet, too. It's a safe bet that there are jeans at least two sizes smaller than what you currently wear hiding in there. Give them to someone who can enjoy them now instead of waiting for the day you hope to wear them again.

Then, assess your furniture. You probably have pieces that don't fit in your smaller home, so before donating or selling them, see if a family member would enjoy them. You never know if the old armoire from Aunt Irene has sentimental value to someone else in the family and would be a cherished and appreciated piece in their home.

Rule of Thumb:
If you haven't used it in a year, then get rid of it. Scaling down is meant to simplify your life, not complicate it.

As you begin going through things that have been stored in the basement and elsewhere, you will be shocked to see what you were saving. In fact, you may not have seen many of these things for years. And there's a reason why — you didn't need them! So, if your children are long gone, but you still have their high school trophies and mementos, then it's time to send them their way. Or, if you're a young family just starting out, unless you plan on having more children, donate or sell toys and clothing as they are outgrown.

No matter how organized you are, if there is no room, there is simply no room. So, if you're downsizing, or you've decided to build a small home, assess your belongings and consider creative storage ideas like hooks, floor-to-ceiling shelving, and storage under the stairs. Open shelving instead of closed cabinets creates the illusion of more space. And, don't forget to utilize your vertical storage capacity! Oftentimes, we neglect to fill up the available vertical space and try to cram everything in at eye level or below. You may need to keep a footstool nearby, but it will be well worth it.

Parting with belongings isn't easy, but it will move you in the direction of less stressful surroundings. It represents change and, that for many, is a physically and emotionally draining process. But afterwards, you can look forward to a clean, clutter-free home that requires less maintenance. The key to successful downsizing is good design, and an efficient small home that has the functionality you need in less space allows you to feel at peace in the small space rather than restricted.

Plan #F07-032D-1107

Dimensions:	35' W x 33' D
Heated Sq. Ft.:	1,050
Bonus Sq. Ft.:	1,050
Bedrooms: 2	**Bathrooms:** 1
Exterior Walls:	2" x 6"

Foundation: Basement standard; crawl space or monolithic slab available for an additional fee

See index for more information

Features

- An attractive Modern Farmhouse style exterior greets guests and offers simple, understated curb appeal

- The living room, dining room and kitchen combination create the open-concept layout that is so desirable

- Two bedrooms provide the perfect quiet place to relax and unwind with a well-appointed master bedroom featuring a walk-in closet in one corner

- The optional lower level has an additional 1,050 square feet of living area

First Floor
1,050 sq. ft.

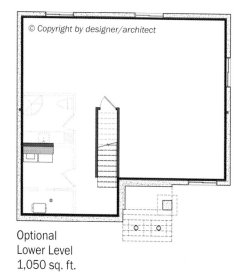

Optional
Lower Level
1,050 sq. ft.

Images provided by designer/architect

Plan #F07-032D-0932

Dimensions:	38' W x 30' D
Heated Sq. Ft.:	1,102
Bonus Sq. Ft.:	1,102
Bedrooms: 2	Bathrooms: 1
Exterior Walls:	2" x 6"

Foundation: Basement standard; crawl space, floating slab or monolithic slab available for an additional fee

See index for more information

Features

- The living room has a fireplace centered off the right wall that can be seen by the dining area and kitchen for added coziness
- The master bedroom is spacious and features two closets
- Bedroom 2 is modest in size, but includes a large walk-in closet
- The kitchen features a functional island with casual dining space
- The optional lower level has an additional 1,102 square feet of living area

First Floor
1,102 sq. ft.

Images provided by designer/architect

© Copyright by designer/architect

Optional Lower Level
1,102 sq. ft.

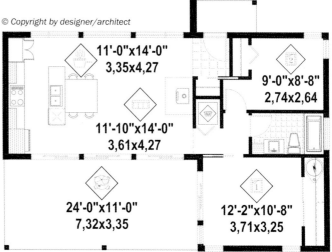

© Copyright by designer/architect

11'-0"x14'-0"
3,35x4,27

9'-0"x8'-8"
2,74x2,64

11'-10"x14'-0"
3,61x4,27

24'-0"x11'-0"
7,32x3,35

12'-2"x10'-8"
3,71x3,25

Plan #F07-126D-1153

Images provided by designer/architect

Dimensions:	40' W x 26' D
Heated Sq. Ft.:	776
Bedrooms: 2	Bathrooms: 1
Exterior Walls:	2" x 6"
Foundation:	Slab

See index for more information

CLO
6 x 6

BEDRM #2
12 x 10

STACKED
LAUNDRY

BATH #1
5 x 12

PULL
DN
STAIR

DN

BEDRM #1
10 x 12

CLO
5 x 5

CLO
3 x 6

Second Floor
505 sq. ft.

© Copyright by
designer/architect

DINING
9 x 10

KITCHEN
9 x 10

1/2
BATH
3 x 7

FAMILY
ROOM
15 x 16

PORCH
5 x 5

UP

First Floor
494 sq. ft.

Plan #F07-141D-0250

Images provided by designer/architect

Dimensions:	19'4" W x 26'8" D
Heated Sq. Ft.:	999
Bedrooms: 2	Bathrooms: 1½
Foundation:	Slab standard; crawl space, basement or walk-out basement available for an additional fee

See index for more information

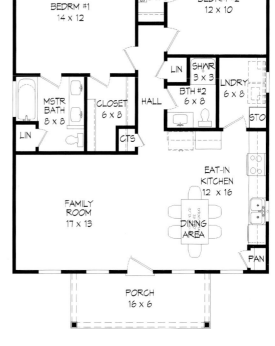

Plan #F07-141D-0066

Images provided by designer/architect

Dimensions: 30' W x 41' D
Heated Sq. Ft.: 1,050
Bedrooms: 2   **Bathrooms:** 2
Foundation: Slab standard; crawl space, basement or walk-out basement available for an additional fee

See index for more information

Plan #F07-077D-0208

Images provided by designer/architect

Dimensions: 50' W x 43' D
Heated Sq. Ft.: 1,200
Bedrooms: 3   **Bathrooms:** 2
Foundation: Crawl space or slab, please specify when ordering; for basement version, see Plan #077D-0246 at houseplansandmore.com

See index for more information

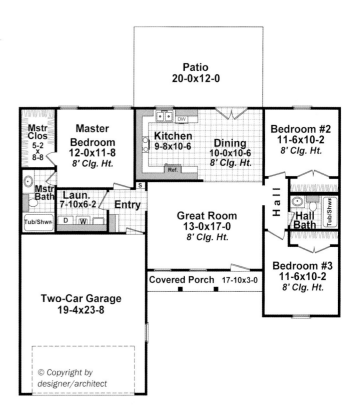

© Copyright by designer/architect

OUTDOOR LIVING 12/0 X 19/0

LIVING 14/0 X 23/0 (10' CLG.)

B.R. 12/6 X 15/10 (10' CLG.)

FOYER 7/0 X 7/0 (11' CLG.)

Images provided by designer/architect

Plan #F07-011D-0291

Dimensions:	49'6" W x 31'6" D
Heated Sq. Ft.:	972
Bedrooms: 1	**Bathrooms:** 1
Exterior Walls:	2" x 6"

Foundation: Crawl space or slab standard; basement available for an additional fee

See index for more information

PATIO 14'-0" X 10'-0"

GARAGE 13'-0" X 20'-0"

KIT. 9'-0" X 11'-8"

BED RM. 2 9'-4" X 11'-4"

BED RM. 3 12'-0" X 9'-0"

BATH

GREAT ROOM 14'-2" X 18'-8"

MASTER BEDROOM 13'-4" X 12'-6"

© Copyright by designer/architect

Images provided by designer/architect

Plan #F07-155D-0171

Dimensions:	53'8" W x 41'4" D
Heated Sq. Ft.:	1,131
Bedrooms: 3	**Bathrooms:** 2

Foundation: Crawl space or slab, please specify when ordering

See index for more information

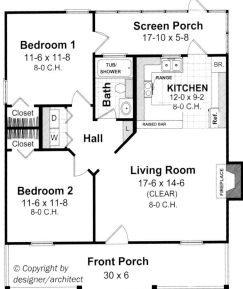

Images provided by designer/architect

Screen Porch
17-10 x 5-8

Bedroom 1
11-6 x 11-8
8-0 C.H.

TUB/SHOWER

RANGE

BR.

KITCHEN
12-0 x 9-2
8-0 C.H.

Ref.

Bath

RAISED BAR

Closet

D

W

Closet

Hall

Bedroom 2
11-6 x 11-8
8-0 C.H.

Living Room
17-6 x 14-6
(CLEAR)
8-0 C.H.

FIREPLACE

© Copyright by designer/architect

Front Porch
30 x 6

Plan #F07-077D-0009

Dimensions: 30' W x 36' D
Heated Sq. Ft.: 800
Bedrooms: 2   Bathrooms: 1
Foundation: Slab or crawl space, please specify when ordering; for basement version, see Plan #077D-0116 at houseplansandmore.com

See index for more information

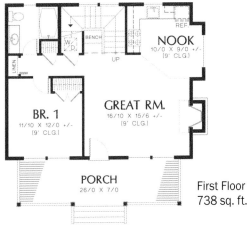

Images provided by designer/architect

OPEN TO BELOW

DN.

DESK

LOFT
12/0 X 13/2
(9' CLG.)

Second Floor
212 sq. ft.

© Copyright by designer/architect

REF.

BENCH

W/D

UP

LINEN

NOOK
10/0 X 9/0 +/-
(9' CLG.)

BR. 1
11/10 X 12/0 +/-
(9' CLG.)

GREAT RM.
16/10 15/6 +/-
(9' CLG.)

PORCH
26/0 X 7/0

First Floor
738 sq. ft.

Plan #F07-011D-0359

Dimensions: 32' W x 31' D
Heated Sq. Ft.: 950
Bedrooms: 1   Bathrooms: 1
Exterior Walls: 2" x 6"
Foundation: Crawl space or slab standard; basement available for an additional fee

See index for more information

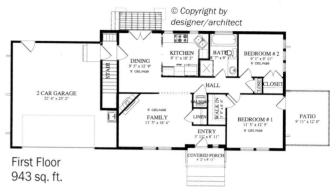

2 CAR GARAGE
22' 4" x 23' 2"

STAIR

DINING
9' 5" x 12' 9"
9' CEILINGS

KITCHEN
9' 1" x 10' 2"

BATH
8' 7" x 9'

BEDROOM # 2
9' 1" x 9' 11"
9' CEILINGS

CLOSET

HALL

FAMILY
11' 5" x 16' 4"
9' CEILINGS

LAUNDRY

LINEN

WALK IN

ENTRY
3' 11" x 8' 11"

BEDROOM # 1
11' 5" x 12' 5"
9' CEILINGS

PATIO
9' 11" x 12' 0"

COVERED PORCH
4' 2" x 8' 11"

First Floor
943 sq. ft.

Plan #F07-172D-0020

Dimensions:	61' W x 25'6" D
Heated Sq. Ft.:	943
Bonus Sq. Ft.:	931
Bedrooms: 2	**Bathrooms:** 1
Exterior Walls:	2" x 6"

Foundation: Basement standard; craw space, monolithic slab, stem wall slab, daylight basement or walk-out basement available for an additional fee

See index for more information

Images provided by designer/architect

DINING
10' 0" x 13' 0"

KITCHEN
9' 1" x 13' 0"

BATH
11' x 10'

BEDROOM # 1
10' 9" x 10' 11"

STAIR

FAMILY
12' 3" x 35' 6"

8' CEILINGS

CLOSET

Optional
Lower Level
931 sq. ft.

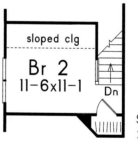

sloped clg

Br 2
11-6x11-1

Dn

Second Floor
168 sq. ft.

Plan #F07-040D-0028

Images provided by designer/architect

Dimensions:	28' W x 31'6" D
Heated Sq. Ft.:	828
Bedrooms: 2	**Bathrooms:** 1
Foundation:	Crawl space

See index for more information

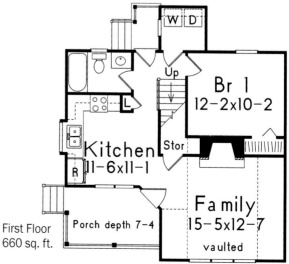

W D

Up

Br 1
12-2x10-2

Kitchen
11-6x11-1

Stor

Family
15-5x12-7

Porch depth 7-4

vaulted

First Floor
660 sq. ft.

Plan #F07-058D-0009

Images provided by
designer/architect

Dimensions:	16' W x 32' D
Heated Sq. Ft.:	448
Bedrooms: 1	Bathrooms: 1
Foundation:	Slab

See index for more information

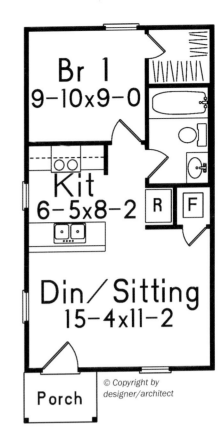

Br 1
9-10x9-0

Kit
6-5x8-2

R   F

Din/Sitting
15-4x11-2

Porch

© Copyright by
designer/architect

Plan #F07-121D-0033

Images provided by
designer/architect

Dimensions:	32' W x 34' D
Heated Sq. Ft.:	944
Bedrooms: 2	Bathrooms: 1

Foundation: Basement standard;
crawl space or slab available for an
additional fee

See index for more information

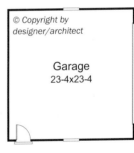

© Copyright by
designer/architect

Garage
23-4x23-4

MBr
13-0x11-7

Br 2
10-2x11-7

Great Rm
16-8x13-5

Kitchen/
Dining
13-4x17-9

Porch

OFFICE / STUDIO
16/6 X 11/4
(8' CLG)

OPEN SHLVS

FOLD'G WALL
HUNG TABLE

W
D

© Copyright by designer/architect

PATIO

Images provided by designer/architect

Plan #F07-011D-0603

Dimensions:	26' W x 12' D
Heated Sq. Ft.:	312
Bedrooms: 1	**Bathrooms:** 1
Exterior Walls:	2" x 6"

Foundation: Crawl space or slab standard; basement available for an additional fee

See index for more information

Plan #F07-032D-0872

Images provided by designer/architect

Dimensions:	24' W x 28' D
Heated Sq. Ft.:	629
Bedrooms: 2	**Bathrooms:** 1
Exterior Walls:	2" x 6"

Foundation: Monolithic slab standard; crawl space or floating slab available for an additional fee

See index for more information

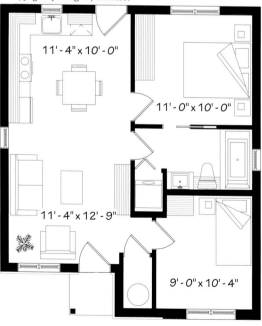

© Copyright by designer/architect

11' - 4" x 10' - 0"

11' - 0" x 10' - 0"

11' - 4" x 12' - 9"

9' - 0" x 10' - 4"

Plan #F07-077D-0088

Dimensions:	30' W x 36' D
Heated Sq. Ft.:	800
Bedrooms: 2	Bathrooms: 1
Foundation:	Slab

See index for more information

Images provided by designer/architect

Bedroom 1
11-6 x 11-8
8-0 C.H.

Screen Porch
17-10 x 5-8

BR.

TUB/SHOWER

Bath

Kitchen
12-0 x 9-2
8-0 C.H.

DW

Ref.

Closet

D

W

Closet

RAISED BAR

Hall

Bedroom 2
11-6 x 11-8
8-0 C.H.

Living Room
8-0 C.H.
17-6 x 14-6
(CLEAR)

Front Porch
30 x 6

© Copyright by designer/architect

Plan #F07-144D-0015

Dimensions:	25'6" W x 38' D
Heated Sq. Ft.:	967
Bedrooms: 3	Bathrooms: 2
Exterior Walls:	2" x 6"

Foundation: Crawl space or slab, please specify when ordering

See index for more information

Images provided by designer/architect

© Copyright by designer/architect

DOUBLE

QUEEN

BED - 2
10'0 X 10'0

W.I.C.

M. BEDROOM
10'4 X 10'11

DRESSER

DRESSER

LINEN

DRESSER

39" HALL

BATH
4'11 X 8'1

M. BATH
4'11 X 8'1

BED - 3
10'0 X 10'0

DOUBLE

W/D

H/W

BUILT-IN

FIRE PLACE

BUILT-IN

LIVING RM.
15'1 X 13'11

KITCHEN
9'3 X 14'7

30 FR

DW

OPEN DECK
16 X 8

Plan #F07-028D-0057

Images provided by designer/architect

Dimensions: 33' W x 36' D
Heated Sq. Ft.: 1,007
Bedrooms: 2 **Bathrooms:** 1
Foundation: Crawl space or slab, please specify when ordering

See index for more information

MASTER BEDROOM
13'-0" X 16'-6"

CLO.
8'-0" X 6'-6"

LAUNDRY
9'-8" X 6'-6"

STOR.

WH

LINEN

KITCHEN
12'-0" X 10'-0"

LINEN

SNACK BAR

BEDROOM 2
13'-0" X 10'-0"

GREAT ROOM
20'-0" X 14'-0"

COVERED PORCH

© Copyright by designer/architect

Plan #F07-141D-0001

Images provided by designer/architect

Dimensions: 24' W x 27'4" D
Heated Sq. Ft.: 561
Bedrooms: 1 **Bathrooms:** 1
Foundation: Crawl space standard; slab or basement available for an additional fee

See index for more information

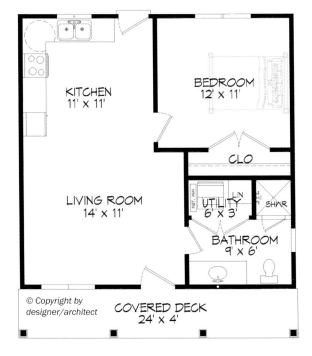

KITCHEN
11' x 11'

BEDROOM
12' x 11'

CLO

LIVING ROOM
14' x 11'

UTILITY
6' x 3'

LIN

SHWR

BATHROOM
9' x 6'

© Copyright by designer/architect

COVERED DECK
24' x 4'

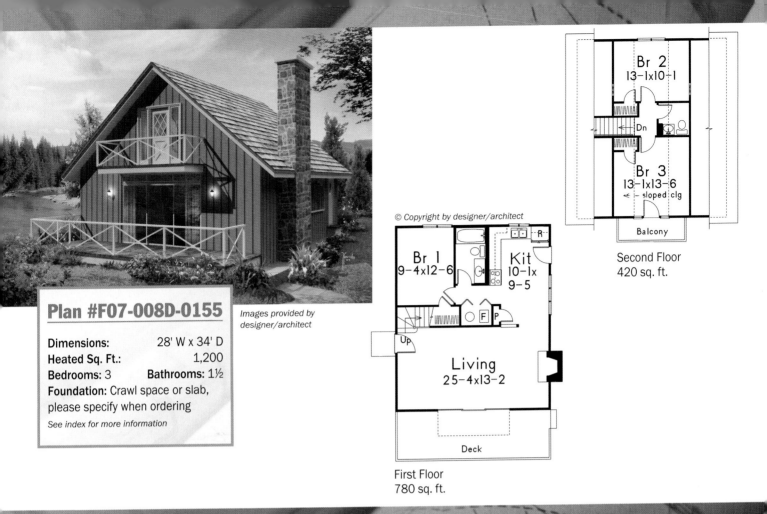

Plan #F07-008D-0155

Images provided by designer/architect

Dimensions: 28' W x 34' D
Heated Sq. Ft.: 1,200
Bedrooms: 3   **Bathrooms:** 1½
Foundation: Crawl space or slab, please specify when ordering

See index for more information

© Copyright by designer/architect

Br 2
13-1x10-1

Dn

Br 3
13-1x13-6
← sloped clg

Balcony

Second Floor
420 sq. ft.

Br 1
9-4x12-6

Kit
10-1x
9-5

R

Up
F P

Living
25-4x13-2

Deck

First Floor
780 sq. ft.

Plan #F07-111D-0034

Images provided by designer/architect

Dimensions: 28' W x 34' D
Heated Sq. Ft.: 1,200
Bedrooms: 2   **Bathrooms:** 2½
Foundation: Slab standard; crawl space or basement available for an additional fee

See index for more information

ATTIC SPACE   ATTIC SPACE

M. BATH   WIC   LINEN   BATH 2

MASTER BEDROOM
11² x 14⁴

READING NOOK

BEDRM 2
9¹⁰ x 14⁴

SLOPE   SEAT   SLOPE

Second Floor
548 sq. ft.

PANTRY

KITCHEN
11⁸ x 9⁰

HALL

PWDR.

DINING
14⁰ x 14⁰

LIVING
14⁰ x 14⁰

ENTRY

PORCH

© Copyright by designer/architect

First Floor
652 sq. ft.

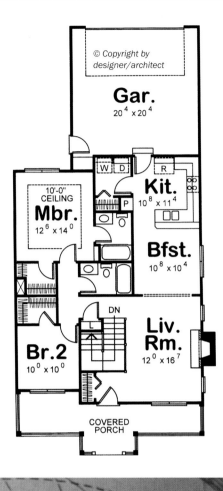

© Copyright by designer/architect

Gar.
20⁴ x 20⁴

Mbr.
10'-0" CEILING
12⁶ x 14⁰

Kit.
10⁸ x 11⁴

Bfst.
10⁸ x 10⁴

Br.2
10⁰ x 10⁰

Liv. Rm.
12⁰ x 16⁷

DN

COVERED PORCH

Plan #F07-026D-0972

Images provided by designer/architect

Dimensions: 30'4" W x 59'8" D
Heated Sq. Ft.:   1,142
Bedrooms: 2   **Bathrooms:** 2
Foundation: Basement standard; crawl space, slab or walk-out basement available for an additional fee

See index for more information

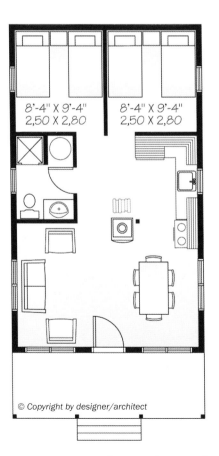

8'-4" X 9'-4"
2,50 X 2,80

8'-4" X 9'-4"
2,50 X 2,80

© Copyright by designer/architect

Plan #F07-032D-0710

Images provided by designer/architect

Dimensions: 18' W x 30' D
Heated Sq. Ft.:   540
Bedrooms: 2   **Bathrooms:** 1
Exterior Walls: 2" x 6"
Foundation: Screw pile standard; crawl space, floating slab or monolithic slab available for an additional fee

See index for more information

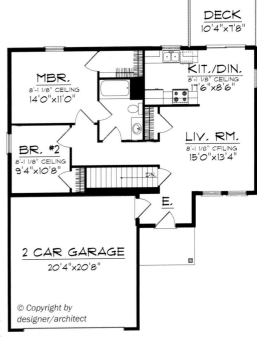

DECK
10'4"x7'8"

MBR.
8'-1 1/8" CEILING
14'0"x11'0"

KIT./DIN.
8'-1 1/8" CEILING
17'6"x8'6"

BR. #2
8'-1 1/8" CEILING
9'4"x10'8"

LIV. RM.
8'-1 1/8" CEILING
15'0"x13'4"

DN.

E.

2 CAR GARAGE
20'4"x20'8"

Plan #F07-051D-0889

Dimensions:	40' W x 44' D
Heated Sq. Ft.:	967
Bedrooms: 2	Bathrooms: 1
Exterior Walls:	2" x 6"

Foundation: Basement standard; crawl space or slab available for an additional fee

See index for more information

Plan #F07-001D-0081

Dimensions:	44' W x 28' D
Heated Sq. Ft.:	1,160
Bedrooms: 3	Bathrooms: 1½

Foundation: Crawl space standard; basement or slab available for an additional fee

See index for more information

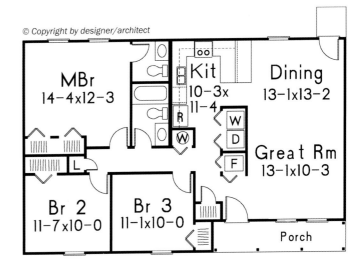

MBr
14-4x12-3

Kit
10-3x
11-4

Dining
13-1x13-2

R

W
D

F

Great Rm
13-1x10-3

L

Br 2
11-7x10-0

Br 3
11-1x10-0

Porch

Plan #F07-007D-0148

Images provided by designer/architect

Dimensions:	28' W x 30' D
Heated Sq. Ft.:	1,167
Bedrooms: 2	Bathrooms: 2½
Foundation:	Basement

See index for more information

Features

- An attractive exterior is enhanced with multiple gables
- The sizable living room features a separate entry foyer and view to the covered front porch
- The functional U-shaped kitchen has a breakfast room with a bay window that includes sliding glass doors to a patio, a built-in pantry, and a laundry room with a half bath
- The master bedroom offers three closets and a luxury bath
- 1-car front entry garage

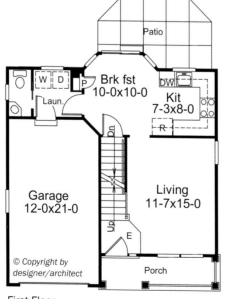

First Floor
476 sq. ft.

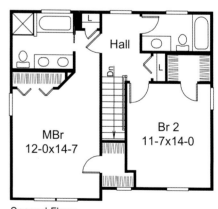

Second Floor
691 sq. ft.

Plan #F07-130D-0363

Dimensions: 16' W x 29' D
Heated Sq. Ft.: 597
Bedrooms: 1   **Bathrooms:** 1
Foundation: Slab standard; crawl space or basement available for an additional fee

See index for more information

Features

- This charming tiny home has a clerestory window brightening the interior
- The living room has a sloped ceiling that allows it to enjoy the clerestory window above, which greatly adds speciousness to the entire first floor
- The kitchen has an eating bar with seating for three people to dine right near the dinette
- The bedroom enjoys a private location on the second floor and has a ceiling that vaults to 8' and a walk-in closet

Images provided by designer/architect

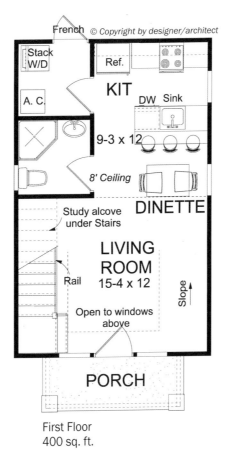

First Floor
400 sq. ft.

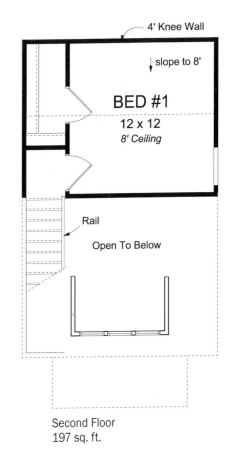

Second Floor
197 sq. ft.

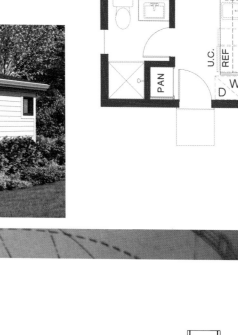

VAULTED
LIVING
11/0 X 10/4

FOLD-DN TABLE

STOR. CAB.

PAN

U.C.

REF

D W

Images provided by designer/architect

Plan #F07-012D-7510

Dimensions:	12' W x 23' D
Heated Sq. Ft.:	276
Bedrooms: Studio	**Bathrooms:** 1
Exterior Walls:	2" x 6"

Foundation: Crawl space or slab standard; basement available for an additional fee

See index for more information

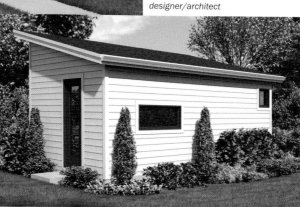

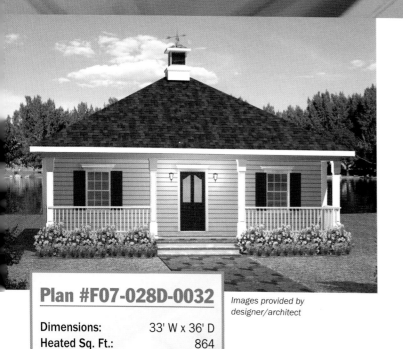

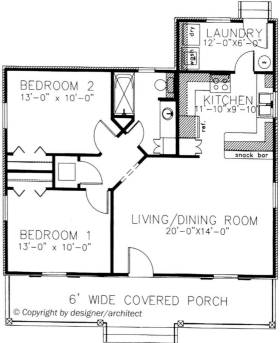

LAUNDRY
12'-0"X6'-9"

BEDROOM 2
13'-0" x 10'-0"

KITCHEN
11'-10"x9'-10"

ref.

snack bar

BEDROOM 1
13'-0" x 10'-0"

LIVING/DINING ROOM
20'-0"X14'-0"

6' WIDE COVERED PORCH

Plan #F07-028D-0032

Images provided by designer/architect

Dimensions:	33' W x 36' D
Heated Sq. Ft.:	864
Bedrooms: 2	**Bathrooms:** 1

Foundation: Slab or crawl space, please specify when ordering

See index for more information

Plan #F07-032D-0725

Dimensions: 32' W x 28' D
Heated Sq. Ft.: 896
Bedrooms: 2   Bathrooms: 1
Exterior Walls: 2" x 6"
Foundation: Basement standard; crawl space, floating slab or monolithic slab available for an additional fee

See index for more information

Plan #F07-141D-0315

Dimensions: 25' W x 40' D
Heated Sq. Ft.: 750
Bedrooms: 1   Bathrooms: 1
Exterior Walls: 2" x 6"
Foundation: Pier

See index for more information

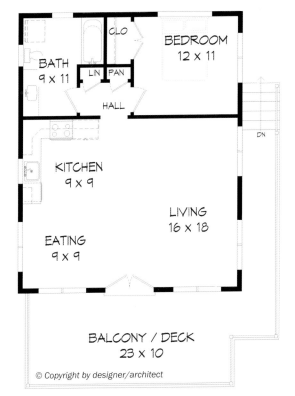

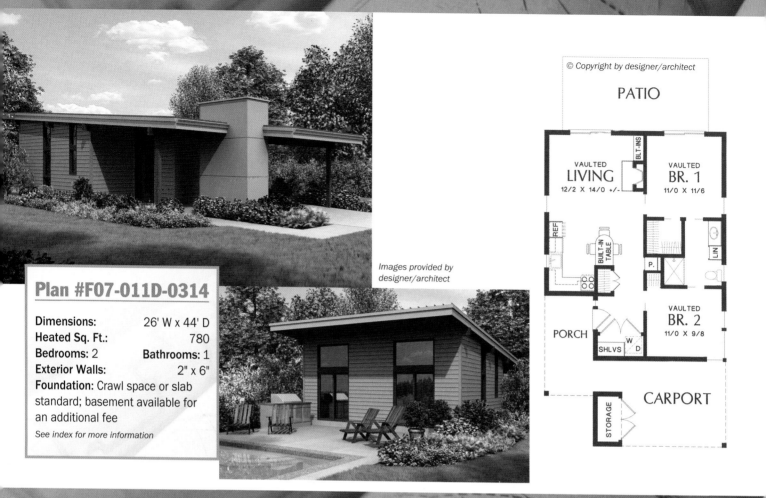

Plan #F07-011D-0314

Dimensions:	26' W x 44' D
Heated Sq. Ft.:	780
Bedrooms: 2	**Bathrooms:** 1
Exterior Walls:	2" x 6"

Foundation: Crawl space or slab standard; basement available for an additional fee

See index for more information

Images provided by designer/architect

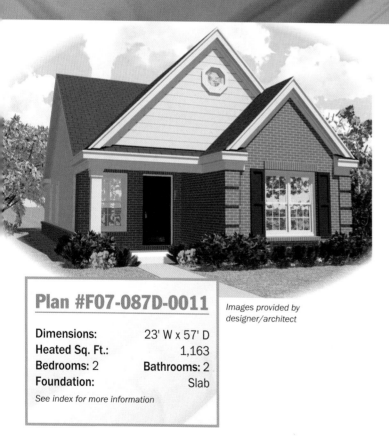

Plan #F07-087D-0011

Images provided by designer/architect

Dimensions:	23' W x 57' D
Heated Sq. Ft.:	1,163
Bedrooms: 2	**Bathrooms:** 2
Foundation:	Slab

See index for more information

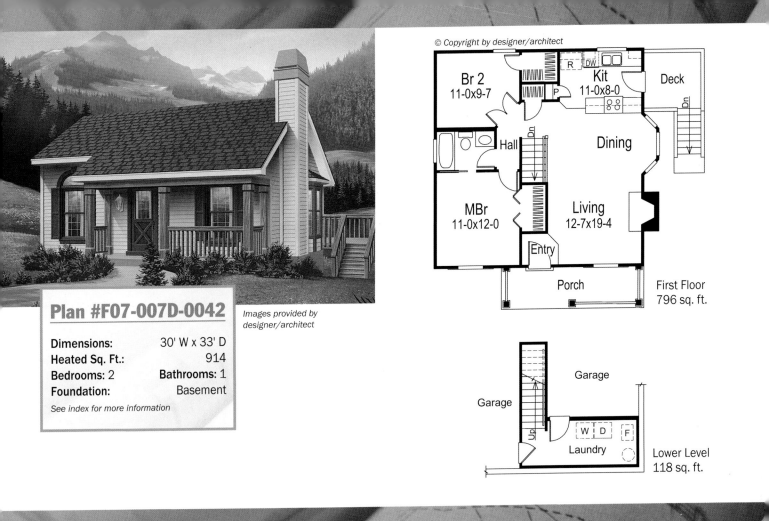

© Copyright by designer/architect

First Floor
796 sq. ft.

Br 2
11-0x9-7

Kit
11-0x8-0

Deck

Hall

Dining

MBr
11-0x12-0

Living
12-7x19-4

Entry

Porch

Lower Level
118 sq. ft.

Garage

Garage

Garage

W D F

Laundry

Plan #F07-007D-0042

Images provided by designer/architect

Dimensions:	30' W x 33' D
Heated Sq. Ft.:	914
Bedrooms: 2	Bathrooms: 1
Foundation:	Basement

See index for more information

© Copyright by designer/architect

br 2
11 x 10

clo

mbr
13 x 13

clo

clo

clo

HEAT BAC

hall

bath

bath

lin

sto 8x4

br 3
11 x 10

lin

clo

ATTIC STAIRS

living
19 x 14

WH

ref

rng

w

slope clg

kit 13 x 9

d

carport
21 x 12

ent

bar

dining
12 x 10

Plan #F07-020D-0030

Images provided by designer/architect

Dimensions:	40' W x 42' D
Heated Sq. Ft.:	1,168
Bedrooms: 3	Bathrooms: 1½
Exterior Walls:	2" x 6"
Foundation:	Slab standard; crawl space available for an additional fee

See index for more information

Images provided by designer/architect

Plan #F07-080D-0001

Dimensions:	24' W x 36' D
Heated Sq. Ft.:	583
Bedrooms: 1	**Bathrooms:** 1
Exterior Walls:	2" x 6"
Foundation:	Crawl space

See index for more information

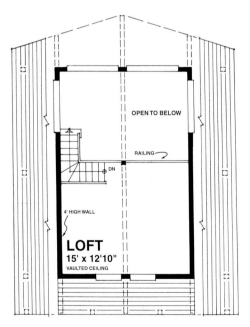

Features

- A large two-story window wall commands full attention upon entering the living area
- A compact, yet convenient eating bar offers a quick meal option in the kitchen
- The second floor sleeping loft enjoys lots of natural sunlight and a vaulted ceiling creating a more spacious feel

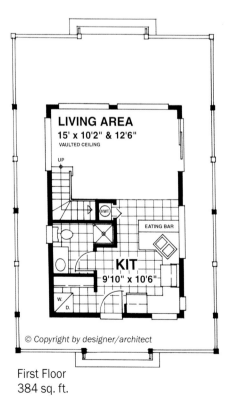

LIVING AREA
15' x 10'2" & 12'6"
VAULTED CEILING

UP

HWT

EATING BAR

KIT
9'10" x 10'6"

W.
D.

© Copyright by designer/architect

First Floor
384 sq. ft.

OPEN TO BELOW

RAILING

DN

4' HIGH WALL

LOFT
15' x 12'10"
VAULTED CEILING

Second Floor
199 sq. ft.

Plan #F07-058D-0214

Dimensions: 23' W x 42'8" D
Heated Sq. Ft.: 866
Bedrooms: 1   Bathrooms: 1½
Foundation: Basement

See index for more information

Images provided by designer/architect

© Copyright by designer/architect

Deck
12-0x6-0

W D

Laundry

Pantry

Kit./Brk.
13-4x14-0

R

Cl.

Dn

Sitting
13-6x14-10

Up

Covered
Porch
16-8x6-8

First Floor
599 sq. ft.

Bedroom
11-8x14-0

Open To
Below

Second Floor
267 sq. ft.

Plan #F07-011D-0312

Dimensions: 22' W x 32' D
Heated Sq. Ft.: 544
Bedrooms: 1   Bathrooms: 1
Exterior Walls: 2" x 6"
Foundation: Crawl space or slab standard; basement available for an additional fee

See index for more information

Images provided by designer/architect

© Copyright by designer/architect

VAULTED
GUEST BR.
12/2 X 11/2

W/D

LINEN

PAN

U.C.
REF

PORCH

VAULTED
LIVING
12/0 X 13/8 +

(8' CLG)

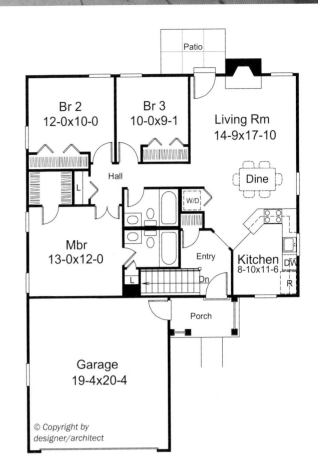

Br 2
12-0x10-0

Br 3
10-0x9-1

Living Rm
14-9x17-10

Hall

Dine

Mbr
13-0x12-0

Entry

Kitchen
8-10x11-6

Porch

Garage
19-4x20-4

© Copyright by
designer/architect

Plan #F07-007D-0181

*Images provided by
designer/architect*

Dimensions: 38' W x 52'8" D
Heated Sq. Ft.: 1,140
Bedrooms: 3 **Bathrooms:** 2
Foundation: Basement standard;
crawl space or slab available for an
additional fee

See index for more information

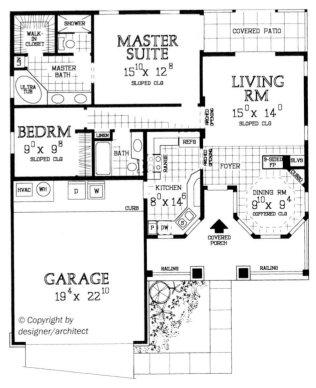

WALK-IN CLOSET

SHOWER

MASTER SUITE
15-10 x 12-8
SLOPED CLG

COVERED PATIO

MASTER BATH

ULTRA TUB

LIN

BEDRM
9-0 x 9-8
SLOPED CLG

LINEN

BATH

REFG

RANGE

LIVING RM
15-0 x 14-0
SLOPED CLG

ARCHED OPENING

ARCHED OPENING

FOYER

9-SIDED FP

CURIO

HVAC WH

D W

KITCHEN
8-0 x 14-6

DINING RM
9-10 x 9-4
COFFERED CLG

CURB

P DW S

COVERED PORCH

GARAGE
19-4 x 22-10

RAILING

RAILING

© Copyright by
designer/architect

Plan #F07-049D-0007

*Images provided by
designer/architect*

Dimensions: 44'4" W x 47'4" D
Heated Sq. Ft.: 1,118
Bedrooms: 2 **Bathrooms:** 2
Exterior Walls: 2" x 6"
Foundation: Slab

See index for more information

Images provided by designer/architect

Plan #F07-122D-0001

Dimensions:	33' W x 35' D
Heated Sq. Ft.:	1,105
Bedrooms: 2	Bathrooms: 1½
Foundation:	Slab

See index for more information

Features

- This fresh, modern design enjoys sleek lines and a stucco exterior making it one-of-a-kind
- The compact, yet efficient U-shaped kitchen has plenty of counter space
- A tall sloped ceiling in the two-story living room provides a spacious feel all those who enter will appreciate

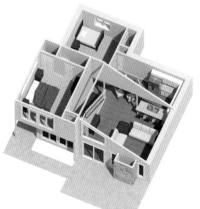

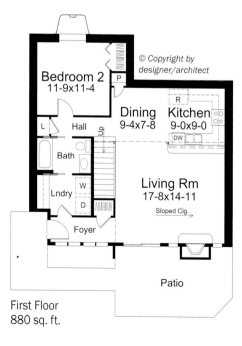

© Copyright by designer/architect

Bedroom 2
11-9x11-4

Dining
9-4x7-8

Kitchen
9-0x9-0

Hall

Bath

Lndry

Living Rm
17-8x14-11

Sloped Clg.

Foyer

Patio

First Floor
880 sq. ft.

Bath

Bedroom 1
11-10x14-2

Open

Second Floor
225 sq. ft.

Alternate Cedar Shake Exterior

Images provided by designer/architect

Plan #F07-011D-0447

Dimensions:	26' W x 42' D
Heated Sq. Ft.:	1,076
Bedrooms: 2	**Bathrooms:** 2½
Exterior Walls:	2" x 6"

Foundation: Crawl space or slab standard; basement available for an additional fee

See index for more information

Features

- The deep covered front porch and side covered porch offer outdoor living space that's beyond compare
- The combination dining/living area has a corner fireplace for added coziness and access to the small covered porch on the right side of the home
- The U-shaped kitchen has a handy pass-through to the dining/living area, plenty of counter space, an oversized closet for a washer and a dryer, and a convenient half bath
- The second floor consists of two vaulted bedrooms, each with their own full bath

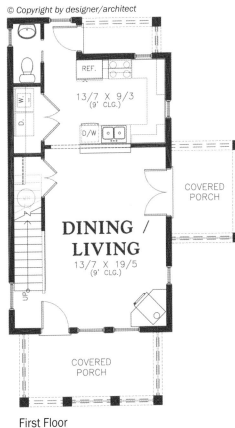

© Copyright by designer/architect

First Floor
572 sq. ft.

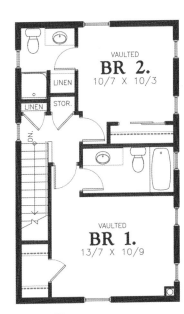

Second Floor
504 sq. ft.

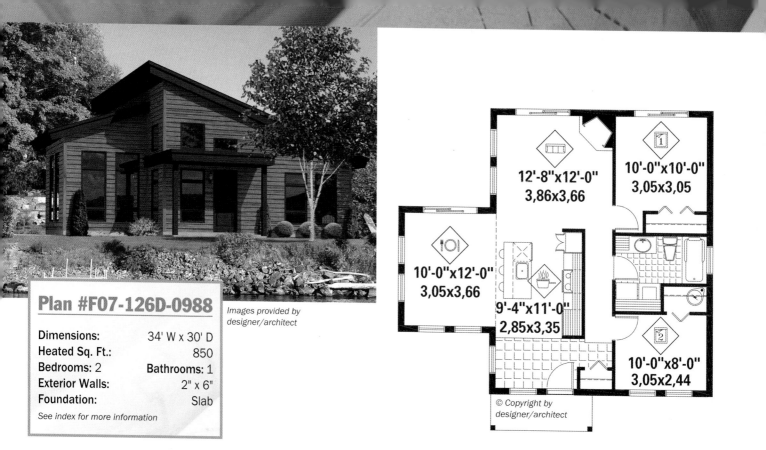

Plan #F07-126D-0988

Dimensions:	34' W x 30' D
Heated Sq. Ft.:	850
Bedrooms: 2	Bathrooms: 1
Exterior Walls:	2" x 6"
Foundation:	Slab

See index for more information

Images provided by designer/architect

12'-8"x12'-0"
3,86x3,66

10'-0"x10'-0"
3,05x3,05

10'-0"x12'-0"
3,05x3,66

9'-4"x11'-0"
2,85x3,35

10'-0"x8'-0"
3,05x2,44

© Copyright by designer/architect

Plan #F07-126D-1152

Dimensions:	38' W x 18' D
Heated Sq. Ft.:	599
Bedrooms: 1	Bathrooms: 1
Exterior Walls:	2" x 6"
Foundation:	Piers

See index for more information

Images provided by designer/architect

© Copyright by designer/architect

8'-0"x12'-6"
2,44x3,81

18'-0"x11'-8"
5,49x3,56

10'-6"x10'-2"
3,20x3,10

19'-0"x8'-0"
5,79x2,44

Plan #F07-051D-0847

Dimensions:	40' W x 46' D
Heated Sq. Ft.:	1,047
Bedrooms: 2	Bathrooms: 1
Exterior Walls:	2" x 6"

Foundation: Basement standard; slab or crawl space available for an additional fee

See index for more information

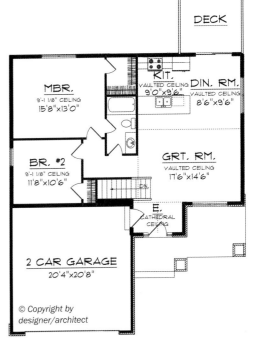

Images provided by designer/architect

DECK

MBR.
9'-1 1/8" CEILING
15'8"x13'0"

KIT.
VAULTED CEILING
9'0"x9'6"

DIN. RM.
VAULTED CEILING
8'6"x9'6"

BR. #2
9'-1 1/8" CEILING
11'8"x10'6"

GRT. RM.
VAULTED CEILING
17'6"x14'6"

CATHEDRAL CEILING

2 CAR GARAGE
20'4"x20'8"

Plan #F07-144D-0016

Images provided by designer/architect

Dimensions:	25'6" W x 38' D
Heated Sq. Ft.:	967
Bedrooms: 3	Bathrooms: 2
Exterior Walls:	2" x 6"
Foundation:	Crawl space

See index for more information

BED - 2
10'0 X 10'0
DOUBLE
DRESSER

W.I.C.

M. BEDROOM
10'4 X 10'11
QUEEN
DRESSER

DRESSER
LINEN

39" Hall

M. BATH
4'11 X 8'1

BATH
4'11 X 8'1

BED - 3
10'0 X 10'0
DOUBLE

W/D

H/W

FIRE PLACE

BUILT-IN

BUILT-IN

LIVING RM.
15'1 X 13'11

KITCHEN
9'3 X 14'7

30 FR

DW

OPEN DECK
16 X 8

Plan #F07-123D-0173

Dimensions:	37' W x 55' D
Heated Sq. Ft.:	1,192
Bonus Sq. Ft.:	839
Bedrooms: 2	**Bathrooms:** 2

Foundation: Basement standard; slab, crawl space or walk-out basement available for an additional fee

See index for more information

Features

- This charming country style home has a great split bedroom floor plan with an open layout in between the private bedrooms, perfect for entertaining
- Enter from the 2-car garage into a mud room and find a laundry room to the right for convenience
- The open kitchen enjoys an island with dining space and additional dining space nearby in the dining area with deck views
- The family room has a cozy fireplace as a focal point
- The optional lower level has an additional 839 square feet of living area
- 2-car front entry garage

First Floor
1,192 sq. ft.

© Copyright by designer/architect

Optional
Lower Level
839 sq. ft.

Images provided by designer/architect

Plan #F07-156D-0014

Dimensions:	25' W x 28' D
Heated Sq. Ft.:	551
Bedrooms: 1	Bathrooms: 1
Foundation:	Slab

See index for more information

Features

- This charming cottage would make an ideal in-law suite or guest house
- An entire wall of windows fills the interior with plenty of natural light
- The kitchen is completely open to the living area
- Tucked in the back of the house is a comfortable bedroom and a full bath with space for a stackable washer and dryer

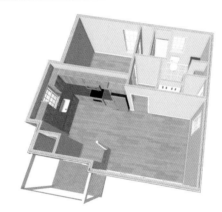

Images provided by designer/architect

© Copyright by
designer/architect

Plan #F07-156D-0003

Dimensions: 25'6" W x 30' D
Heated Sq. Ft.: 664
Bedrooms: 1   **Bathrooms:** 1
Foundation: Slab standard; crawl space available for an additional fee

See index for more information

Images provided by designer/architect

© Copyright by designer/architect

Plan #F07-155D-0100

Dimensions: 24' W x 56'6" D
Heated Sq. Ft.: 970
Bedrooms: 3   **Bathrooms:** 1
Foundation: Crawl space or slab, please specify when ordering

See index for more information

Images provided by designer/architect

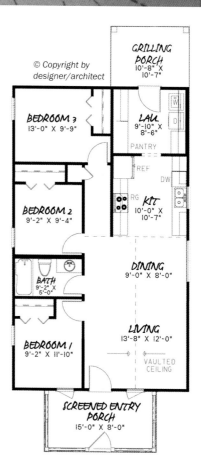

© Copyright by designer/architect

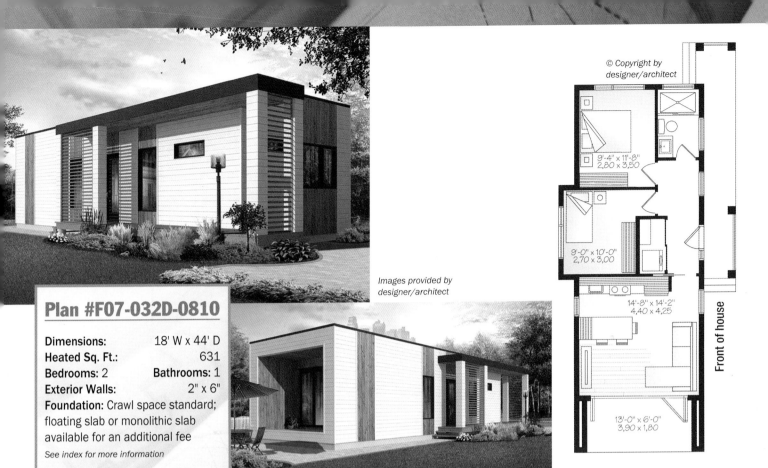

Images provided by designer/architect

9'-4" x 11'-8"
2,80 x 3,50

9'-0" x 10'-0"
2,70 x 3,00

14'-8" x 14'-2"
4,40 x 4,25

Front of house

13'-0" x 6'-0"
3,90 x 1,80

Plan #F07-032D-0810

Dimensions: 18' W x 44' D
Heated Sq. Ft.: 631
Bedrooms: 2   **Bathrooms:** 1
Exterior Walls: 2" x 6"
Foundation: Crawl space standard; floating slab or monolithic slab available for an additional fee

See index for more information

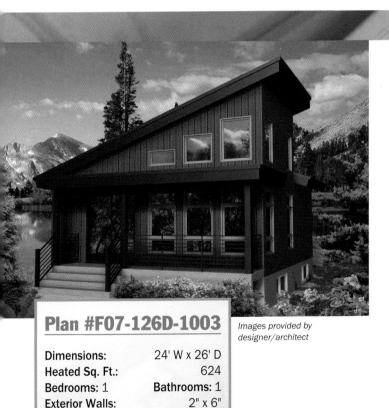

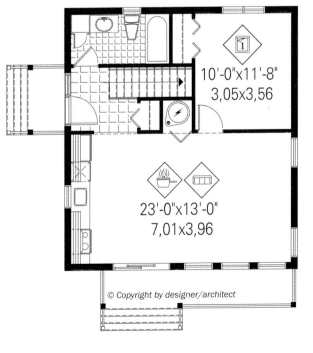

Images provided by designer/architect

Plan #F07-126D-1003

Dimensions: 24' W x 26' D
Heated Sq. Ft.: 624
Bedrooms: 1   **Bathrooms:** 1
Exterior Walls: 2" x 6"
Foundation: Basement

See index for more information

10'-0"x11'-8"
3,05x3,56

23'-0"x13'-0"
7,01x3,96

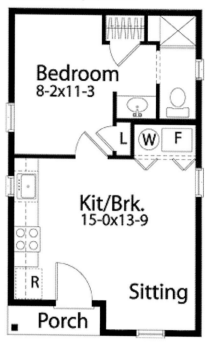

Bedroom
8-2x11-3

Kit/Brk.
15-0x13-9

R

Sitting

■ **Porch**

Plan #F07-058D-0228

Images provided by designer/architect

Dimensions:	16' W x 26'4" D
Heated Sq. Ft.:	403
Bedrooms: 1	Bathrooms: 1
Exterior Walls:	2" x 6"
Foundation:	Slab

See index for more information

VAULTED
LIVING
13/0 X 11/4

FOLD-DN TABLE

BUILT-IN

WARDROBE CAB.

PAN

U.C.

REF

D   W

Images provided by designer/architect

Plan #F07-012D-7507

Dimensions:	14' W x 23' D
Heated Sq. Ft.:	322
Bedrooms: 1	Bathrooms: 1
Exterior Walls:	2" x 6"
Foundation:	Crawl space or slab standard; basement available for an additional fee

See index for more information

Plan #F07-084D-0051

Images provided by designer/architect

Dimensions:	51' W x 28' D
Heated Sq. Ft.:	815
Bedrooms: 1	**Bathrooms:** 1

Foundation: Slab standard; crawl space available for an additional fee

See index for more information

Patio

Bath 11-10x7-5 9' ceiling

Laun. 7-0x7-5 9' ceiling

Kitchen/ Dining 11-10x10-0 9' ceiling

Carport 12-0x17-10 9' ceiling

Storage 5-6x16-4

Closet 7-0x7-8

Bedroom 11-10x15-7 9' ceiling

Living 11-10x13-0 9' ceiling

Foyer 7-0x7-7

Porch

© Copyright by designer/architect

Plan #F07-013D-0248

Dimensions:	24' W x 36' D
Heated Sq. Ft.:	1,137
Bedrooms: 1	**Bathrooms:** 2

Foundation: Crawl space standard; basement or slab available for an additional fee

See index for more information

Second Floor
426 sq. ft.

MECH.

8' HIGH CEILINGS

5' HIGH KNEE WALL   5' HIGH KNEE WALL

LOFT / OFFICE
12'-0" x 23'-2"

Images provided by designer/architect

DN

DECK
23'-5" x 9'-8"

LAUNDRY

KITCHEN
9'-9" x 8'-0"

STOR./ MECH.   PANTRY

UP

9' HIGH CEILINGS

FLEX ROOM
23'-2" x 17'-1"

PORCH
23'-2" x 5'-7"

DN

First Floor
711 sq. ft.

© Copyright by designer/architect

Plan #F07-144D-0024

Dimensions:	32' W x 32' D
Heated Sq. Ft.:	1,024
Bedrooms: 1	**Bathrooms:** 1½
Exterior Walls:	2" x 6"

Foundation: Basement or daylight basement standard; crawl space, slab or walk-out basement available for an additional fee

See index for more information

Features

- This compact Craftsman Modern Farmhouse style home design has an efficiently designed floor plan that utilizes barns and pocket style doors that minimize wasted space
- Step into an open living room that has a kitchen attached that features a large breakfast bar
- To the left is a side entry with a powder room nearby
- A huge walk-in pantry is centrally located
- The laundry room has a large closet for extra storage
- The master bedroom enjoys its own private bath with a roll-in shower, ideal for someone with a disability
- A huge walk-in closet keeps the homeowner organized

© Copyright by designer/architect

Images provided by designer/architect

Plan #F07-032D-0809

Dimensions:	30' W x 21' D
Heated Sq. Ft.:	924
Bedrooms: 2	Bathrooms: 2
Exterior Walls:	2" x 6"

Foundation: Floating slab standard; crawl space or monolithic slab available for an additional fee

See index for more information

Features

- Step into the main entrance and discover a vestibule for removing your coat before entering the home
- The open kitchen features enough room for a table that seats four people
- Sliding glass doors lead to the backyard and offer views while dining
- The second floor offers a spacious private bedroom with an open bath layout and sliding glass doors to the huge terrace

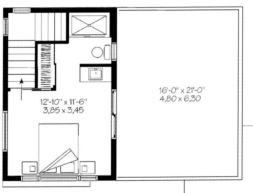

12'-10" x 11'-6"
3,85 x 3,45

16'-0" x 21'-0"
4,80 x 6,30

Second Floor
294 sq. ft.

Images provided by designer/architect

13'-4" x 9'-0"
4,00 x 2,70

9'-8" x 10'-8"
2,90 x 3,20

11'-10" x 10'-8"
3,55 x 3,20

First Floor
630 sq. ft.

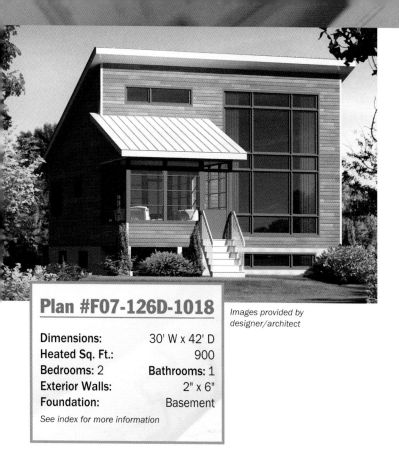

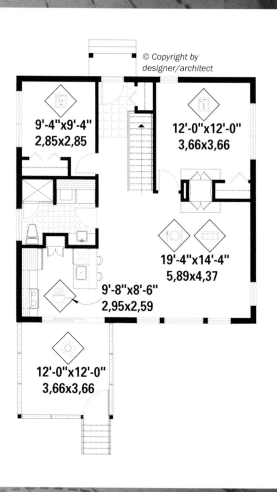

© Copyright by
designer/architect

9'-4"x9'-4"
2,85x2,85

12'-0"x12'-0"
3,66x3,66

19'-4"x14'-4"
5,89x4,37

9'-8"x8'-6"
2,95x2,59

12'-0"x12'-0"
3,66x3,66

Plan #F07-126D-1018

Images provided by
designer/architect

Dimensions:	30' W x 42' D
Heated Sq. Ft.:	900
Bedrooms: 2	Bathrooms: 1
Exterior Walls:	2" x 6"
Foundation:	Basement

See index for more information

15'-0" x 13'-6"
4,50 x 4,05

9'-0" x 11'-0"
2,70 x 3,30

11'-3" x 11'-0"
3,37 x 3,30

12'-8" x 11'-5"
3,80 x 3,42

© Copyright by designer/architect

Plan #F07-032D-0833

Images provided by
designer/architect

Dimensions:	40'8" W x 26' D
Heated Sq. Ft.:	1,007
Bedrooms: 2	Bathrooms: 1
Exterior Walls:	2" x 6"

Foundation: Basement standard;
crawl space, floating slab or monolithic slab available for an additional fee

See index for more information

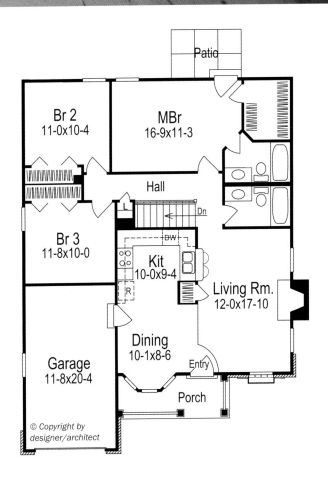

Plan #F07-007D-0110

Dimensions:	37'4" W x 46'8" D
Heated Sq. Ft.:	1,169
Bedrooms: 3	**Bathrooms:** 2
Foundation:	Basement

See index for more information

Images provided by designer/architect

© Copyright by designer/architect

Plan #F07-013D-0257

Dimensions:	40'3" W x 42'4" D
Heated Sq. Ft.:	1,059
Bedrooms: 2	**Bathrooms:** 1½

Foundation: Basement standard; crawl space or slab available for an additional fee

See index for more information

Images provided by designer/architect

© Copyright by designer/architect

Plan #F07-028D-0108

Dimensions:	33' W x 40' D
Heated Sq. Ft.:	890
Bedrooms: 2	Bathrooms: 1
Exterior Walls:	2" x 6"

Foundation: Crawl space or slab, please specify when ordering

See index for more information

Images provided by designer/architect

Features

- If you're dreaming of your very own modern farmhouse, then look no further - this home has the curb appeal you're looking for

- Step inside from the covered front porch and discover a great room with a fireplace

- A galley-style kitchen is tucked between the great room and kitchen/dining space, perfect when entertaining

- The two bedrooms are located away from the main living areas for privacy

- There is a rear covered porch that is ideal for enjoying the outdoors without direct sunlight

© Copyright by designer/architect

PORCH 8'-0" DEEP

KITCHEN/ DINING 12-0 X 16-6

BEDROOM 2 14-0 X 10-0

BATH 7-0 X 10-0

GREAT ROOM 20-0 X 14-0

BEDROOM 1 13-0 X 10-0

VENTLESS GAS FIREPLACE

PORCH 8'-0" DEEP

Plan #F07-013D-0243

Dimensions:	28' W x 26' D
Heated Sq. Ft.:	514
Bedrooms: 1	Bathrooms: 1
Exterior Walls:	2" x 6"

Foundation: Slab standard; basement or crawl space available for an additional fee

See index for more information

Images provided by designer/architect

Features

- This charming Craftsman cottage offers two covered porches for plenty of outdoor living space
- Enter the living area and discover a large fireplace centered between the living area and kitchen for added coziness
- The bedroom is a roomy size and has a large walk-in closet and direct access to the full bath for convenience
- Sliding glass doors in the kitchen lead to the back covered porch

© Copyright by designer/architect

COVERED PORCH
27'-4" X 7'-7"

EAT-IN KITCHEN
13' X 17'

PANTRY

BATH
8'-3" X 5'-0"

CLOSET
5'-0" X 5'-0"

LIVING

BEDROOM
13'-8" X 11'-8"

COVERED PORCH
14'-0" X 6'-0"

Plan #F07-159D-0017

Dimensions:	44' W x 48' D
Heated Sq. Ft.:	1,200
Bonus Sq. Ft.:	1,284
Bedrooms: 2	Bathrooms: 2
Exterior Walls:	2" x 6"

Foundation: Walk-out basement or basement, please specify when ordering

See index for more information

Images provided by designer/architect

Optional Second Floor
420 sq. ft.

ATTIC STORAGE 13' x 11'

BED 3 17'-3" x 14'

DECK 12' x 12'

Optional Lower Level
864 sq. ft.

FAMILY ROOM 15'-5" x 17'
BED 5 / OFFICE 10'-3" x 11'-5"
BED 4 10'-6" x 12'-9"
STORAGE 16'-10" x 9'-3"
TOY ROOM 11'-9" x 13'-3"

First Floor
1,200 sq. ft.

BED 1 12'-6" x 14'
W.I.C. 8'-1" x 6'-4"
GREAT ROOM
DINING 21' x 15'-2"
FOYER
BED 2 10'-1" x 11'-5"
KITCHEN 10' x 10'
PORCH
2-CAR GARAGE 23'-4" x 21'-8"

© Copyright by designer/architect

Plan #F07-011D-0316

Dimensions:	30' W x 48' D
Heated Sq. Ft.:	960
Bedrooms: 1	Bathrooms: 1
Exterior Walls:	2" x 6"

Foundation: Crawl space or slab standard; basement available for an additional fee

See index for more information

Images provided by designer/architect

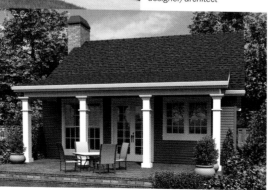

PORCH 26/0 X 8/0
© Copyright by designer/architect
11/0 X 9/0 (9' CLG.)
REF PAN
W/D
GREAT RM. 16/8 X 23/8 (9' CLG.)
LIN
BR. 11/0 X 13/0 (9' CLG.)
SHLVS
BUILT-IN GUEST BED
PORCH 26/0 X 8/0

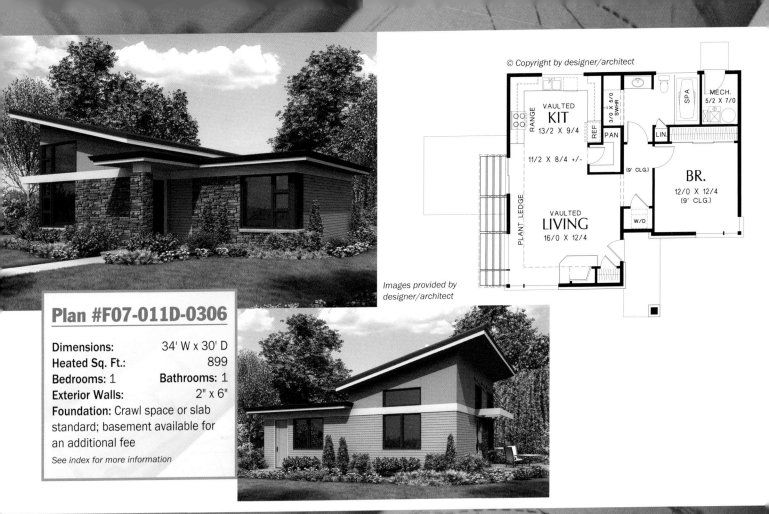

Images provided by
designer/architect

Plan #F07-011D-0306

Dimensions:	34' W x 30' D
Heated Sq. Ft.:	899
Bedrooms: 1	Bathrooms: 1
Exterior Walls:	2" x 6"

Foundation: Crawl space or slab
standard; basement available for
an additional fee

See index for more information

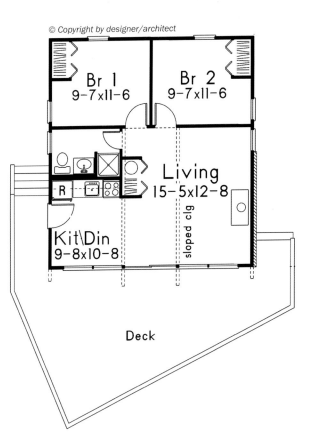

Plan #F07-008D-0133

Images provided by
designer/architect

Dimensions:	26' W x 24' D
Heated Sq. Ft.:	624
Bedrooms: 2	Bathrooms: 1
Foundation:	Pier

See index for more information

Plan #F07-032D-0813

Images provided by designer/architect

Dimensions: 26' W x 26' D
Heated Sq. Ft.: 686
Bedrooms: 2   **Bathrooms:** 1
Exterior Walls: 2" x 6"
Foundation: Monolithic slab standard; crawl space or floating slab available for an additional fee
See index for more information

Features

- If you're looking for a small, modern dwelling, or would love to escape city life but still have all of the amenities, then this home is for you

- Soaring ceilings overhead keeps the interior bright and cheerful

- The openness promotes fun and easy entertaining when friends are over

- You will be thankful for the large covered porch for those days when there's a mist in the air

- This small home is far from boring and has everything you want for comfortable living for today's lifestyle

9' - 0" x 10' - 0"

9' - 11" x 10' - 0"

25' - 0" x 11' - 0"

© Copyright by designer/architect

Plan #F07-123D-0264

Dimensions:	34'8" W x 32' D
Heated Sq. Ft.:	733
Bedrooms: 1	**Bathrooms:** 1

Foundation: Slab standard, crawl space, basement or walk-out basement available for an additional fee

See index for more information

Images provided by designer/architect

Features

- The covered front porch of this charming bungalow style cottage offers a great place outdoors to relax and unwind in the shade
- This stylish little cottage enjoys a kitchen island overlooking the great room featuring a cozy fireplace
- The bedroom has a roomy walk-in closet and is right across the hall from a full bath
- An oversized laundry room is a memorable feature and provides extra space for storage and handling chores

© Copyright by designer/architect

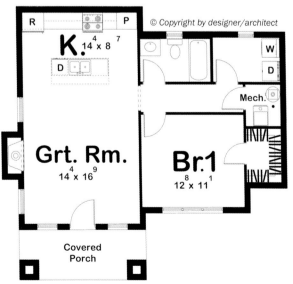

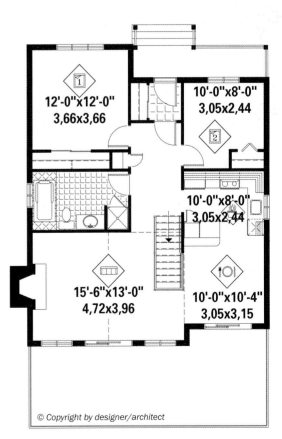

Plan #F07-126D-0984

Images provided by designer/architect

Dimensions:	30' W x 36' D
Heated Sq. Ft.:	992
Bedrooms: 2	Bathrooms: 1
Exterior Walls:	2" x 6"
Foundation:	Basement

See index for more information

Features

- The spacious vaulted great room enjoys a series of arched windows across one wall allowing views of the surroundings to easily be seen, while also warming the interior with sunlight

- The small, yet efficient kitchen handles meals perfectly and includes nearby dining table space and an eating bar

- Two bedrooms share a full bath that features both a spa style tub and a walk-in shower

12'-0"x12'-0"
3,66x3,66

10'-0"x8'-0"
3,05x2,44

10'-0"x8'-0"
3,05x2,44

15'-6"x13'-0"
4,72x3,96

10'-0"x10'-4"
3,05x3,15

© Copyright by designer/architect

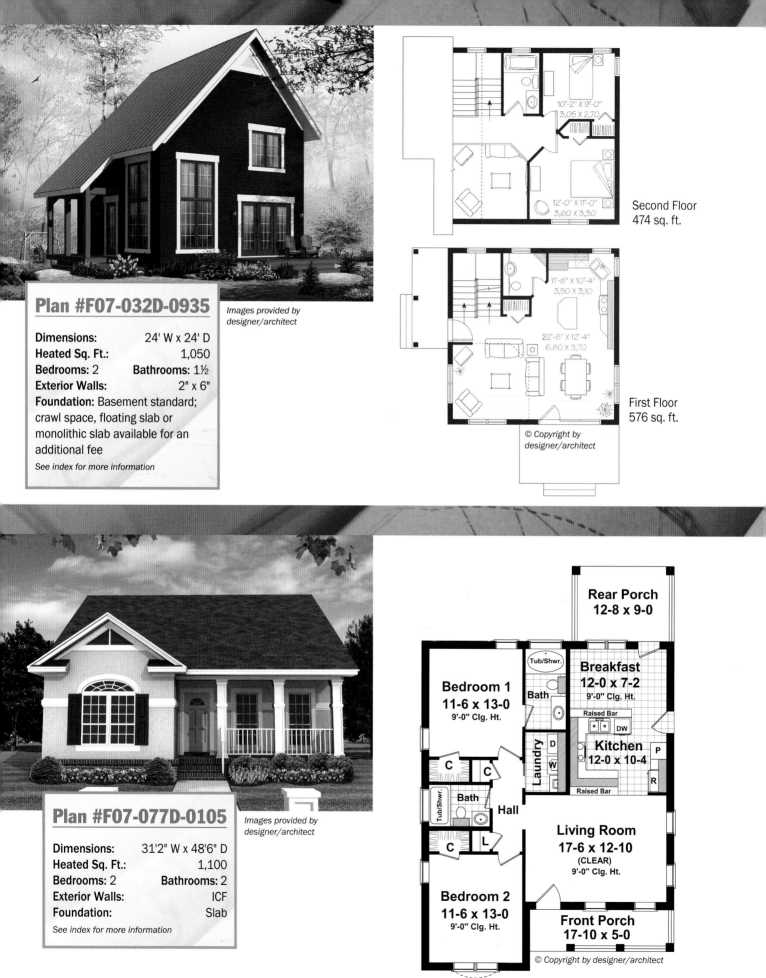

Plan #F07-032D-0935

Images provided by designer/architect

Dimensions: 24' W x 24' D
Heated Sq. Ft.: 1,050
Bedrooms: 2   **Bathrooms:** 1½
Exterior Walls: 2" x 6"
Foundation: Basement standard; crawl space, floating slab or monolithic slab available for an additional fee

See index for more information

Second Floor
474 sq. ft.

First Floor
576 sq. ft.

10'-2" X 9'-0"
3,05 X 2,70

12'-0" X 11'-0"
3,60 X 3,30

11'-8" X 10'-4"
3,50 X 3,10

22'-8" X 12'-4"
6,80 X 3,70

© Copyright by designer/architect

Plan #F07-077D-0105

Images provided by designer/architect

Dimensions: 31'2" W x 48'6" D
Heated Sq. Ft.: 1,100
Bedrooms: 2   **Bathrooms:** 2
Exterior Walls: ICF
Foundation: Slab

See index for more information

Rear Porch
12-8 x 9-0

Bedroom 1
11-6 x 13-0
9'-0" Clg. Ht.

Tub/Shwr.

Bath

Breakfast
12-0 x 7-2
9'-0" Clg. Ht.

Raised Bar

Kitchen
12-0 x 10-4

DW

Laundry

D

W

P

R

Raised Bar

Bath

Tub/Shwr.

C

C

Hall

L

Living Room
17-6 x 12-10
(CLEAR)
9'-0" Clg. Ht.

Bedroom 2
11-6 x 13-0
9'-0" Clg. Ht.

Front Porch
17-10 x 5-0

© Copyright by designer/architect

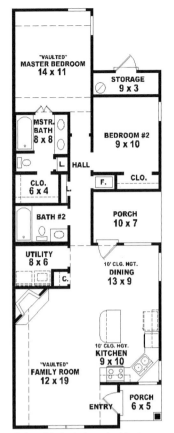

© Copyright by designer/architect

Plan #F07-087D-0002

Dimensions:	23' W x 59' D
Heated Sq. Ft.:	1,057
Bedrooms: 2	Bathrooms: 2
Foundation:	Slab

See index for more information

Images provided by designer/architect

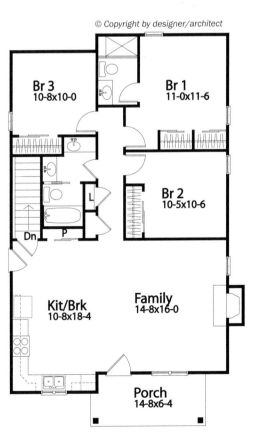

© Copyright by designer/architect

Plan #F07-058D-0221

Dimensions:	30' W x 48' D
Heated Sq. Ft.:	1,181
Bedrooms: 3	Bathrooms: 2
Foundation:	Basement

See index for more information

Images provided by designer/architect

Plan #F07-041D-0006

Images provided by designer/architect

Dimensions:	36' W x 35'8" D
Heated Sq. Ft.:	1,189
Bedrooms: 3	**Bathrooms:** 2½
Foundation:	Basement

See index for more information

Features

- The vaulted great room is spacious and features windows allowing views of the front yard and backyard
- All of the bedrooms are located on the second floor for added privacy
- The dining room and kitchen both have views of the patio
- The convenient half bath is located near the kitchen
- The vaulted master bedroom has a private bath
- 2-car front entry garage

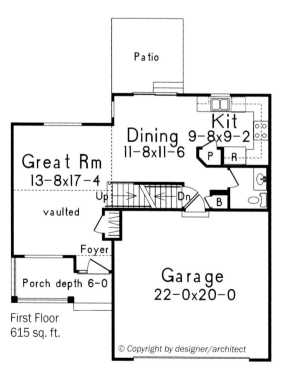

Patio

Kit
Dining 9-8x9-2
11-8x11-6
P   R

Great Rm
13-8x17-4
Up   Dn   B
vaulted

Foyer

Porch depth 6-0

Garage
22-0x20-0

First Floor
615 sq. ft.

© Copyright by designer/architect

Br 2   Br 3
10-6x9-0   10-6x10-0

L
Dn

MBr
12-8x11-3
vaulted

Second Floor
574 sq. ft.

Plan #F07-032D-0835

Dimensions:	40' W x 30' D
Heated Sq. Ft.:	1,146
Bedrooms: 2	Bathrooms: 1
Exterior Walls:	2" x 6"

Foundation: Basement standard; floating slab available for an additional fee

See index for more information

Images provided by designer/architect

Features

- Rustic and Contemporary collide to create a modern-day vacation retreat that definitely stands out
- Take a couple of stairs up to the open living area that perfectly combines with the dining area and kitchen to create a home that maximizes all of its square footage perfectly
- Two sizable bedrooms provide plenty of comfort and are located near the full bath featuring a spa style tub, a walk-in shower and the washer and dryer
- Sliding glass doors lead to the outdoors from the kitchen and dining area

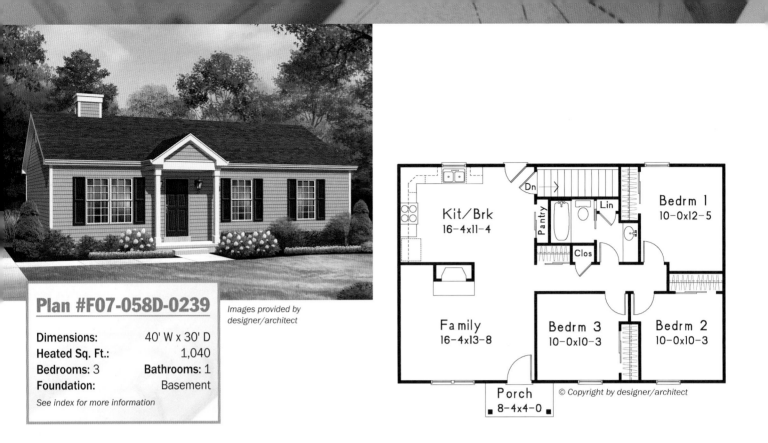

Plan #F07-058D-0239

Images provided by designer/architect

Dimensions:	40' W x 30' D
Heated Sq. Ft.:	1,040
Bedrooms: 3	Bathrooms: 1
Foundation:	Basement

See index for more information

Kit/Brk
16-4x11-4

Pantry

Lin

Bedrm 1
10-0x12-5

Clos

Family
16-4x13-8

Bedrm 3
10-0x10-3

Bedrm 2
10-0x10-3

Porch
8-4x4-0

© Copyright by designer/architect

Plan #F07-026D-1667

Images provided by designer/architect

Dimensions:	30' W x 50'4" D
Heated Sq. Ft.:	1,091
Bedrooms: 2	Bathrooms: 2

Foundation: Basement standard; crawl space, slab or walk-out basement available for an additional fee

See index for more information

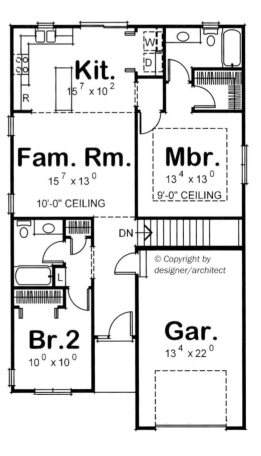

Kit.
15⁷ x 10²

Fam. Rm.
15⁷ x 13⁰
10'-0" CEILING

Mbr.
13⁴ x 13⁰
9'-0" CEILING

DN

© Copyright by designer/architect

Br.2
10⁰ x 10⁰

Gar.
13⁴ x 22⁰

Plan #F07-032D-0357

Dimensions:	36' W x 24' D
Heated Sq. Ft.:	874
Bedrooms: 2	Bathrooms: 1
Exterior Walls:	2" x 6"

Foundation: Crawl space standard; floating slab or monolithic slab available for an additional fee

See index for more information

Images provided by designer/architect

FRONT PORCH

BEDROOM 1
10-0 X 11-2

BATH ROOM

FOYER

BEDROOM 2
10-2 X 8-0

FAMILY ROOM
18-6 X 11-2

KITCHEN
16-2 X 11-2

© Copyright by designer/architect

TERRACE

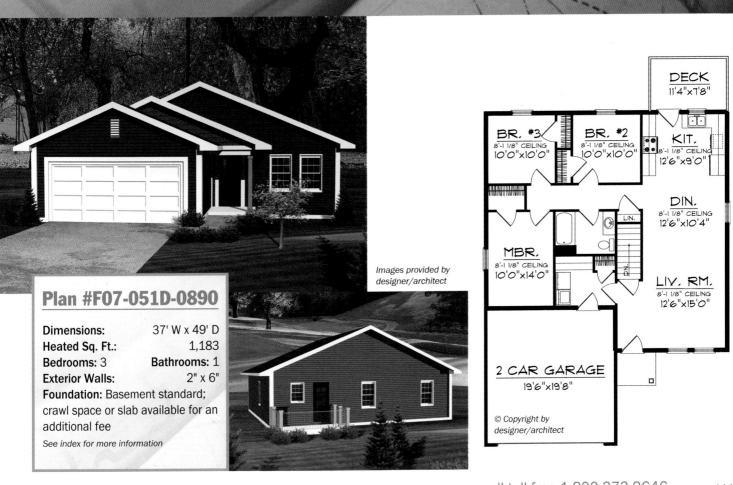

Plan #F07-051D-0890

Dimensions:	37' W x 49' D
Heated Sq. Ft.:	1,183
Bedrooms: 3	Bathrooms: 1
Exterior Walls:	2" x 6"

Foundation: Basement standard; crawl space or slab available for an additional fee

See index for more information

Images provided by designer/architect

DECK
11'4"x7'8"

BR. #3
8'-1 1/8" CEILING
10'0"x10'0"

BR. #2
8'-1 1/8" CEILING
10'0"x10'0"

KIT.
8'-1 1/8" CEILING
12'6"x9'0"

DIN.
8'-1 1/8" CEILING
12'6"x10'4"

MBR.
8'-1 1/8" CEILING
10'0"x14'0"

LIN.

LIV. RM.
8'-1 1/8" CEILING
12'6"x15'0"

2 CAR GARAGE
19'6"x19'8"

© Copyright by designer/architect

Plan #F07-032D-0403

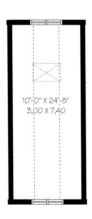

Dimensions: 60' W x 30' D
Heated Sq. Ft.: 1,073
Bonus Sq. Ft.: 281
Bedrooms: 2   **Bathrooms:** 1
Exterior Walls: 2" x 6"
Foundation: Basement standard; crawl space, floating slab or monolithic slab available for an additional fee

See index for more information

Images provided by designer/architect

Features

- The center island in the kitchen creates dining for three and is perfect for serving buffet style meals

- A cozy living room has been achieved by adding a corner fireplace

- Two bedrooms with a fully equipped bath are conveniently located on the first floor

- Extra counter space will be enjoyed in the laundry room

- The optional second floor has an additional 281 square feet of living area

- 2-car front entry garage

10'-0" X 24'-8"
3,00 X 7,40

Optional
Second Floor
281 sq. ft.

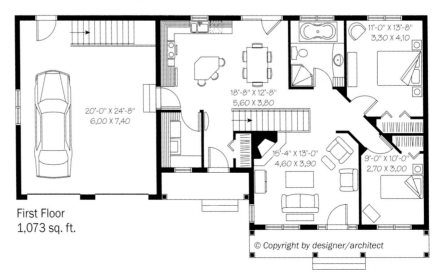

First Floor
1,073 sq. ft.

20'-0" X 24'-8"
6,00 X 7,40

11'-0" X 13'-8"
3,30 X 4,10

18'-8" X 12'-8"
5,60 X 3,80

15'-4" X 13'-0"
4,60 X 3,90

9'-0" X 10'-0"
2,70 X 3,00

© Copyright by designer/architect

Right and Rear View

Images provided by designer/architect

Front and Right View

Plan #F07-032D-0588

Dimensions:	22' W x 26'4" D
Heated Sq. Ft.:	1,077
Bedrooms: 3	**Bathrooms:** 1
Exterior Walls:	2" x 6"

Foundation: Basement standard; crawl space, floating slab or monolithic slab available for an additional fee

See index for more information

Features

- Stylish country farmhouse enjoys a massive amount of outdoor living space that wraps around three sides of the home

- The open concept floor plan greets you as you enter the front door and offers an spacious feeling to the first floor

- The first floor has an open L-shaped kitchen with enough space for a dining table

- The second floor enjoys three bedrooms all in close proximity to one another

11'-8" X 11'-0"
3,50 X 3,30

15'-4" 14'-0"
4,60 X 4,20

© Copyright by designer/architect

First Floor
550 sq. ft.

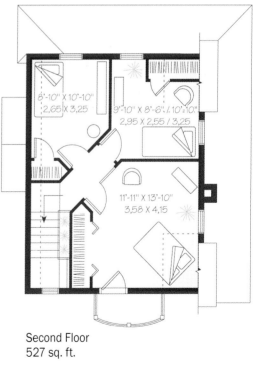

8'-10" X 10'-10"
2,65 X 3,25

9'-10" X 8'-6" /. 10'-10"
2,95 X 2,55 / 3,25

11'-11" X 13'-10"
3,58 X 4,15

Second Floor
527 sq. ft.

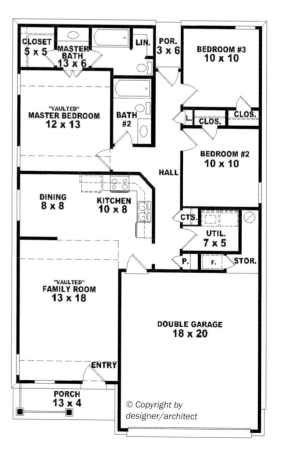

10'-4"x9'-6"
3,15x2,90

10'-0"x9'-0"
3,05x2,74

13'-4"x8'-0"
4,06x2,44

13'-4"x11'-0"
4,06x3,35

11'-0"x11'-0"
3,35x3,35

Plan #F07-126D-0563

Images provided by designer/architect

Dimensions:	28'10" W x 30' D
Heated Sq. Ft.:	821
Bedrooms: 2	Bathrooms: 1
Exterior Walls:	2" x 6"
Foundation:	Basement

See index for more information

Plan #F07-087D-0016

Images provided by designer/architect

Dimensions:	33' W x 53' D
Heated Sq. Ft.:	1,199
Bedrooms: 3	Bathrooms: 2
Foundation:	Slab

See index for more information

CLOSET 5 x 5

MASTER BATH 13 x 6

LIN.

POR. 3 x 6

BEDROOM #3 10 x 10

"VAULTED" MASTER BEDROOM 12 x 13

BATH #2

BEDROOM #2 10 x 10

HALL

DINING 8 x 8

KITCHEN 10 x 8

CTS.

UTIL. 7 x 5

"VAULTED" FAMILY ROOM 13 x 18

DOUBLE GARAGE 18 x 20

ENTRY

PORCH 13 x 4

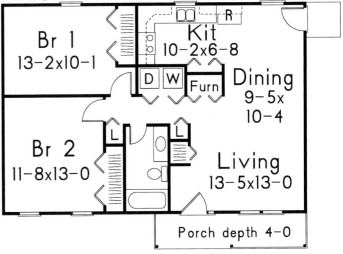

Br 1
13-2x10-1

Kit
10-2x6-8

R

D W Furn

Dining
9-5x
10-4

Br 2
11-8x13-0

L L

Living
13-5x13-0

Porch depth 4-0

Plan #F07-001D-0040

Images provided by designer/architect

Dimensions: 36' W x 28' D
Heated Sq. Ft.: 864
Bedrooms: 2   **Bathrooms:** 1
Foundation: Crawl space standard; basement or slab available for an additional fee

See index for more information

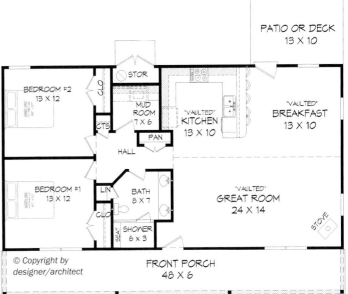

PATIO OR DECK
13 X 10

BEDROOM #2
13 X 12

STOR

CLO

MUD ROOM
7 X 6

PAN

"VAULTED"
KITCHEN
13 X 10

"VAULTED"
BREAKFAST
13 X 10

HALL

BEDROOM #1
13 X 12

LIN

BATH
8 X 7

"VAULTED"
GREAT ROOM
24 X 14

CLO

SEAT

SHOWER
6 X 3

STOVE

FRONT PORCH
48 X 6

Plan #F07-141D-0232

Images provided by designer/architect

Dimensions: 48' W x 25' D
Heated Sq. Ft.: 1,185
Bedrooms: 2   **Bathrooms:** 1
Foundation: Slab or crawl space, please specify when ordering

See index for more information

Plan #F07-032D-0963

Dimensions:	34' W x 38' D
Heated Sq. Ft.:	1,178
Bonus Sq. Ft.:	1,178
Bedrooms: 1	**Bathrooms:** 1
Exterior Walls:	2" x 6"

Foundation: Basement standard; crawl space, floating slab or monolithic slab available for an additional fee

See index for more information

Images provided by designer/architect

Features

- Step into this modern one-story and immediately enjoy the light, airy interior with an open floor plan
- The great room, dining and kitchen are designed to merge together and create one large space for relaxing or entertaining
- The spacious bedroom is near an oversized bath with a free-standing tub as well as a large walk-in shower
- A compact office is ideal when working from home
- The optional lower level has an additional 1,178 square feet of living area

© Copyright by designer/architect

Optional Lower Level
1,178 sq. ft.

First Floor
1,178 sq. ft.

Plan #F07-032D-0754

Dimensions:	42' W x 40' D
Heated Sq. Ft.:	1,054
Bonus Sq. Ft.:	300
Bedrooms: 1	**Bathrooms: 1**
Exterior Walls:	2" x 6"

Foundation: Basement standard; crawl space, floating slab or monolithic slab available for an additional fee

See index for more information

Images provided by designer/architect

BONUS
15'-0" X 16'-0"
4.50 X 4.80

Optional
Second Floor
300 sq. ft.

14'-0" X 13'-0"
4.20 X 3.90

11'-0" X 11'-0"
3.30 X 3.30

15'-0" X 26'-4"
4.50 X 7.90

10'-6" X 11'-0"
3.15 X 3.30

14'-0" X 12'-0"
4.20 X 3.60

First Floor
1,054 sq. ft.

© Copyright by
designer/architect

Plan #F07-069D-0109

Dimensions:	36' W x 41' D
Heated Sq. Ft.:	1,013
Bedrooms: 2	**Bathrooms: 2**

Foundation: Crawl space or slab, please specify when ordering

See index for more information

Images provided by designer/architect

PORCH
25 x 8

© Copyright by designer/architect

BEDRM. 1
15 x 12

UTILITY

CLOS.

D   DW

D.W.   Sink

KIT'N/ DINING
15 x 12

Range

Refrig.

HALL

BATH #1   BATH #2

CLOS.   LIN

HVAC

W/H

LIVING RM.
15 x 14

CLOS.

BEDRM. 2
12 x 12

CLOS.

PORCH
5 x 8

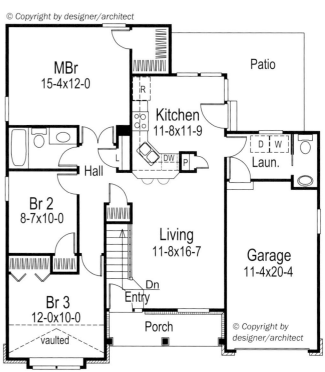

© Copyright by designer/architect

Images provided by designer/architect

MBr
15-4x12-0

Patio

Kitchen
11-8x11-9

Laun.

Hall

Br 2
8-7x10-0

Living
11-8x16-7

Garage
11-4x20-4

Br 3
12-0x10-0

Entry

Dn

vaulted

Porch

© Copyright by designer/architect

Plan #F07-007D-0031

Dimensions:	40'4" W x 42' D
Heated Sq. Ft.:	1,092
Bedrooms: 3	Bathrooms: 1½

Foundation: Basement, standard; crawl space or slab available for an additional fee

See index for more information

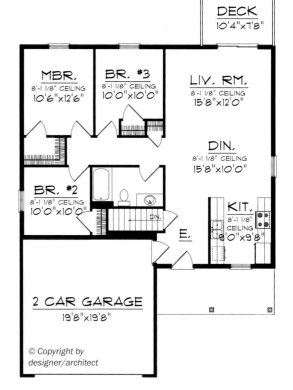

DECK
10'4"x7'8"

MBR.
8'-1 1/8" CEILING
10'6"x12'6"

BR. #3
8'-1 1/8" CEILING
10'0"x10'0"

LIV. RM.
8'-1 1/8" CEILING
15'8"x12'0"

DIN.
8'-1 1/8" CEILING
15'8"x10'0"

BR. #2
8'-1 1/8" CEILING
10'0"x10'0"

DN.

KIT.
8'-1 1/8" CEILING
8'0"x9'8"

E.

2 CAR GARAGE
19'8"x19'8"

© Copyright by designer/architect

Images provided by designer/architect

Plan #F07-051D-0891

Dimensions:	38' W x 48' D
Heated Sq. Ft.:	1,139
Bedrooms: 3	Bathrooms: 1
Exterior Walls:	2" x 6"

Foundation: Basement standard; crawl space or slab available for an additional fee

See index for more information

First Floor
720 sq. ft.

© Copyright by designer/architect

Optional Lower Level
720 sq. ft.

Plan #F07-148D-0047

*Images provided by
designer/architect*

Dimensions:	30' W x 24' D
Heated Sq. Ft.:	720
Bonus Sq. Ft.:	720
Bedrooms: 1	Bathrooms: 1
Exterior Walls:	2" x 6"
Foundation:	Basement

See index for more information

Plan #F07-156D-0004

*Images provided by
designer/architect*

Dimensions:	31' W x 29' D
Heated Sq. Ft.:	600
Bedrooms: 1	Bathrooms: 1

Foundation: Slab standard; crawl
space available for an additional
fee

See index for more information

© Copyright by
designer/architect

PORCH
26/0 X 8/0

© Copyright by designer/architect

11/0 X 9/0
(9' CLG)

REF PAN

W/D

GREAT RM.
16/8 X 23/8
(9' CLG.)

LIN

BR.
11/0 X 13/0
(9' CLG.)

SHLVS

BUILT-IN
GUEST BED

PORCH
26/0 X 8/0

*Images provided by
designer/architect*

Plan #F07-011D-0315

Dimensions:	30' W x 48' D
Heated Sq. Ft.:	960
Bedrooms: 1	Bathrooms: 1
Exterior Walls:	2" x 6"

Foundation: Crawl space or slab standard; basement available for an additional fee

See index for more information

DECK

MBR.
9'-1 1/8" CEILING
11'6"x12'6"

BR. #3
9'-1 1/8" CEILING
10'0"x10'0"

GRT. RM.
9'-1 1/8" CEILING
15'8"x12'8"

DIN. RM.
9'-1 1/8" CEILING
15'8"x8'8"

BR. #2
9'-1 1/8" CEILING
11'0"x10'0"

DN.

KIT.
1/8" CEIL.
9'0"x10'0"

E.

2 CAR GARAGE
20'8"x19'8"

© Copyright by
designer/architect

*Images provided by
designer/architect*

Plan #F07-051D-0849

Dimensions:	39' W x 48' D
Heated Sq. Ft.:	1,170
Bedrooms: 3	Bathrooms: 1
Exterior Walls:	2" x 6"

Foundation: Basement standard; slab or crawl space available for an additional fee

See index for more information

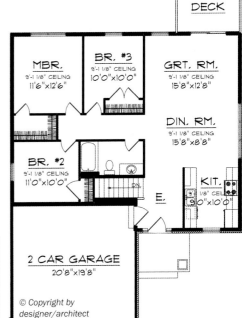

Images provided by designer/architect

Plan #F07-144D-0013

Dimensions:	24' W x 36' D
Heated Sq. Ft.:	624
Bedrooms: 1	Bathrooms: 1
Exterior Walls:	2" x 6"

Foundation: Slab standard; crawl space available for an additional fee

See index for more information

Features

- This charming Craftsman home has a tremendous amount of curb appeal
- The large covered front porch has enough space for relaxing outdoors
- The living room has an open feel to the kitchen
- The kitchen has a large island with snack bar space
- Behind a pocket door is the mud room with closetspace and direct access into a full bath
- The bedroom also offers direct access into the bath

PORCH

COATS

BRM.

BATH
6' 0" x 11' 6"

BEDROOM
10' 4" x 9' 4"

MUDRM
6' 0" x 12' 0"

D

W

TOWELS

LIN.   CLOSET

PANTRY

F

KITCHEN
9' 7" x 13' 0"

SNACK BAR

LIVING ROOM
13' 6" x 13' 0"

DW

PORCH
15' 0" x 6' 0"

© Copyright by designer/architect

Plan #F07-008D-0162

Images provided by designer/architect

Dimensions:	26' W x 36' D
Heated Sq. Ft.:	865
Bedrooms: 2	**Bathrooms:** 1
Foundation:	Pier

See index for more information

Features

- The central living area provides an enormous amount of space for gathering around the fireplace
- The outdoor ladder on the wrap-around deck connects the top deck with the main deck
- The kitchen is bright and cheerful with lots of windows and access to the deck
- Two bedrooms comprise the second floor and both have their own sliding glass doors that lead onto the second floor wrap-around balcony, perfect for unobstructed views

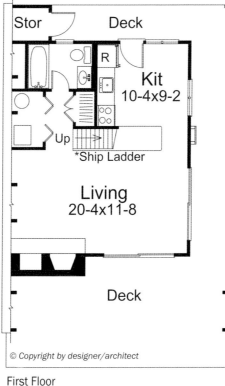

First Floor
495 sq. ft.

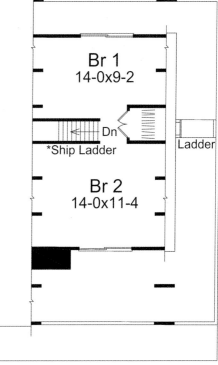

Second Floor
370 sq. ft.

Plan #F07-032D-0561

Dimensions:	27' W x 23'6" D
Heated Sq. Ft.:	1,181
Bedrooms: 2	Bathrooms: 1½
Exterior Walls:	2" x 6"

Foundation: Basement standard; crawl space, floating slab or monolithic slab available for an additional fee

See index for more information

Second Floor
581 sq. ft.

11'-0" X 14'-10"
3,30 X 4,45

11'-0" X 10'-8"
3,30 X 3,20

First Floor
600 sq. ft.

11'-0" X 8'-4"
3,30 X 2,50

11'-0" X 15'-3"
3,30 X 4,58

11'-0" X 11'-6"
3,30 X 3,45

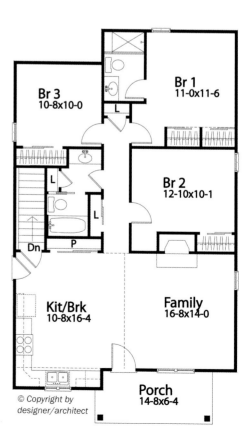

Plan #F07-058D-0223

Dimensions:	28' W x 48' D
Heated Sq. Ft.:	1,149
Bedrooms: 3	Bathrooms: 2
Foundation:	Basement

See index for more information

Br 3
10-8x10-0

Br 1
11-0x11-6

Br 2
12-10x10-1

Dn

Kit/Brk
10-8x16-4

Family
16-8x14-0

Porch
14-8x6-4

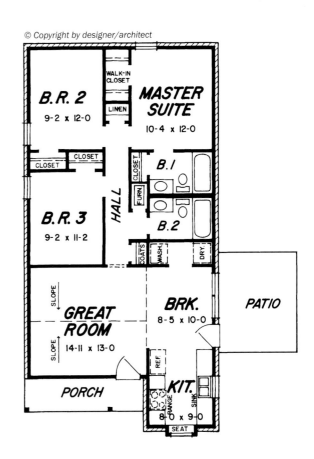

WALK-IN CLOSET

B.R. 2
9-2 x 12-0

MASTER SUITE
10-4 x 12-0

LINEN

CLOSET   CLOSET

HALL

B.R. 3
9-2 x 11-2

CLOSET

FURN

B.I

B.2

COATS   WASH.   DRY.

SLOPE

GREAT ROOM
14-11 x 13-0

SLOPE

BRK.
8-5 x 10-0

PATIO

REF.

PORCH

RANGE

KIT.
8-5 x 9-0

SINK

SEAT

Plan #F07-060D-0013

Images provided by designer/architect

Dimensions:	24'9" W x 46'9" D
Heated Sq. Ft.:	1,053
Bedrooms: 3	**Bathrooms:** 2
Foundation: Crawl space or slab, please specify when ordering	

See index for more information

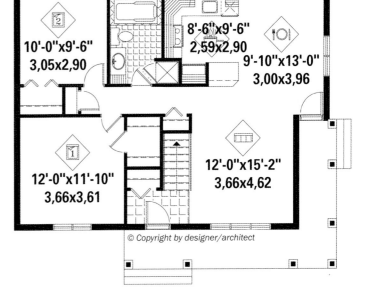

10'-0"x9'-6"
3,05x2,90

8'-6"x9'-6"
2,59x2,90

9'-10"x13'-0"
3,00x3,96

12'-0"x11'-10"
3,66x3,61

12'-0"x15'-2"
3,66x4,62

Plan #F07-126D-0562

Images provided by designer/architect

Dimensions:	36' W x 26' D
Heated Sq. Ft.:	894
Bedrooms: 2	**Bathrooms:** 1
Exterior Walls:	2" x 6"
Foundation:	Basement

See index for more information

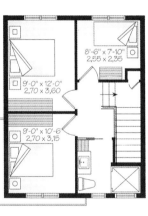

Rear View

Plan #F07-032D-0807

Images provided by designer/architect

Dimensions: 19' W x 24' D
Heated Sq. Ft.: 1,015
Bedrooms: 3   **Bathrooms:** 1½
Exterior Walls: 2" x 6"
Foundation: Floating slab standard;
crawl space or monolithic slab
available for an additional fee
See index for more information

Features

- Contemporary living has never looked so fresh as it does in this three level home with a sleek exterior that would suit many smaller urban lots
- The first floor includes a 1-car garage and laundry room
- The second floor offers an open concept floor plan with enough space for gathering, cooking, and dining and it includes access to two outdoor balconies
- The third floor remains private with three bedrooms and a full bath featuring an oversized walk-in shower
- 1-car front entry garage

Second Floor
394 sq. ft.

Third Floor
456 sq. ft.

First Floor
165 sq. ft.

© Copyright by
designer/architect

Plan #F07-011D-0430

Dimensions:	27' W x 29'6" D
Heated Sq. Ft.:	1,105
Bedrooms: 1	**Bathrooms:** 2
Exterior Walls:	2" x 6"
Foundation:	Basement

See index for more information

Images provided by designer/architect

Features

- The perfect plan for a get-away location that has a sloping lot
- The second floor has a bath with a shower, a huge living area with a cozy fireplace, nearby built-in window seat, and a media center
- The U-shaped kitchen can handle meals with ease
- The third floor is dominated by the master suite, which has a vaulted ceiling with built-in bookcases and a window seat, a vaulted bath with a spa style tub, a separate shower and a huge walk-in closet
- An alcove on the third floor provides space for a stackable washer/dryer for ease with this frequent chore
- 2-car rear entry drive under garage

First Floor
652 sq. ft.

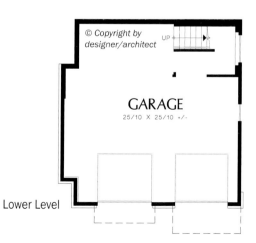

© Copyright by
designer/architect

Lower Level

Second Floor
453 sq. ft.

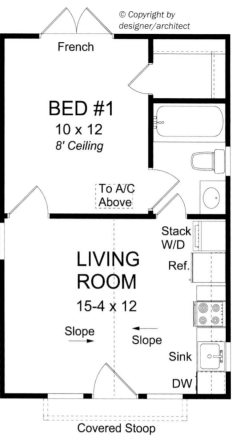

French

BED #1
10 x 12
8' Ceiling

To A/C
Above

Stack
W/D

Ref.

**LIVING
ROOM**
15-4 x 12

Slope

Slope

Sink

DW

Covered Stoop

Plan #F07-130D-0362

*Images provided by
designer/architect*

Dimensions: 16' W x 24'8" D
Heated Sq. Ft.: 395
Bedrooms: 1 **Bathrooms:** 1
Foundation: Slab standard; crawl
space or basement available for an
additional fee
See index for more information

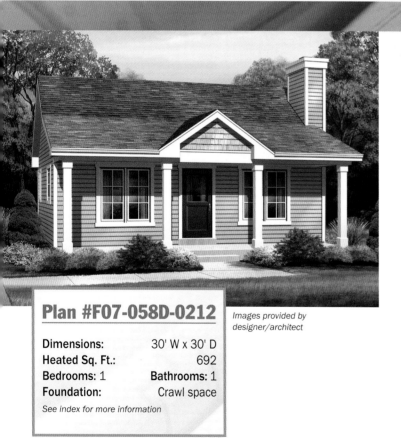

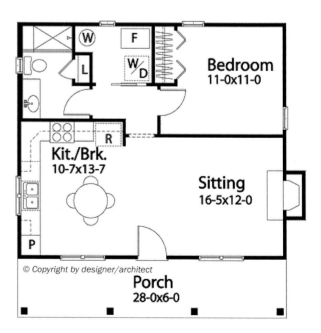

W

F

W/D

L

Bedroom
11-0x11-0

R

Kit./Brk.
10-7x13-7

Sitting
16-5x12-0

P

Porch
28-0x6-0

Plan #F07-058D-0212

*Images provided by
designer/architect*

Dimensions: 30' W x 30' D
Heated Sq. Ft.: 692
Bedrooms: 1 **Bathrooms:** 1
Foundation: Crawl space
See index for more information

First Floor
1,167 sq. ft.

DECK
12-0 X 6-0

DINING ROOM
9-0 X 13-0

LIVING ROOM
13-4 X 14-10

KITCHEN
11-0 X 13-0

BATHROOM
+ LAUNDRY

MASTER BED.
13-6 X 12-0

BED. 2
10-0 X 10-0

FOYER
6-2 X 6-2

FRONT PORCH
20-10 X 4-6

© Copyright by designer/architect

Optional Lower Level
1,167 sq. ft.

Plan #F07-032D-1113

Images provided by designer/architect

Dimensions:	34' W x 34'4" D
Heated Sq. Ft.:	1,167
Bonus Sq. Ft.:	1,167
Bedrooms: 2	Bathrooms: 1
Exterior Walls:	2" x 6"

Foundation: Basement standard; crawl space, floating slab or monolithic slab available for an additional fee

See index for more information

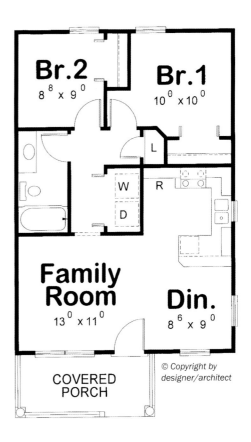

Br.2
8⁸ x 9⁰

Br.1
10⁰ x 10⁰

L

W

D

R

Family Room
13⁰ x 11⁰

Din.
8⁶ x 9⁰

COVERED PORCH

© Copyright by designer/architect

Plan #F07-026D-2053

Images provided by designer/architect

Dimensions:	22' W x 37' D
Heated Sq. Ft.:	682
Bedrooms: 2	Bathrooms: 1
Foundation:	Slab

See index for more information

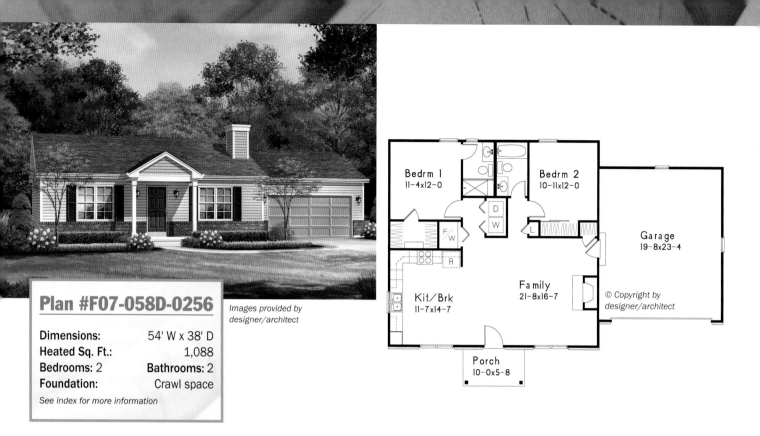

Plan #F07-058D-0256

Dimensions:	54' W x 38' D
Heated Sq. Ft.:	1,088
Bedrooms: 2	**Bathrooms:** 2
Foundation:	Crawl space

See index for more information

Images provided by designer/architect

Plan #F07-130D-0361

Dimensions:	21'8" W x 35' D
Heated Sq. Ft.:	550
Bedrooms: 1	**Bathrooms:** 1

Foundation: Slab standard; crawl space or basement available for an additional fee

See index for more information

Images provided by designer/architect

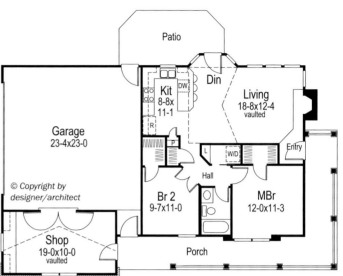

Plan #F07-007D-0135

Images provided by designer/architect

Dimensions:	57' W x 36'4" D
Heated Sq. Ft.:	801
Bedrooms: 2	Bathrooms: 1
Foundation:	Slab

See index for more information

Patio
Kit 8-8x 11-1
Din
Living 18-8x12-4 vaulted
DW
Garage 23-4x23-0
R
Entry
© Copyright by designer/architect
P
L
W/D
Hall
Br 2 9-7x11-0
MBr 12-0x11-3
Shop 19-0x10-0 vaulted
Porch

First Floor
988 sq. ft.

Optional Lower Level 988 sq. ft.

18'-0" x 12'-4"
© Copyright by designer/architect
17'-4" x 28'-8"
10'-0" x 11'-4"
18'-8" x 12'-0"
12'-0" x 13'-0"
21'-0" x 4'-0"
8'-8" x 9'-8"

Plan #F07-032D-0985

Images provided by designer/architect

Dimensions:	56' W x 30' D
Heated Sq. Ft.:	988
Bonus Sq. Ft.:	988
Bedrooms: 2	Bathrooms: 1
Exterior Walls:	2" x 6"

Foundation: Basement standard; crawl space, floating slab or monolithic slab available for an additional fee

See index for more information

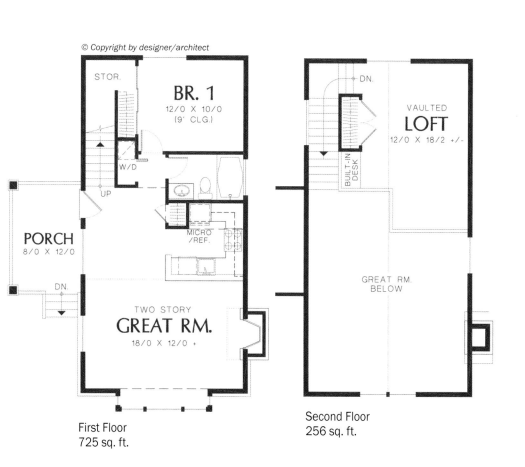

Plan #F07-011D-0358

Images provided by designer/architect

Dimensions: 27' W x 39' D
Heated Sq. Ft.: 981
Bedrooms: 1   **Bathrooms:** 1
Exterior Walls: 2" x 6"
Foundation: Crawl space or slab standard; basement available for an additional fee
See index for more information

Features

- With the porch entry on the side, a large box bay window provides an unobstructed view out the front of this cozy vacation home
- The heart of the home is the two-story great room with its fireplace and a wall of windows where family will want to gather on chilly evenings next to the fire and close to the efficient kitchen
- The bedroom and the bath are located in the rear of the home to provide more privacy, but remain easily accessible to all areas of the home
- The second floor vaulted loft creates an additional area for children to bunk with a closet and built-in desk, all while overlooking the great room

© Copyright by designer/architect

STOR.

BR. 1
12/0 X 10/0
(9' CLG.)

W/D

UP

PORCH
8/0 X 12/0

DN.

MICRO /REF.

TWO STORY
GREAT RM.
18/0 X 12/0 +

First Floor
725 sq. ft.

DN.

VAULTED
LOFT
12/0 X 18/2 +/-

BUILT-IN DESK

GREAT RM. BELOW

Second Floor
256 sq. ft.

DESIGNAMERICA

SEE YOUR HOME ON YOUR LOT BEFORE IT'S BUILT.

Selecting the right home design for your needs and lifestyle requires a lot of thought as your new home is an investment in both the present and the future. The site for your new home will have a definite impact on the home plan you select. It's a good idea to select a home design that will complement your site. And you've come to the right place to make this happen! With the Design America Innovative 3D App you can see your home on your lot before it's built. Simply follow the instructions on page 134 and look for the Design America 3D logo on the pages of plans that you can view in 3D.

Let your Dream Home come to life in 3D!

Install the Design America 3D app and get started!

Instructions:
How to use the 3D App:

Finding your dream home just got a little easier. We, at Design America, have been bringing the best in residential design to homeowners for over 30 years. To help you in your search for that perfect home, we're introducing 3D technology to 2D home plans. Now, even before you purchase any blueprints, you can actually view your dream home on your lot, from any direction. Just follow the easy steps below. It's a great tool...and it's fun!

#1 Download the 3D Design America Application from the Apple or Android App Store on your mobile phone or tablet. Once installed, open the app. You must allow the app to access your camera in order for it to work.

#2 Allow the app to open the camera and begin scanning for an image. If you point the camera at any of the plans in this book, the house will appear in 3D on the screen of your mobile device. HELPFUL TIP: To work properly, make sure your camera is pointed at the front image of the home, not the floor plan.

FOLLOW THESE 4 EASY STEPS

#4 When scanning stops, press the button to select a photo of your lot from your photo library. Then, use conventional finger commands to move, rotate, and scale the 3D house to fit your site. HELPFUL TIP: Start scanning again by pressing the 3D button.

#3 Press the center 3D button to stop the camera from scanning and to keep the scanned 3D house on your mobile device's screen.

THE SMALL ICONS ON THE BOTTOM BAR OF THE 3D APP PERFORM DIFFERENT FUNCTIONS:

Turn shadows on and off, and rotate the sun's position.

View the 3D house with the live camera in the background, or with a gray flat background.

Start, stop, or resume scanning the front image of the homes in this book.

Select a photo from your photo library, such as a photo of your lot, and use it as the background for the 3D house.

Take a screenshot of the 3D house and save it in your photo library on your mobile device.

Images provided by designer/architect

Plan #F07-007D-0108

Dimensions: 25' W x 60' D
Heated Sq. Ft.: 983
Bedrooms: 3 **Bathrooms:** 2
Foundation: Crawl space standard; slab available for an additional fee

See index for more information

Features

- This home is the ideal design for a narrow lot
- The spacious front porch leads you into the relaxing living and dining areas that are open to the well designed kitchen with a convenient breakfast bar
- A small patio with a privacy fence creates an awesome private exterior space and is accessed from the open living room
- The comfortable master bedroom includes a large walk-in closet and its own private full bath
- 2-car front entry garage

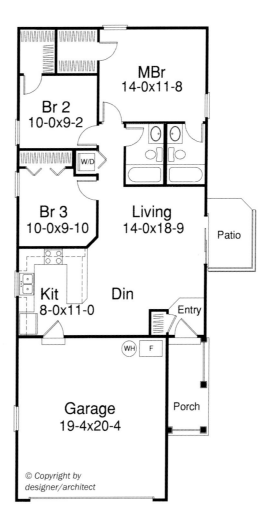

MBr
14-0x11-8

Br 2
10-0x9-2

W/D

Br 3
10-0x9-10

Living
14-0x18-9

Patio

Kit
8-0x11-0

Din

Entry

WH F

Garage
19-4x20-4

Porch

© Copyright by
designer/architect

Images provided by designer/architect

Plan #F07-007D-0105

Dimensions:	35' W x 40'8" D
Heated Sq. Ft.:	1,084
Bedrooms: 2	**Bathrooms:** 2

Foundation: Basement standard; crawl space or slab available for an additional fee

See index for more information

Features

- This home's delightful country porch is perfect for quiet evenings
- The living room offers a front feature window which invites the sun and includes a fireplace and dining area with a private patio
- The U-shaped kitchen features lots of cabinets and a bayed breakfast room with a built-in pantry
- Both bedrooms have walk-in closets and access to their own bath

© Copyright by designer/architect

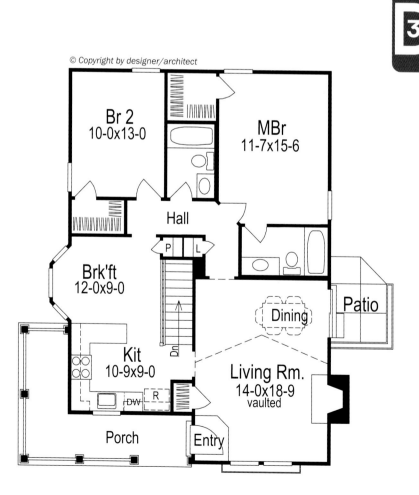

houseplansandmore.com

Plan #F07-001D-0088

Dimensions:	32' W x 25' D
Heated Sq. Ft.:	800
Bedrooms: 2	Bathrooms: 1

Foundation: Crawl space standard;
slab available for an additional fee

See index for more information

Features

- This cozy plan has an excellent compact floor plan
- The large living room boasts a handy coat closet located near the entry door
- An efficient kitchen includes a side entrance to the outdoors, a closet that is perfect for a pantry, and also a convenient laundry closet
- The lovely master bedroom features a walk-in closet and private access to the bath

Images provided by designer/architect

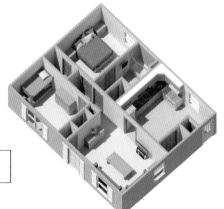

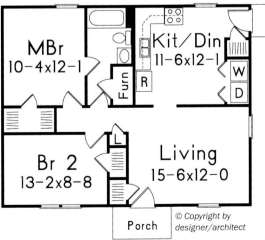

MBr
10-4x12-1

Kit/Din
11-6x12-1

Br 2
13-2x8-8

Living
15-6x12-0

Porch

© Copyright by
designer/architect

Plan #F07-007D-0043

Dimensions:	40' W x 22' D
Heated Sq. Ft.:	647
Bedrooms: 1	Bathrooms: 1

Foundation: Crawl space standard;
slab available for an additional fee

See index for more information

Features

- Large Palladian style windows adorn each end of the cottage creating a cheerful atmosphere throughout

- A large vaulted room for living/sleeping features plant shelves on each end, a stone fireplace, and wide glass doors for views

- The roomy kitchen is vaulted and has a bayed dining area and fireplace

- Step down into a sunken and vaulted bath featuring a whirlpool tub-in-a-bay with shelves at each end for storage

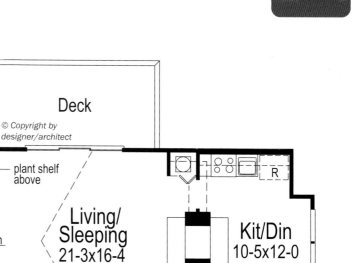

Deck

© Copyright by designer/architect

plant shelf above

sunken bath

Dn

Living/ Sleeping
21-3x16-4
vaulted

plant shelf above

Kit/Din
10-5x12-0

R

P

Entry

Porch

Images provided by designer/architect

Plan #F07-007D-0128

Dimensions:	52' W x 40'8" D
Heated Sq. Ft.:	1,072
Bonus Sq. Ft.:	345
Bedrooms: 2	Bathrooms: 2
Foundation:	Walk-out basement

See index for more information

Features

- Integrated open and screened front porches guarantee comfortable summer enjoyment
- An oversized garage includes an area for a shop and miscellaneous storage
- The U-shaped kitchen and breakfast area is adjacent to the vaulted living room and has access to the screened porch through sliding glass doors
- The optional lower level has an additional 345 square feet of living area
- 2-car side entry garage with workshop

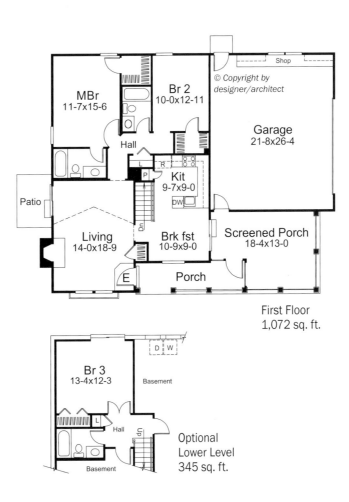

© Copyright by designer/architect

First Floor
1,072 sq. ft.

Optional
Lower Level
345 sq. ft.

Images provided by designer/architect

Plan #F07-007D-0029

Dimensions: 24' W x 30' D
Heated Sq. Ft.:   576
Bedrooms: 1   Bathrooms: 1
Foundation: Crawl space standard;
slab available for an additional fee

See index for more information

Features

- This perfect country retreat features a vaulted welcoming entry and an impressive living room with skylights and a plant shelf above
- The well designed kitchen offers generous storage and a pass-through breakfast bar as well as a handy eating bar for casual meals
- A stately double-door entry leads to the comfortable vaulted bedroom with bath access and a useful closet for organization

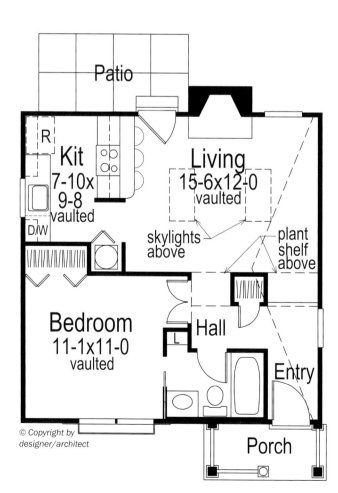

Patio

Kit
7-10x
9-8
vaulted

R

D/W

Living
15-6x12-0
vaulted

skylights
above

plant
shelf
above

Bedroom
11-1x11-0
vaulted

Hall

L

Entry

Porch

© Copyright by
designer/architect

Plan #F07-001D-0085

Dimensions:	28' W x 38' D
Heated Sq. Ft.:	720
Bedrooms: 2	Bathrooms: 1

Foundation: Crawl space standard; slab available for an additional fee

See index for more information

Features

- Abundant windows in the kitchen/dining area and the living area provide generous amounts of sunlight throughout both of these fantastic spaces

- The U-shaped kitchen with large breakfast bar opens into the living area creating the feel of an open floor plan

- The large covered deck offers plenty of outdoor living space

- The secluded laundry area features a handy storage closet

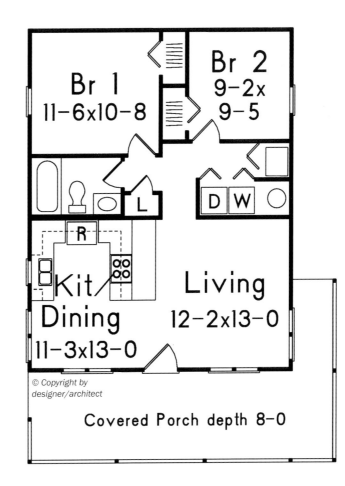

Br 1
11-6x10-8

Br 2
9-2x
9-5

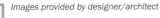

L

D W

Kit
Dining
11-3x13-0

R

Living
12-2x13-0

© Copyright by
designer/architect

Covered Porch depth 8-0

Plan #F07-001D-0041

Dimensions: 40' W x 25' D
Heated Sq. Ft.: 1,000
Bedrooms: 3 **Bathrooms:** 1
Foundation: Crawl space standard; basement or slab available for an additional fee

See index for more information

Features

- As soon as you enter this home, you will find a handy coat closet
- The L-shaped kitchen/dining area provides easy access outdoors
- The bath includes a convenient closeted laundry area
- The master bedroom includes double closets and private access to the bath
- Two secondary bedrooms each include ample closetspace

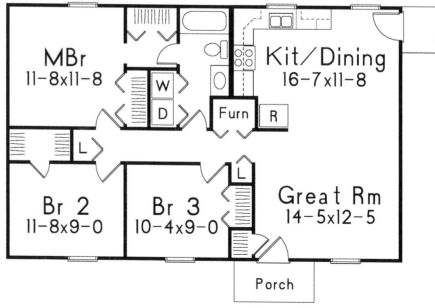

MBr
11-8x11-8

Kit/Dining
16-7x11-8

Furn

Br 2
11-8x9-0

Br 3
10-4x9-0

Great Rm
14-5x12-5

Porch

Plan #F07-032D-0808

Dimensions:	32' W x 24' D
Heated Sq. Ft.:	900
Bedrooms: 2	Bathrooms: 1½
Exterior Walls:	2" x 6"

Foundation: Basement standard; crawl space, floating slab or monolithic slab available for an additional fee

See index for more information

Features

- The open floor plan is fantastic in this Craftsman style home
- The entrance foyer includes plenty of closet space when guests arrive
- The kitchen and family room merges to maximize floor space
- The washer and dryer are located on the first floor for convenience
- The second floor consists of two generously-sized bedrooms with large closets plus a full bath with a double-bowl vanity that is easily shared
- 1-car front entry garage

10'-8" x 10'-5"
3,20 x 3,12

12'-8" x 9'-8"
3,80 x 2,90

Second Floor
420 sq. ft.

20'-0" x 12'-0"
6,00 x 3,60

11'-4" x 20'-8"
3,40 x 6,20

First Floor
480 sq. ft.

Images provided by designer/architect

Plan #F07-013D-0133

Dimensions: 36' W x 42'4" D
Heated Sq. Ft.: 953
Bedrooms: 2 **Bathrooms:** 1½
Foundation: Crawl space standard; basement or slab available for an additional fee

See index for more information

Features

- Relax on the rocking chairs and enjoy the two covered porches

- With two large bedrooms that have oversized closets, a spacious kitchen, and a family room with a fireplace, this home has everything you need to enjoy a vacation get-away, or cozy small home living

- The kitchen has a sunny corner double sink, a roomy center island/snack bar and shares a vaulted ceiling with the spacious and open family room

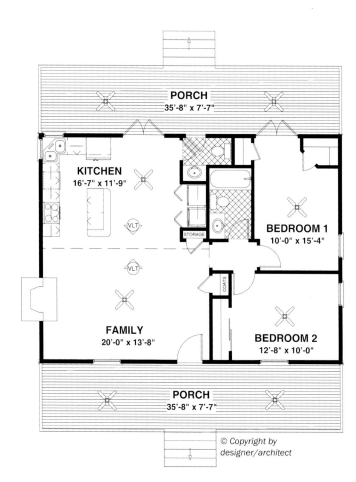

PORCH
35'-8" x 7'-7"

KITCHEN
16'-7" x 11'-9"

BEDROOM 1
10'-0" x 15'-4"

STORAGE

FAMILY
20'-0" x 13'-8"

COATS

BEDROOM 2
12'-8" x 10'-0"

PORCH
35'-8" x 7'-7"

© Copyright by designer/architect

Plan #F07-008D-0153

Dimensions: 24' W x 42' D
Heated Sq. Ft.: 792
Bedrooms: 2 **Bathrooms:** 1
Foundation: Crawl space standard; slab available for an additional fee

See index for more information

Features

- The attractive exterior features wood posts and beams, a wrap-around deck with railing and glass sliding doors with transoms
- The kitchen/dining area and living area enjoy sloped ceilings, a cozy fireplace, and views of the covered deck
- Two bedrooms share a bath just off the hall and are separated from the entertainment areas for convenience and privacy

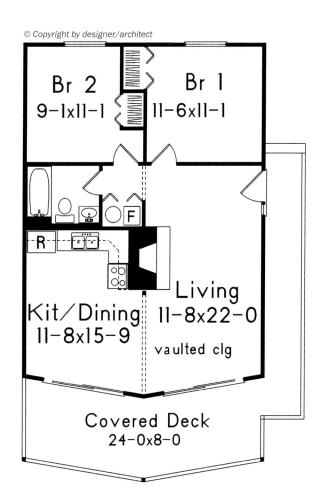

Images provided by designer/architect

Plan #F07-007D-0040

Dimensions:	28' W x 26' D
Heated Sq. Ft.:	632
Bedrooms: 1	**Bathrooms:** 1
Foundation:	Slab

See index for more information

Features

- A porch leads to a vaulted entry and stairs with feature window, coat closet and access to the garage/laundry
- The cozy living room offers a vaulted ceiling, fireplace, large Palladian window and pass-through to kitchen
- The kitchen features an eating bar for two perfect for casual meal
- Bedroom #1 has a sizable closet and is close to a roomy bath with garden tub and an arched window
- 2-car front entry garage

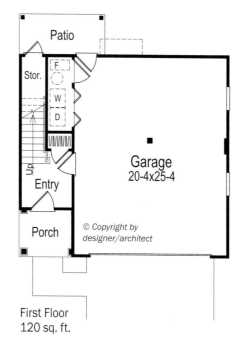

Patio

Stor.

Garage
20-4x25-4

Entry

Porch

© Copyright by designer/architect

First Floor
120 sq. ft.

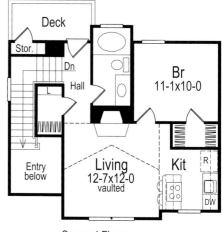

Deck

Stor.

Dn

Hall

Br
11-1x10-0

Entry below

Living
12-7x12-0
vaulted

Kit

Second Floor
512 sq. ft.

Images provided by designer/architect

Plan #F07-032D-1108

Dimensions:	40' W x 33'8" D
Heated Sq. Ft.:	1,188
Bonus Sq. Ft.:	843
Bedrooms: 2	**Bathrooms:** 2
Exterior Walls:	2" x 6"

Foundation: Basement standard; crawl space, floating slab or monolithic slab for an additional fee

See index for more information

Second Floor
345 sq. ft.

Features

- The attractive exterior features wood posts and beams, a wrap-around deck with railing and glass sliding doors with transoms
- The kitchen/dining area and living area enjoy sloped ceilings, a cozy fireplace, and views of the covered deck
- Two bedrooms share a bath just off the hall and are separated from the entertainment areas for convenience and privacy
- The optional lower level has an additional 843 square feet of living area
- 1-car front entry garage

© Copyright by designer/architect

Optional
Lower Level
843 sq. ft.

First Floor
843 sq. ft.

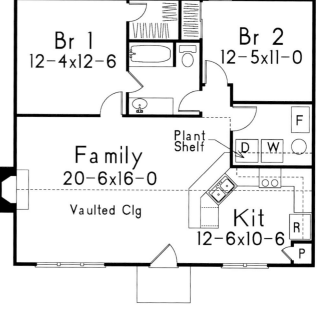

Plan #F07-051D-0848

Dimensions: 39' W x 51' D
Heated Sq. Ft.:   1,069
Bedrooms: 2   Bathrooms: 1
Exterior Walls: 2" x 6"
Foundation: Basement standard;
slab or crawl space available for an
additional fee

See index for more information

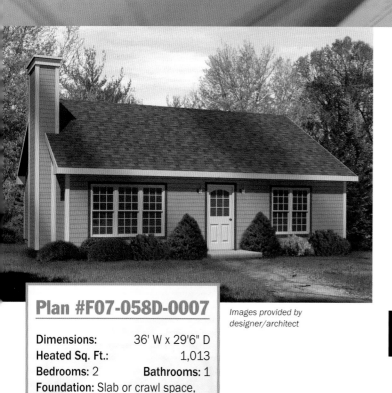

Plan #F07-058D-0007

Dimensions: 36' W x 29'6" D
Heated Sq. Ft.:   1,013
Bedrooms: 2   Bathrooms: 1
Foundation: Slab or crawl space,
please specify when ordering

See index for more information

9'-6" x 10'-0"

9'-0" x 9'-0"

9'-8" x 12'-0"

© Copyright by designer/architect

19'-0" x 12'-4"

Plan #F07-032D-0815

Images provided by designer/architect

Dimensions: 20'4" W x 32' D
Heated Sq. Ft.: 643
Bedrooms: 2 **Bathrooms:** 1
Exterior Walls: 2" x 6"
Foundation: Monolithic slab standard; crawl space or floating slab available for an additional fee

See index for more information

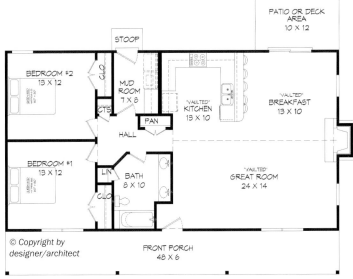

PATIO OR DECK AREA
10 X 12

STOOP

BEDROOM #2
13 X 12

CLO.

MUD ROOM
7 X 8

CTS.

KITCHEN
13 X 10

"VAULTED" BREAKFAST
13 X 10

PAN.

HALL

BEDROOM #1
13 X 12

LIN.

BATH
8 X 10

CLO.

"VAULTED" GREAT ROOM
24 X 14

© Copyright by designer/architect

FRONT PORCH
48 X 6

Plan #F07-141D-0013

Images provided by designer/architect

Dimensions: 50' W x 33' D
Heated Sq. Ft.: 1,200
Bedrooms: 2 **Bathrooms:** 1
Foundation: Slab standard; crawl space, basement or walk-out basement available for an additional fee

See index for more information

© Copyright by designer/architect

STORAGE
14'-2" X 10'-8"

PORCH

CARPORT
14'-0" X 25'-4"

KIT/DINING
13'-10" X
13'-4"

BEDROOM 1
13'-8" X 13'-0"

GREAT ROOM
20'-4" X 14'-6"

BEDROOM 2
13'-8" X 11'-6"

PORCH

Images provided by
designer/architect

Plan #F07-028D-0058

Dimensions: 48' W x 36' D
Heated Sq. Ft.: 1,152
Bedrooms: 2   Bathrooms: 2
Foundation: Slab or crawl space,
please specify when ordering

See index for more information

Plan #F07-046D-0095

Dimensions: 47' W x 43'4" D
Heated Sq. Ft.: 1,077
Bedrooms: 3   Bathrooms: 1
Foundation: Basement

See index for more information

Images provided by
designer/architect

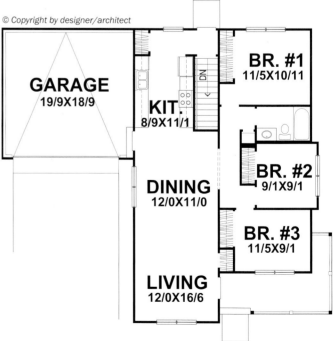

© Copyright by designer/architect

GARAGE
19/9X18/9

KIT.
8/9X11/1

DINING
12/0X11/0

LIVING
12/0X16/6

BR. #1
11/5X10/11

BR. #2
9/1X9/1

BR. #3
11/5X9/1

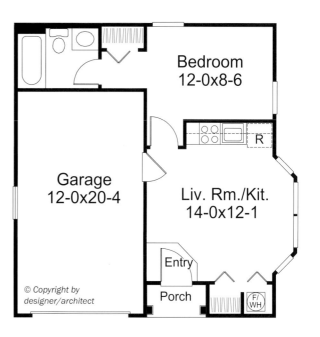

Plan #F07-007D-0196

Images provided by designer/architect

Dimensions:	27' W x 27' D
Heated Sq. Ft.:	421
Bedrooms: 1	Bathrooms: 1
Foundation:	Slab

See index for more information

Bedroom
12-0x8-6

Garage
12-0x20-4

Liv. Rm./Kit.
14-0x12-1

Entry

Porch

© Copyright by designer/architect

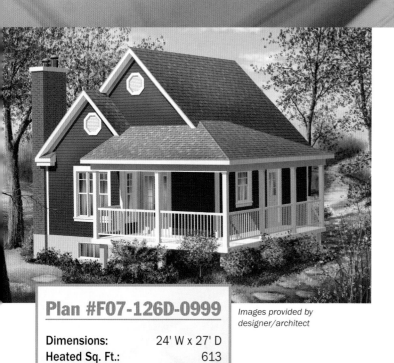

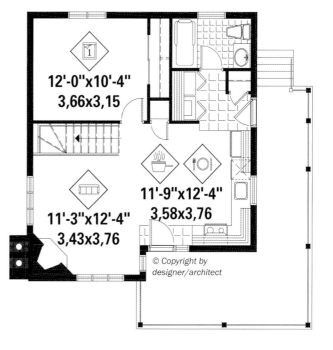

Plan #F07-126D-0999

Images provided by designer/architect

Dimensions:	24' W x 27' D
Heated Sq. Ft.:	613
Bedrooms: 1	Bathrooms: 1
Exterior Walls:	2" x 6"
Foundation:	Basement

See index for more information

12'-0"x10'-4"
3,66x3,15

11'-3"x12'-4"
3,43x3,76

11'-9"x12'-4"
3,58x3,76

© Copyright by designer/architect

no excuses... it's time to
get organized

PLEASE REMAIN CALM

Does the thought of downsizing to a smaller home put you in a state of panic? Where will you possibly put all of your stuff? Just the thought of having to fit all of your things into a smaller space can be completely overwhelming. How do you choose what to get rid of? What do you decide to keep?

Today's first-time homeowners are starting out smarter; they're learning sometimes too much of a good thing is literally too much. In fact, scaling down your surroundings, being conscientious of how much you acquire, and filling a smaller ecological footprint are often on the top of many first-time home buyers checklists. But, that doesn't mean small is a sacrifice. In many ways, living in a smaller space creates the opportunity for more financial freedom, time to travel and enjoy hobbies, and spend quality time with family and friends. And, when it comes to all of your possessions, there are many clever ways to make good use of the space you do have.

BE TRUE TO YOURSELF

Be honest with yourself and just get rid of it! Donate, reuse, or recycle if at all possible, but if not, then discard it. The next step is to look at each room and make a plan. What items do you use daily? What can be stored away for occasional use? Which spaces are wasting potential? If you could have your storage set up any way you wanted, how would it be?

Whether you're just starting out, or you're scaling back to something smaller after many years of living in a larger home, here's some amazing ways to maximize space and organize your small home so you can keep the things you love and keep them organized and ready to use at your fingertips.

Ask Yourself
How many things do you no longer need?
How many things do you actually use?
How many things do you just want?

How To Maximize Space Room-by-Room

MAKE AN ENTRANCE

The entryway of a home is the first thing your guests see. No matter what the size of the entry, there is an organized solution for this favorite dumping ground. First, make sure to scale the furniture to the space so there is plenty of room to open the door as well as room for comfortable greeting. For a home with a designated foyer, add a bench that serves as storage as well as a place to put on, or take off shoes. If the seat of the bench can be lifted to include a hidden storage spot, even better. For smaller entry halls, store in style with a tall, narrow shelf or chest that has baskets, drawers and doors. If you mix storage with good style then no one will notice how functional it is. Another great option is to frame the doorway with built-in bookcases. This fun and custom looking idea adds tons of personality to your front entry hall without sacrificing much space.

DOWN & DIRTY ORGANIZATION IN THE MUD ROOM

It is easy for the mud room to become cluttered and unorganized because it is the first room family members typically enter. The laundry and mud rooms are spaces that may be combined or separated, but they're always busy and working hard to keep families on the move organized. These spaces are best outfitted with flexible storage solutions. Baskets are great to assign to family members. Each person has their own basket to toss in gloves, hats, shoes and laundry. It's decorative, yet corrals the clutter simply. The same can be said for designated hooks and built-in cubbies. Or, create a locker for each family member. The kids can hang coats, keep backpacks and their shoes right there by the door. If you do not have enough wall space for lockers, a built-in shelf with smart phone plug-ins, and a drawer for a wallet or purse is a great way to store phones, keys, and all those belongings you will need as you are running out the door and are often easily forgotten.

HAPPY PUP, HAPPY HOME

The mud room/laundry room is also the spot for your furry family member to feel at home. Build a nook or cozy area for your pet in this space and organize their food, toys, and leash so it feels like home for them.

Another spot often near the laundry room are the stairs. For steep stairs, there is sufficient room to add a cozy reading nook, or even a computer niche. If your stairs are not steep, there are a few creative effects you can execute to not waste any space like building shelves, drawers or wine storage.

MUST-HAVE SMART STORAGE

The family room generates the most traffic and yesterday's family rooms are now today's open living spaces that combine dining, gathering and cooking. The typical family gathering space is often littered with electronic gadgets, books, toys and games. Floor-to-ceiling entertainment centers or built-ins offer the perfect mix of open shelving and storage cabinets. The key is to avoid over stuffing them. Then, they become visually distracting making your room appear even smaller. Hide small knick-knacks behind cabinet doors and keep a few items on the shelves for decoration. Make the most of this multi-purpose space by making it visually uncluttered. Avoid oversized furniture that can overwhelm. Stick with light colors and smaller scaled furniture pieces that have more than one function. Add a couch that can be opened up to become a bed, or a table that folds up. Add casters so pieces can be moved easily offering the multi-function perfect for smaller homes. Make those furniture pieces' work for you!

154

MESSY ROOMS NO MORE

Bedroom storage is all about finding ways to create clean surfaces so it's a restful uncluttered place to unwind and de-stress. New technology like charging spots can be added to furniture helping to keep the nightstand free of cords and clutter. Under the bed storage, large dressers, and closed armoires are excellent options. Or, choose a tall bed frame so you can utilize under-the-bed storage boxes. A well-organized closet is a must and plastic bins are a cheap, easy organization solution for clothes and toys. Moving the hanging rod up higher and adding another below it in the closet doubles your hanging capabilities. Add a chest or ottoman at the end of the bed for pillow and blanket storage. And, in the kid's bedrooms, go vertical and opt for bunk beds. This allows for possibly a desk underneath the bed, or twice as much sleeping space, all while keeping the floor space open for other activities.

Whether you like the idea of a more expensive customized storage system, or you want to create your own with baskets and shelves, keep in mind sensible storage is flexible and adapts to your ever-changing life. With these easy tips and a new perspective on the stuff you truly need, your home can be organized, functional and clutter-free.

Don't Forget

Take your storage pieces to new heights and select pieces that go all the way to the ceiling to make a room feel larger and add that extra storage you can't live without.

Unless noted, all images copyrighted by the designer/architect; Page 154, top to bottom: ClosetMaid® slide-out wire storage in mud room pet space, closetmaid.com; Do-it-yourself hidden dog bowl storage cabinet, freshome.com; Deriba Furniture built-in under the stair storage, deriba.co.uk; Ivy Design Premium Folding Table, ivydesign-furniture.com; Maximize vertical space with a tall, narrow bookcase unit like Ikea's GNEDBY Bookcase, Item# 402.771.43, ikea.com; Page 155, top, left: Double your closetspace by hanging two rows instead of one, ClosetMaid®, closetmaid.com; top, right: Bunk beds and built-ins make this small bedroom super functional and comfortable, Plan #011S-0003; middle: Mockett Illuminated Wireless Charging Grommet®, Item# PCS79/WC, mockett.com; See more photos and purchase plans at houseplansandmore.com.

bathroom STORAGE SOLVED

Storage space in bathrooms is usually non-existent. So, anytime you can find a way to utilize what little space you do have, then by all means go for it! A couple of easy ideas for adding some precious extra space include incorporating tall, vertical freestanding shelves or cubbies to store toilet paper, towels and other bathroom necessities. Or, if the bathroom is small, over the toilet shelving and cabinets are ideal for providing a place for frequently used items like toothpaste and mouthwash. This frees up the smaller and somewhat awkward under-sink space for long-term storage of toilet paper, cleaning supplies, etc. Where bathroom storage is concerned, it is also smart to look outside the immediate space for storage options, too. Storing extra towels in the hall linen closet or laundry room makes more sense and is easier to access than squeezing them under the bathroom sink.

The three major problems to address when trying to reduce bathroom clutter:

Problem #1
THROW IT OUT

Unused products is the largest source of clutter in most bathrooms. Everyone has purchased toiletries they dislike. So, toss anything past the expiration date, or that hasn't been used in more than 12 months. Always make certain that potentially harmful products are disposed of properly. And, consider donating good, but unwanted items to shelters.

Problem #2
MAKE ROOM

Whether organizing a spacious master bath, or a small mud room half-bath, homeowners always need to make the most of the space available. Both functional and aesthetically pleasing, baskets or glass jars are great ways to keep cabinets tidy and countertops clean. Plus, baskets are the perfect option for the humid environment since they allow the contents to breathe. As previously mentioned above, utilizing vertical space in smaller bathrooms is key. A floating shelf above a toilet or sink is an ideal choice. Or, build shelves between the studs and create tiny wall niches for towels and other necessities. Don't forget the importance of "off-site" storage, too! Hall closets are great for storing extra rolls of toilet paper, towels, and other surplus until needed.

Problem #3
GET A ROUTINE

Once the clutter has been removed and the amount of storage space has been determined, find everything a place. Don't rush putting things back. Determine a sensible system for storing commonly used toiletries, and keep them in a spot easiest to reach. No more than four objects should remain on the counter, so put everything else in cabinets or on shelves. It may take some time for a new system to become habit, but it will be completely worth it when you have a functional and uncluttered bathroom.

Remember...
Try to have no more than four objects on the counter.

banish kitchen clutter FOREVER

FEELING TRAPPED?

Every homeowner knows the importance of storage space in the kitchen. It is the most popular room in the house where guests gather and family constantly come and go, so it's best to keep it looking great and free of unwanted clutter. Everyday life is greatly improved when this key entertaining space has all its contents in their proper place. But, inadequate storage in the kitchen is still a common problem in most households. Even the smallest kitchens can be arranged to suitably store kitchen items properly. In many kitchens, it is the little things that are constantly in the way. Bulky spice racks, small appliances, items that don't fit in the pantry, and cookware that can't be manipulated into a standard sized cabinet often remain homeless and sitting on the counter. It's easy to see why built-in kitchen storage walls and backsplashes, and kitchen islands with extra cabinets are so popular for making the most of a kitchen's square footage. Extra counter space is every chef's dream. Creating space in the kitchen can be difficult, and cooking meals in a cluttered kitchen is even harder. Evaluate your daily routine and note the things you actually use. Try the tip below to get started!

Try This.

Use removable labels for a week and every time you use a kitchen item, put a label on it. Chances are, at the end of the week, very few items will have a label on them. A handful of glasses, some silverware, utensils, and a few pots and pans most likely will be all you need to run a functional kitchen and still treat family and friends to amazing meals.

20 Kitchen Organizing Tips

1 Clear everything out of the kitchen. Dispose of items you don't use by donating or selling. Then, clean everything you plan to keep.

2 Plan a place for everything BEFORE putting it back. Group like items; baking supplies, grilling equipment, etc.

3 Arrange kitchenware by frequency of use. Keep dishes for special occasions in high cabinets, store everyday tableware on shelves easiest to reach. Keep utensils near the stove.

4 Use dividers and drawer organizers to keep items visible. Avoid cutting yourself by separating cutlery from utensils.

5 Use clear containers for large utensils and odd-shaped gadgets.

6 Store cutting boards or cookie sheets in skinny cabinets sideways.

7 Store small appliances, such as coffee grinders, blenders, and hand held mixers in corner cabinets equipped with a Lazy Susan, so they're easy to reach. Or, install hooks to hang pots and pans in there. This allows easy visibility in this typically hard to reach corner.

8 Hang pots, pans and utensils from hooks above the island, counter, or stove to free up cabinets. Still need space? Move small appliances to a nearby closet, or the basement if rarely used. How often do you make waffles? Or, homemade ice cream? Get these appliances out seasonally only.

9 Use baskets for storage container lids, or if your kitchen is small, place storage containers one inside another. If you tend to lose the lids easily, keep them on the container when storing if space permits.

10 Cabinets with glass doors showcase dishes or crystal, adding style and personality. Hooks in the cabinets can add more display space.

11 Install pull-out shelves to make deep cabinets accessible.

12 Install shelves inches below the ceiling around the perimeter of the kitchen to add display and storage space that's out of the way.

13 Install drawer slides and insert a drawer where the kickboard is located under your cabinets. Find drawers that match your existing cabinetry for a seamless look.

14 Label baskets and shelves. Keep like items together and use wire baskets to easily see the contents.

15 Make a pantry door message center with magnetic, dry erase, or cork board. Or, paint the inside of the door with blackboard paint. An over-the-door rack is perfect for spices, oil and vinegar inside, too.

16 Store dry goods in jars, canisters and baskets.

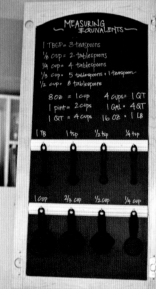

17 Shelves and caddies are great for under the kitchen sink. Buckets are excellent for storing cleaning supplies and are easy to grab when ready to use. Use a waterproof mat to prevent water damage under your sink.

18 Carts are excellent for storing large appliances like stand mixers and microwaves. Small cart designs are portable islands that can easily be rolled out for parties. A cart can also function as prep space and serve buffet style meals.

19 Use a hutch in the dining area. Hutches can fit in a wide hallway or corridor, too. A hutch is an elegant storage solution that's beautiful and versatile.

20 Eliminate the dreaded "junk drawer." But, many experts say maintain drawer space for this necessity. It's good practice to go through the drawer every few months and reorganize it.

Whether you have a luxury home, or a small cottage style abode, kitchen storage space is always important real estate. With organization being key to properly maintaining a kitchen, it's important to have a place for everything and everything in its place so your kitchen will remain neat and functional daily, or when entertaining.

Unless noted, all images copyrighted by the designer/architect; Page 156, top to bottom: Narrow open bookcase, Ikea, ikea.com; ClosetMaid® built-in laundry hamper, closetmaid.com; Teak storage tower, signaturehardware.com; Page 157, top, right: Plan #101D-0045, Warren Diggles Photography; bottom, left: ClosetMaid® track pantry shelves, closetmaid.com; bottom, right: Kitchen storage wall, shelterness.com; Page 158, left, top to bottom: ClosetMaid® kitchen storage solution, closetmaid.com; Ikea Variera Bamboo Flatware Tray, ikea.com; YouCopia StoreMore Adjustable Bakeware Rack, amazon.com; Perfect overhead storage, Plan #128D-0004; Glass cabinets done right, Plan #011S-0005; top to bottom, right: ClosetMaid® Pro Cuisine Organization, closetmaid.com; The Family Handyman® Do-it-yourself under the cabinet storage drawer, familyhandyman.com; Chalkboard in cabinet, homeandhues.com; Elfa® Wire utility door and wall rack, elfa.com; Page 159, top to bottom: Hanging utensils near the stovetop, istockphoto.com; Ikea 365+ Dry Food Jar with Lid, Item #800.667.23, ikea.com; IdeaWorks Adjustable Under Sink Storage Shelf, amazon.com; Chamberlin Kitchen Cart by Trent Austin Design, wayfair.com; See more photos and purchase plans at houseplansandmore.com.

pantry organization 101

How come it always seems your pantry is so full, but there's nothing to cook or eat? Organize your pantry and see the meal possibilities!

- Remove food and crumbs and clean shelves
- Separate misplaced items
- Check the freshness dates on the food you keep
- Donate fresh, unwanted items to a local food bank, or church
- Combine similar items if two packages or more are open
- Arrange items in categories - baking, snacks, cereal etc.
- Place flour, sugar and pastas in airtight containers
- Store wrapped items like granola bars in wire bins
- Put items rarely used on top shelf
- Put like items away with the newest item in back
- Organize canned goods with risers
- Put frequently made recipe ingredients together for easy meal prep
- Put oils and vinegars that fit on door racks
- Put coffee and tea in a cabinet near your coffeemaker
- Put heavy items, dog food, or bottled water, on the floor
- Label shelves so it's easy for anyone to put groceries away

Besides making you feel like you accomplished and tackled an overdue task, organizing your kitchen pantry can result in savings at the grocery store, more creative meals, and accidental stockpiling.

159

Plan #F07-001D-0043

Images provided by designer/architect

Dimensions: 44' W x 26' D
Heated Sq. Ft.: 1,104
Bedrooms: 3   Bathrooms: 2
Foundation: Crawl space standard; slab or basement available for an additional fee

See index for more information

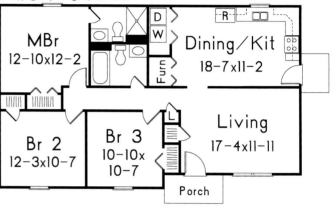

© Copyright by designer/architect

MBr
12-10x12-2

Dining/Kit
18-7x11-2

Furn

Br 2
12-3x10-7

Br 3
10-10x
10-7

Living
17-4x11-11

Porch

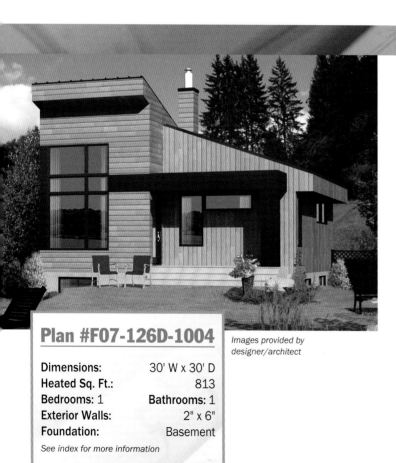

Plan #F07-126D-1004

Images provided by designer/architect

Dimensions: 30' W x 30' D
Heated Sq. Ft.: 813
Bedrooms: 1   Bathrooms: 1
Exterior Walls: 2" x 6"
Foundation: Basement

See index for more information

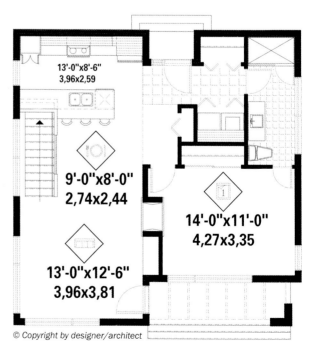

13'-0"x8'-6"
3,96x2,59

9'-0"x8'-0"
2,74x2,44

14'-0"x11'-0"
4,27x3,35

13'-0"x12'-6"
3,96x3,81

© Copyright by designer/architect

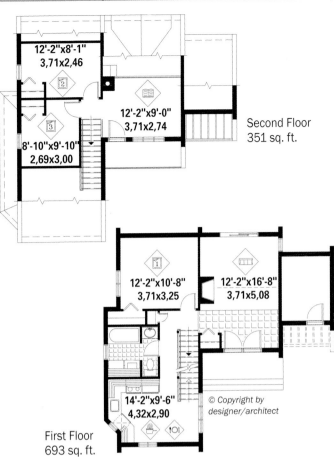

Second Floor
351 sq. ft.

12'-2"x8'-1"
3,71x2,46

12'-2"x9'-0"
3,71x2,74

8'-10"x9'-10"
2,69x3,00

12'-2"x10'-8"
3,71x3,25

12'-2"x16'-8"
3,71x5,08

14'-2"x9'-6"
4,32x2,90

© Copyright by
designer/architect

First Floor
693 sq. ft.

Plan #F07-126D-0174

Images provided by designer/architect

Dimensions:	36' W x 32' D
Heated Sq. Ft.:	1,044
Bedrooms: 3	Bathrooms: 1
Exterior Walls:	2" x 6"
Foundation:	Basement

See index for more information

© Copyright by designer/architect

12'-0"x9'-6"
3,66x2,90

13'-6"x11'-2"
4,12x3,40

12'-0"x8'-0"
3,66x2,44

15'-4"x13'-4"
4,67x4,06

10'-0"x10'-2"
3,05x3,10

Plan #F07-126D-0356

Images provided by designer/architect

Dimensions:	29' W x 31' D
Heated Sq. Ft.:	845
Bedrooms: 2	Bathrooms: 1
Exterior Walls:	2" x 6"
Foundation:	Basement

See index for more information

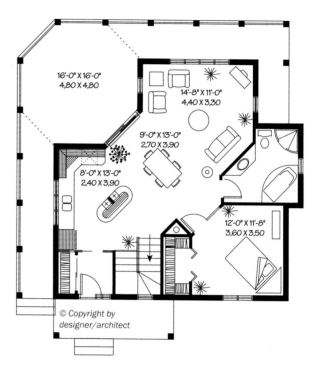

Plan #F07-032D-0050

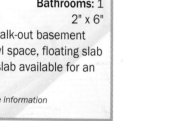

Images provided by designer/architect

Dimensions:	33' W x 31' D
Heated Sq. Ft.:	840
Bedrooms: 1	Bathrooms: 1
Exterior Walls:	2" x 6"

Foundation: Walk-out basement standard; crawl space, floating slab or monolithic slab available for an additional fee

See index for more information

© Copyright by designer/architect

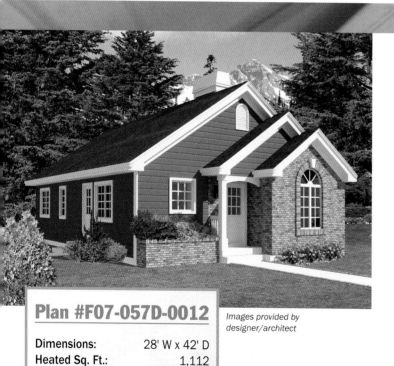

Plan #F07-057D-0012

Images provided by designer/architect

Dimensions:	28' W x 42' D
Heated Sq. Ft.:	1,112
Bedrooms: 3	Bathrooms: 1
Exterior Walls:	2" x 6"
Foundation:	Basement

See index for more information

© Copyright by designer/architect

Images provided by
designer/architect

© Copyright by designer/architect

Plan #F07-077D-0085

Dimensions:	22' W x 32' D
Heated Sq. Ft.:	400
Bedrooms: 1	Bathrooms: 1
Foundation:	Slab

See index for more information

Images provided by
designer/architect

Plan #F07-156D-0006

Dimensions:	25' W x 28' D
Heated Sq. Ft.:	550
Bedrooms: 1	Bathrooms: 1

Foundation: Slab standard; crawl
space available for an additional
fee

See index for more information

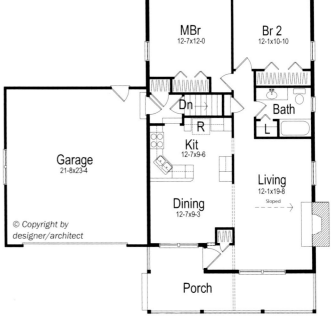

Plan #F07-057D-0033

Images provided by
designer/architect

Dimensions:	50'2" W x 48' D
Heated Sq. Ft.:	1,056
Bedrooms: 2	Bathrooms: 1
Exterior Walls:	2" x 6"
Foundation:	Basement

See index for more information

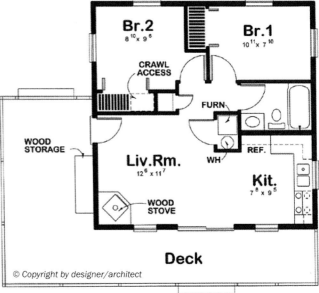

Plan #F07-109D-7500

Images provided by
designer/architect

Dimensions:	24' W x 24' D
Heated Sq. Ft.:	576
Bedrooms: 2	Bathrooms: 1
Exterior Walls:	2" x 6"
Foundation:	Slab

See index for more information

Plan #F07-156D-0012

Dimensions: 22' W x 35'6" D
Heated Sq. Ft.: 621
Bedrooms: 1 **Bathrooms:** 1
Foundation: Slab standard; crawl space available for an additional fee

See index for more information

Images provided by designer/architect

© Copyright by designer/architect

Plan #F07-069D-0108

Dimensions: 30' W x 38' D
Heated Sq. Ft.: 856
Bedrooms: 2 **Bathrooms:** 1
Foundation: Pier

See index for more information

Images provided by designer/architect

© Copyright by designer/architect

Plan #F07-011D-0591

Dimensions:	30' W x 32' D
Heated Sq. Ft.:	960
Bedrooms: 1	**Bathrooms:** 1
Exterior Walls:	2" x 6"

Foundation: Crawl space or slab standard; basement available for an additional fee

See index for more information

Features

- This European style cottage is ideal as a free-standing guest house, or the perfect in-law quarters
- The vaulted great room feels much more spacious than its true size and has French door access onto a covered rear porch and a cozy fireplace
- The compact, yet efficient U-shaped kitchen has plenty of counter space to cook meals easily
- Near the bedroom you'll discover a washer and dryer closet and a full bath with an oversized walk-in shower
- Behind double barn style doors is a unique space with a built-in guest bed, perfect for grandchildren sleeping over, or as a guest space

© Copyright by designer/architect

REAR PORCH
17/6 X 8/0 +/-

12/6 X 9/0
(9' CLG.)

REF | PAN

W/D

VAULTED
GREAT RM.
16/6 X 23/8

LIN

BR.
12/0 X 13/0
(9' CLG.)

(10' CLG)

SHLVS

9/6 X 7/0
(10' CLG)

BUILT-IN GUEST BED

PORCH
9/6 X 4/6

Images provided by designer/architect

Plan #F07-123D-0084

Dimensions:	39' W x 38' D
Heated Sq. Ft.:	831
Bedrooms: 1	Bathrooms: 1

Foundation: Basement standard; crawl space, slab or walk-out basement available for an additional fee

See index for more information

Features

- The footprint for this home will fit almost any lot and the curb appeal will welcome you home
- The covered porch offers an inviting entry into this home
- The open great room is perfect for entertaining
- The bedroom has a roomy walk-in closet not usually found in homes this size, a beautiful trayed ceiling, and a full bath nearby
- 2-car front entry garage

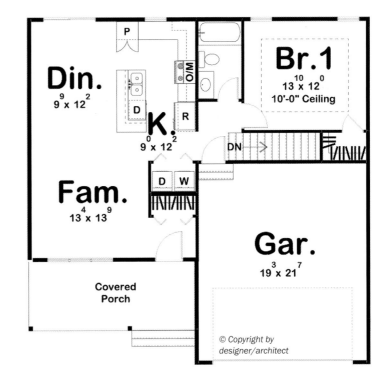

Din.
9 x 12²

K.
9 x 12

Br.1
13 x 12⁰
10'-0" Ceiling

DN

Fam.
13 x 13⁹

Gar.
19³ x 21⁷

Covered Porch

© Copyright by designer/architect

Plan #F07-144D-0022

Images provided by designer/architect

Dimensions:	32' W x 28' D
Heated Sq. Ft.:	896
Bedrooms: 1	**Bathrooms:** 1½
Exterior Walls:	2" x 6"

Foundation: Crawl space or slab, please specify when ordering

See index for more information

Features

- Great sleek style and a narrow is perfect for a small lot and definitely makes this home stand out from the rest

- The open living area has direct patio access and merges nicely with the kitchen that features a breakfast bar and huge walk-in pantry

- There's a handy powder room/laundry room combination that is quite efficient

- The master bedroom features a an oversized walk-in closet for optimal storage and well a private bath with a roll-in shower making this an ideal floor plan for anyone with a disability

- Pocket doors are used throughout this plan to maximize the home's square footage to the fullest

© Copyright by designer/architect

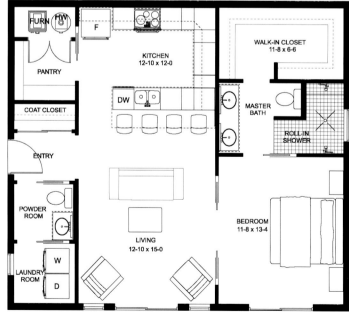

Plan #F07-032D-0863

Dimensions: 27'7" W x 28' D
Heated Sq. Ft.: 1,200
Bedrooms: 2 **Bathrooms:** 2
Exterior Walls: 2" x 6"
Foundation: Crawl space standard; floating slab or monolithic slab available for an additional fee

See index for more information

Rear View

Front View

Features

- A sleek, modern exterior gives way to an open and bright interior with the first floor combining the dining and gathering spaces perfectly

- The large L-shaped kitchen has a built-in table with space for three people and enjoys outdoor access onto a partially covered patio

- A designated space has been created that's hidden away on the first floor for easily accessing utilities

- The second floor has two sizable bedrooms, a full bath, and lovely views of the living and dining area below

- 1-car front entry carport

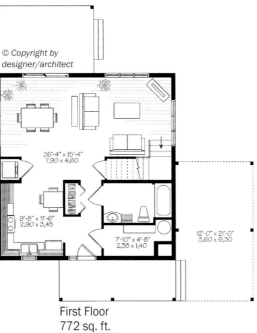

© Copyright by designer/architect

26'-4" x 15'-4"
7,90 x 4,60

9'-8" x 11'-6"
2,90 x 3,45

7'-10" x 4'-8"
2,35 x 1,40

12'-0" x 21'-0"
3,60 x 6,30

First Floor
772 sq. ft.

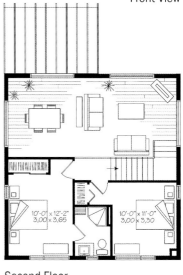

10'-0" x 12'-2"
3,00 x 3,65

10'-0" x 11'-0"
3,00 x 3,30

Second Floor
428 sq. ft.

Plan #F07-057D-0013

Dimensions:	36' W x 28' D
Heated Sq. Ft.:	1,117
Bedrooms: 2	Bathrooms: 1
Exterior Walls:	2" x 6"
Foundation:	Basement

See index for more information

Images provided by designer/architect

Br 1
10-10x12-0

Br 2
10-0x7-6

UP   DN

Living
13-6x11-2

Kit/Brk
10-0x13-10

Deck
19-0x10-0

First Floor
790 sq. ft.

© Copyright by designer/architect

Loft
16-10x12-0

DN

Open to Below

Second Floor
327 sq. ft.

Plan #F07-126D-0993

Images provided by designer/architect

Dimensions:	22' W x 26' D
Heated Sq. Ft.:	572
Bedrooms: 2	Bathrooms: 1
Exterior Walls:	2" x 6"
Foundation:	Pilings

See index for more information

1
9'-2"x9'-8"
2,79x2,95

2
9'-2"x9'-8"
2,79x2,95

15'-8"x15'-0"
4,78x4,57

© Copyright by designer/architect

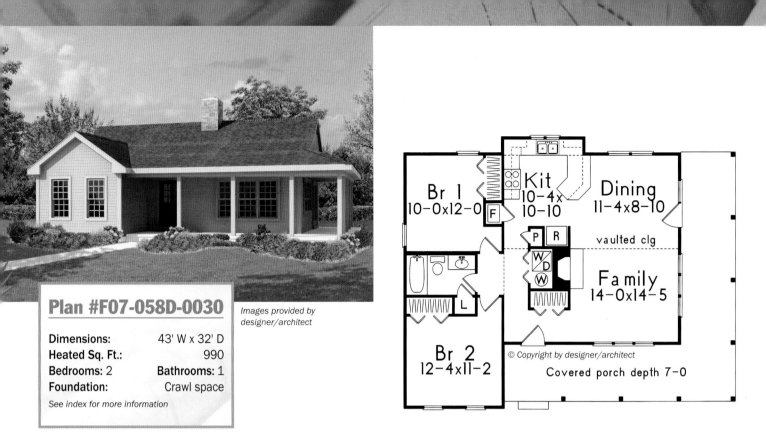

Plan #F07-058D-0030

Images provided by
designer/architect

Dimensions:	43' W x 32' D
Heated Sq. Ft.:	990
Bedrooms: 2	Bathrooms: 1
Foundation:	Crawl space

See index for more information

Br 1
10-0x12-0

Kit
10-4x
10-10

Dining
11-4x8-10

vaulted clg

Family
14-0x14-5

Br 2
12-4x11-2

© Copyright by designer/architect

Covered porch depth 7-0

Plan #F07-007D-0177

Images provided by
designer/architect

Dimensions:	38' W x 51'8" D
Heated Sq. Ft.:	1,102
Bedrooms: 3	Bathrooms: 2

Foundation: Basement standard;
crawl space or slab available for an
additional fee

See index for more information

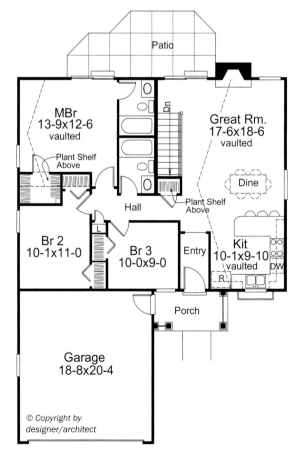

Patio

MBr
13-9x12-6
vaulted

Plant Shelf
Above

Great Rm.
17-6x18-6
vaulted

Dn

Hall

Plant Shelf
Above

Dine

Br 2
10-1x11-0

Br 3
10-0x9-0

Entry

Kit
10-1x9-10
vaulted

DW

Porch

Garage
18-8x20-4

© Copyright by
designer/architect

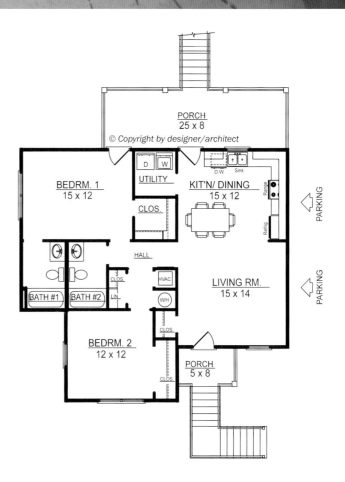

© Copyright by designer/architect

PORCH
25 x 8

BEDRM. 1
15 x 12

UTILITY

CLOS.

KIT'N/ DINING
15 x 12

D W

Sink

Range

Refrig

PARKING

PARKING

BATH #1

BATH #2

HALL

CLOS

LIN

HVAC

W/H

LIVING RM.
15 x 14

BEDRM. 2
12 x 12

CLOS

PORCH
5 x 8

Plan #F07-069D-0110

Images provided by designer/architect

Dimensions:	36' W x 41' D
Heated Sq. Ft.:	1,013
Bedrooms: 2	Bathrooms: 2
Foundation:	Pier

See index for more information

Attic

Sloped Clg.

Dn

Study
10-9x12-0

Firepl.

Sleeping
14-4x12-0

Second Floor
562 sq. ft.

Furn.

Entry

Kit./Brk.
15-5x11-4

R

Garage
14-4x23-4

Porch
6-0x4-4

Sitting
13-1x12-0

Up

© Copyright by designer/architect

First Floor
492 sq. ft.

Plan #F07-058D-0224

Images provided by designer/architect

Dimensions:	38' W x 24' D
Heated Sq. Ft.:	1,054
Bedrooms: 1	Bathrooms: 1½
Foundation:	Basement

See index for more information

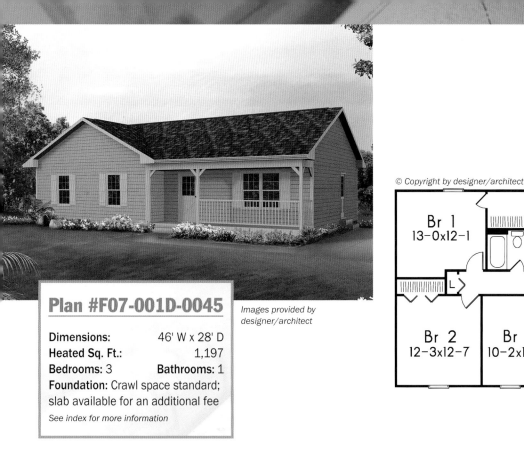

Plan #F07-001D-0045

Images provided by designer/architect

Dimensions: 46' W x 28' D
Heated Sq. Ft.: 1,197
Bedrooms: 3 **Bathrooms:** 1
Foundation: Crawl space standard; slab available for an additional fee

See index for more information

© Copyright by designer/architect

Br 1
13-0x12-1

Dining
10-2x11-0

Kit
10-3x11-0

D
W
F
L

Br 2
12-3x12-7

Br 3
10-2x12-7

Living
20-0x12-1

Porch depth 4-0

Plan #F07-008D-0121

Images provided by designer/architect

Dimensions: 40' W x 24' D
Heated Sq. Ft.: 960
Bedrooms: 3 **Bathrooms:** 1
Foundation: Basement standard; crawl space or slab available for an additional fee

See index for more information

Opt. Storage | Stoop

Bed 1
11-4x11-3

Dn

Family Rm/ Kit
18-9x11-3

R
DW
L

Bed 2
11-4x9-5

Bed 3
9-8x8-5

Living Rm
15-4x11-9

Stoop

© Copyright by designer/architect

Plan #F07-058D-0014

Images provided by
designer/architect

Dimensions: 26' W x 22' D
Heated Sq. Ft.: 416
Bedrooms: 1 **Bathrooms:** 1
Foundation: Footing and foundation wall

See index for more information

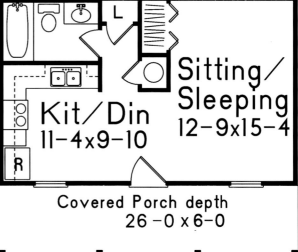

Sitting/Sleeping
12-9x15-4

Kit/Din
11-4x9-10

Covered Porch depth
26-0x6-0

Plan #F07-069D-0105

Images provided by
designer/architect

Dimensions: 27' W x 33' D
Heated Sq. Ft.: 736
Bedrooms: 2 **Bathrooms:** 1
Foundation: Crawl space or slab, please specify when ordering

See index for more information

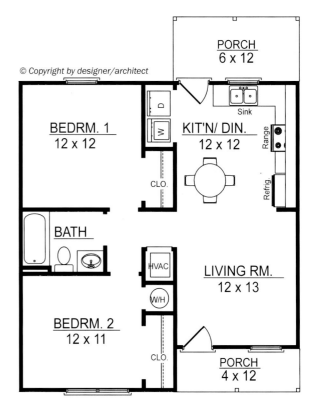

PORCH
6 x 12

BEDRM. 1
12 x 12

KIT'N/ DIN.
12 x 12

Sink

CLO.

BATH

HVAC

W/H

LIVING RM.
12 x 13

BEDRM. 2
12 x 11

CLO.

PORCH
4 x 12

BATH
8'-3" X 4'-11"

CLOSET
2' X 4'-11"

BEDROOM
8'-4" X 8'-4"

W/D

HALL
6'-1" X 3'-1"

REF

KITCHEN
9'-4" X 10'-8"

LIVING
10' X 10'-8"

PORCH
4'-1" X 8'-3"

Images provided by
designer/architect

Plan #F07-156D-0001

Dimensions: 24'4" W x 20' D
Heated Sq. Ft.: 400
Bedrooms: 1 **Bathrooms:** 1
Foundation: Slab standard; crawl
space available for an additional
fee

See index for more information

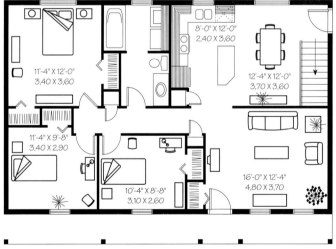

11'-4" X 12'-0"
3,40 X 3,60

8'-0" X 12'-0"
2,40 X 3,60

12'-4" X 12'-0"
3,70 X 3,60

11'-4" X 9'-8"
3,40 X 2,90

10'-4" X 8'-8"
3,10 X 2,60

16'-0" X 12'-4"
4,80 X 3,70

Images provided by
designer/architect

Plan #F07-032D-0001

Dimensions: 42' W x 26' D
Heated Sq. Ft.: 1,092
Bedrooms: 3 **Bathrooms:** 1
Exterior Walls: 2" x 6"
Foundation: Basement standard;
crawl space, floating slab or mono-
lithic slab available for an addition-
al fee

See index for more information

First Floor
810 sq. ft.

© Copyright by
designer/architect

Garage
20-4x29-2

Br 1
15-3x11-6

Kit / Brkfst
15-8x9-6

Sitting
15-4x13-7

Cov'd
Porch

Br 2
14-0x10-10

Unfinished Area
Optional Finish

Lower Level
302 sq. ft.

Plan #F07-058D-0194

*Images provided by
designer/architect*

Dimensions:	44' W x 40' D
Heated Sq. Ft.:	1,112
Bonus Sq. Ft.:	508
Bedrooms: 2	Bathrooms: 2
Foundation:	Basement

See index for more information

Br 2
13-1x10-4

Dn

Br 3
13-1x10-4

Second Floor
434 sq. ft.

Br 1
13'-0"x13'-0"

Kit
12'-0"x9'-4"

Porch

Up

Living/Dining
23'-5"X12'-9"

Deck

© Copyright by designer/architect

First Floor
720 sq. ft.

Plan #F07-001D-0086

*Images provided by
designer/architect*

Dimensions:	28' W x 30' D
Heated Sq. Ft.:	1,154
Bedrooms: 3	Bathrooms: 1½

Foundation: Crawl space standard;
slab or basement available for an
additional fee

See index for more information

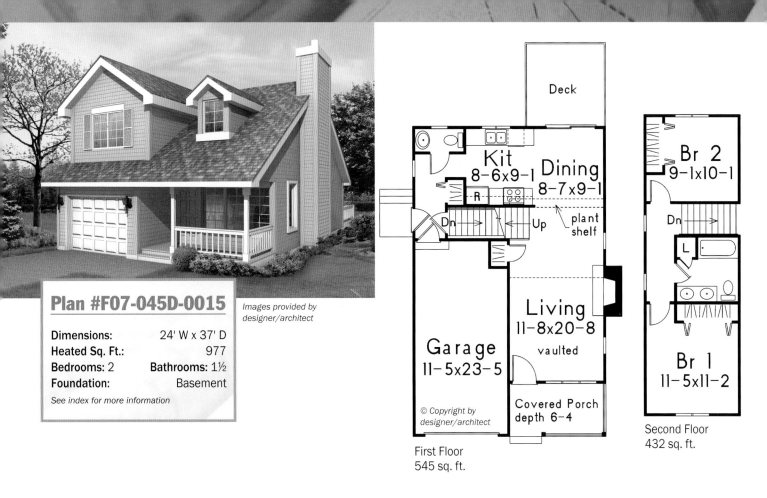

Plan #F07-045D-0015

Images provided by
designer/architect

Dimensions: 24' W x 37' D
Heated Sq. Ft.: 977
Bedrooms: 2   Bathrooms: 1½
Foundation: Basement

See index for more information

Deck

Kit
8-6x9-1

Dining
8-7x9-1

plant
shelf

Dn   Up

R

Living
11-8x20-8
vaulted

Garage
11-5x23-5

© Copyright by
designer/architect

Covered Porch
depth 6-4

First Floor
545 sq. ft.

Br 2
9-1x10-1

Dn

L

Br 1
11-5x11-2

Second Floor
432 sq. ft.

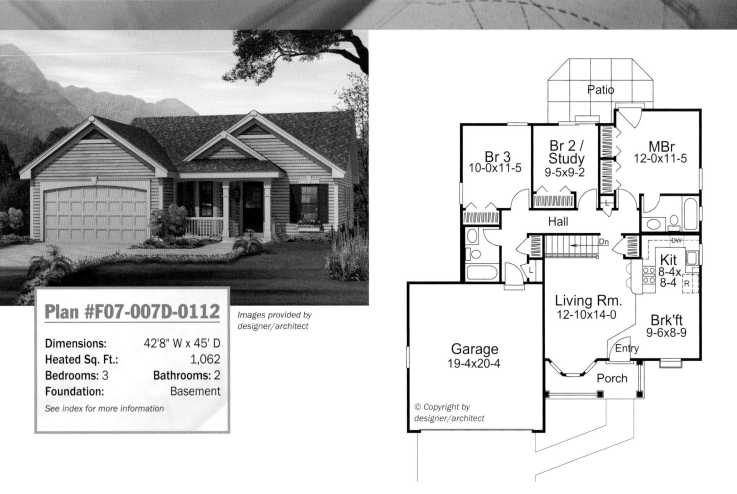

Plan #F07-007D-0112

Images provided by
designer/architect

Dimensions: 42'8" W x 45' D
Heated Sq. Ft.: 1,062
Bedrooms: 3   Bathrooms: 2
Foundation: Basement

See index for more information

Patio

Br 3
10-0x11-5

Br 2 /
Study
9-5x9-2

MBr
12-0x11-5

Hall

Dn

Kit
8-4x
8-4

Garage
19-4x20-4

Living Rm.
12-10x14-0

Entry

Brk'ft
9-6x8-9

Porch

© Copyright by
designer/architect

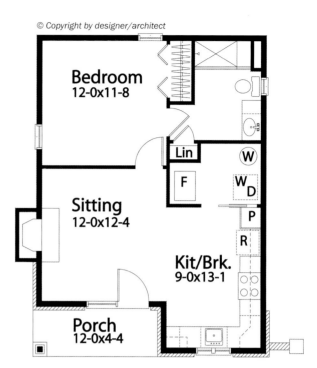

© Copyright by designer/architect

Bedroom
12-0x11-8

Sitting
12-0x12-4

Lin

W

F

W D

P

R

Kit/Brk.
9-0x13-1

Porch
12-0x4-4

Plan #F07-058D-0227

Images provided by designer/architect

Dimensions:	27'8" W x 30' D
Heated Sq. Ft.:	610
Bedrooms: 1	Bathrooms: 1
Exterior Walls:	2" x 6"
Foundation:	Slab

See index for more information

Loft
9-0x9-6

Br
11-6x9-6

Dn

open to below

Second Floor
275 sq. ft.

Porch

Kit
9-6x
12-0

D W

Br
11-6x11-6

Stor.

Up

Stor.

Living/Dining
26-0x11-6

© Copyright by designer/architect

Deck

First Floor
764 sq. ft.

Plan #F07-022D-0001

Images provided by designer/architect

Dimensions:	30' W x 33'5" D
Heated Sq. Ft.:	1,039
Bedrooms: 2	Bathrooms: 1½
Foundation:	Crawl space

See index for more information

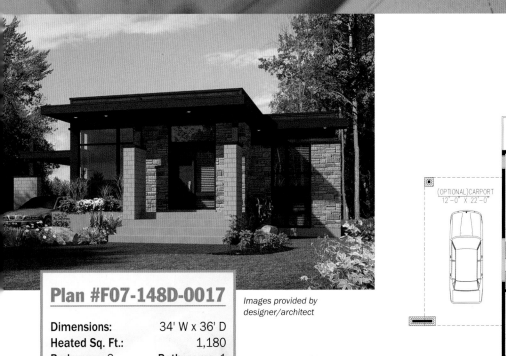

Plan #F07-148D-0017

Images provided by
designer/architect

Dimensions:	34' W x 36' D
Heated Sq. Ft.:	1,180
Bedrooms: 3	Bathrooms: 1
Exterior Walls:	2" x 6"
Foundation:	Basement

See index for more information

© Copyright by designer/architect

Plan #F07-077D-0106

Images provided by
designer/architect

Dimensions:	30' W x 32' D
Heated Sq. Ft.:	1,200
Bedrooms: 3	Bathrooms: 2

Foundation: Slab or crawl space,
please specify when ordering

See index for more information

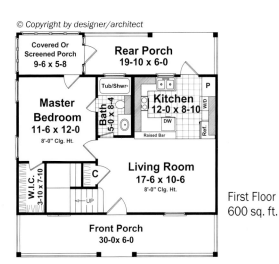

Second Floor
600 sq. ft.

First Floor
600 sq. ft.

Plan #F07-008D-0136

Dimensions:	22' W x 36' D
Heated Sq. Ft.:	1,106
Bedrooms: 2	Bathrooms: 1
Foundation:	Pier

See index for more information

Features

- This delightful A-frame style house design provides exciting vacation-style living all year long
- The deck accesses a large living room with an open soaring ceiling above
- The living room includes a free-standing wood stove for a cozier atmosphere
- An enormous sleeping area is provided on the second floor with a balcony overlook to the living room below
- One bedroom can be found on the first floor and has a bath nearby

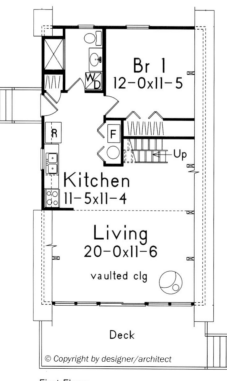

Br 1
12-0x11-5

Kitchen
11-5x11-4

Living
20-0x11-6
vaulted clg

Up

Deck

© Copyright by designer/architect

First Floor
792 sq. ft.

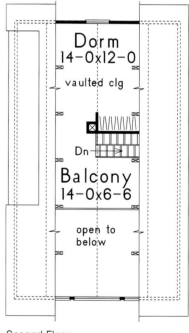

Dorm
14-0x12-0
vaulted clg

Dn

Balcony
14-0x6-6

open to below

Second Floor
314 sq. ft.

Plan #F07-130D-0360

Dimensions:	27' W x 17' D
Heated Sq. Ft.:	664
Bedrooms: 1	Bathrooms: 1½

Foundation: Slab standard; crawl space or basement available for an additional fee

See index for more information

Images provided by designer/architect

Features

- There's a lot of living packed into this small two-story home
- The living room has a sloped ceiling and is steps from the kitchen
- The kitchen enjoys many extras that smaller homes typically do not have including an island with dining space, and an angled sink with a window above
- The dinette enjoys full views through the sliding glass doors
- The second floor bedroom enjoys its privacy and has a full bath right outside its door
- Additional storage can be found both outside as well as under the stairs to the second floor

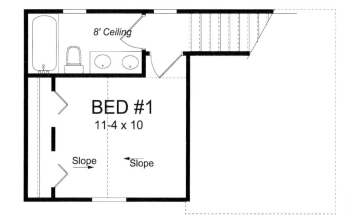

Second Floor
229 sq. ft.

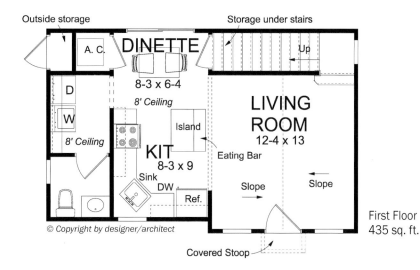

© Copyright by designer/architect

First Floor
435 sq. ft.

what home buyers want:
WIDE OPEN SPACES

When having a party, do you ever feel cut off from your guests as you scurry between rooms? You're trying to take care of kitchen tasks, while maintaining a connection with your guests, but it's a struggle to do so in a floor plan so disconnected. Or, perhaps there are times when work in the kitchen is begging your attention, but so are the children playing in the family room. Too many homeowners can relate with the desire to be in more than one place at one time within their home. Thankfully, today's dream homes offer the luxury of an open floor plan allowing homeowners to feel as though they are in more than one place at a time!

Open floor plans are the answer to this common problem in the past, and luckily open layouts are the future in home design. Open floor plans combine all gathering spaces into one large space. The kitchen, dining area, and great room form one large place where cooking, eating, relaxing, and other tasks can be done together. With as many distractions as there are today, both inside and outside our homes that keep us from being together with family and friends, the open floor plan at least has found a way to bring people together.

Feeling Lonely?

Are there ways to open up your kitchen to your great room in your home? Could columns replace walls? These changes can be customized in a new home, too.

AN OPEN MIND
IS A GOOD PLACE TO START

Today's floor plans are designed with little or no divisions between rooms. But, what if you fall in love with a floor plan that isn't quite as open as you'd like for it to be? There are some creative ways to open it up.

Unless noted, all images copyrighted by the designer/architect; Page 182, Plan #F07-032D-0963 on page 116; Page 183, top: Well designed open living between the kitchen and dining area, Plan #F07-032D-0887 on page 50; open living area, Plan #011D-0313 on page 8; See more photos and purchase plans at houseplansandmore.com.

SPREAD OUT

Even homes with modest square footage can be transformed into airy, open spaces. Wherever possible, eliminate doorways, widen passages, and remove boundaries. Ultimately, you're turning your home into a "universal" home design which means, it suits all people of all ages and accommodates all physical abilities. This is a smart move for resale values and allows all those who enter your home to feel welcome and able to move about freely. Allowing traffic to flow easily from one "room" to another is important in making a home feel more spacious.

LIGHTEN UP

Natural light can make any space inviting and warm. Use large windows and long views to connect with the outdoors and make an open room appear even larger. If window walls are not appropriate, consider skylights and strategically placed mirrors to make the most of some natural light and space.

FAMILY FUNCTIONALITY WITH PERSONALITY

Open floor plans that combine kitchens, dining, and living rooms are imperative for busy families. When open, these spaces transition easily into one another, allowing family members to take on various tasks without being entirely separated, or tripping over one another. A great addition to open kitchens is the snack bar/preparation island. Kids can keep busy and close, while still allowing mom and dad enough room to visit and get meals underway.

There are simple steps homeowners can do to open up their homes

Unless noted, all images copyrighted by the designer/ architect; Page 184, top: Spacious vaulted living area, REAL LOG HOMES®, realloghomes.com, James Ray Spahn, photographer; bottom: ClosetMaid® game room with smart storage ideas, closetmaid.com; Page 185, top: Plan #101D-0149; Plan #101D-0105; Page 186, top, right: Plan #011D-0266, Bob Greenspan, photographer; bottom: Plan #055D-0748; See more photos and purchase plans at houseplansandmore.com.

USE IT OR LOSE IT

It's important to make the most of the space you have, using every corner and nook. The formal dining room is becoming a space of the past in small or moderate sized homes where square footage is a high commodity. If you find a floor plan that includes a formal dining room in addition to a more casual dining space, open up the walls and turn it into a media room, home office, playroom or other space that better suits your families' needs. Most often windows, deck access, fireplaces, and bay windows can be incorporated into these new open spaces making them feel seamless with other areas.

OPEN UP & GET TOGETHER

Like the dining room and kitchen, opening the great room presents numerous benefits to families. This once formally enclosed space sometimes referred to as a den in the past, can now be a spacious area perfect for daily family activities, or ideal for keeping guests comfortable when entertaining.

By building a home with an open floor plan, or customizing a plan to create a more open feel, there is no longer any reason to limit your spaces or banish particular tasks to designated rooms. Your home's floor plan should offer a seamless space where guests and hosts, and parents and children, can all interact and enjoy an area that is completely multi-purpose.

Nowhere To Hide

Not only does your home appear twice as large as it normally would, an open floor plan is a great way to get the entire family into one space, sharing cooking, hobbies and relaxation together.

making your tiny kitchen
FEEL SPACIOUS

Homes being designed today finally get it. The #1 busiest place in the home is the kitchen; it's where everyone wants to be. New homes are designed to handle the challenges a kitchen faces each day. These kitchens include planning desks, center islands, breakfast bars, nearby laundry areas and mud rooms plus built-in appliances. They're equipped for anything and everything. But, for those of us that don't have a brand-new home, or have a small home, this may be far from your reality. Every day you navigate the tight quarters of your kitchen trying to find ways to efficiently cook, serve, and dine, while juggling crowded appliances and zero storage. Face it; your kitchen is too small to be functional. To make matters worse, it looks as small as it feels. Crowded, dysfunctional, and mostly useless, even on its good days. But, don't give up - there are many clever ways to turn a small kitchen into a space to be proud of thanks to some super smart design tricks. Don't let your kitchen be a never-ending battle of space versus function. The solution is making the most of the least.

THINK OUTSIDE THE BOX

So, you think your kitchen is too small to be stylish? That is not so. Small kitchens may have to get creative in order to be considered truly stylish, but often their lack of space affords them the opportunity to use bold elements to make a strong impact. Try scaling down the size of the appliances used in the space. Purchase a sleek, yet smaller refrigerator, a smaller microwave and a stove that includes only two burners. Does anyone use four burners at a time ever anyway? There are also single sinks that offer just as much function as a double basin style sink. Suddenly, you have the same amount of function taking up much less square footage.

Another way to add more space to a small kitchen is to open it up by removing overhead cabinets. If you can pair down your kitchen accessories and get organized, consider installing open shelving for overhead cabinets so the space doesn't seem as closed in. Not only will the shelving give the area a more open and larger feel, it will also allow you to see what is being stored there. Overhead cabinets are many times hard to access anyway, so use open shelving to show off your china, attractive glassware, or colorful platters.

BOLD IS BEAUTIFUL

Just because your kitchen may be small, it doesn't have to be boring. Consider mixing it up a bit with different material choices, or choose a contrasting island or cabinet color. Select a unique, or bold color scheme and have fun picking floors, countertop material and cabinetry. Add a fun and whimsical backsplash design and soon the eyes of guests will be drawn to the fun and playful space with everyone forgetting entirely about the lack of square footage. Adding unique color choices, or a bold color scheme will also take away from the fact that there is not a lot of architectural detail in your small kitchen. Also, fun and colorful lighting options can create a kitchen that is functional and stylish at the same time. Such simple style upgrades can change the overall feel of the room. Diamond patterned flooring, fresh light colored paint, and special lighting are all decorative tricks that can fool the eye into seeing a space as slightly larger. Weeding out all the non-essentials and sprucing up the basics can quickly turn your kitchen space into a dream kitchen – without ever changing the floor plan.

SHOW & TELL

If possible, consider incorporating glass as much as possible throughout the space. Adding glass front cabinets, a kitchen table, or other element will automatically open up the space quite a bit. If doors separate your kitchen from the rest of the home, make sure they are glass and suddenly the space will not feel so divided. Or, better yet, remove the doors and instantly make it feel more open. If your kitchen features a pass-through window into the main living space, keep it open as much as possible. If you don't have this feature, consider adding a pass-through for an open and modern look if the separating wall isn't load-bearing this can often be an easy change. The same goes for mirrors, too. Create a gorgeous backsplash with mirrored mosaics, or use mirrored accessories to add life and spaciousness to a cramped kitchen.

LET THERE BE LIGHT

Create an open kitchen space also by including several types of light sources. Lighting above the cabinets and even at floor level create the illusion of a larger space. Lights directed at cabinetry will increase shadowing of the space and give the area greater visual movement through light and dark contrasts.

BETTER YET, GET COZY

Another advantage of a small space is it can be very easy to make it cozy. So, you've faced the facts that your kitchen is small. Instead of trying every tactic in the book to make it appear larger or choosing to be discouraged by its shortcomings, make the decision to embrace it the way it is and enjoy its cozy atmosphere. Choose a dark rich wall color and add sophisticated accessories that complement the rich background and amp up your kitchen's luxury quotient. Make this a small, yet interesting spot for intimate dining, or cozy coffee chatter with friends.

The kitchen can be a space full of possibilities. You can have a kitchen that sees everything happen from beginning to end. Living in a smaller home with a tiny kitchen doesn't have to be a downfall. Make a conscious effort to embrace this small space, accentuate the positive, add elements to deceive the eye, and suddenly this area of your home will become a true focal point.

Unless noted, all images copyrighted by the designer/architect; Page 187, top: Functional, compact kitchen, istockphoto.com; Small modern kitchen, dreamstime.com; Page 188, Plan #F07-028D-0115 on page 19; Page 189, top to bottom: Great use of open shelving, Plan #028D-0099, houseplansandmore. com; White kitchens feel larger than their true size, istockphoto.com; Small Modern Farmhouse style kitchen, Plan #F07-032D-0963 on page 116; See more photos and purchase plans at houseplansandmore.com.

Plan #F07-032D-0806

Dimensions:	18' W x 30' D
Heated Sq. Ft.:	976
Bedrooms: 3	**Bathrooms:** 1
Exterior Walls:	2" x 6"

Foundation: Screw pile, pilaster or partial crawl space/floating slab standard; crawl space, floating slab or monolithic slab available for an additional fee

See index for more information

Images provided by designer/architect

Features

- Great modern style and a narrow frontage is perfect for a small lot and definitely makes this home stand out from the rest
- The first floor of this home enjoys a covered front porch, a family room, a kitchen with a dining area, and plenty of storage
- There's a handy powder room/laundry room combination that is quite efficient
- Enjoy the outdoors in the sizable rear screened porch
- The master bedroom features a walk-in closet for optimal storage
- Pocket doors were used on two of the bedrooms as well as the second floor bath to maximize the home's square footage to the fullest

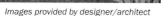

Second Floor
528 sq. ft.

© Copyright by
designer/architect

First Floor
448 sq. ft.

houseplansandmore.com

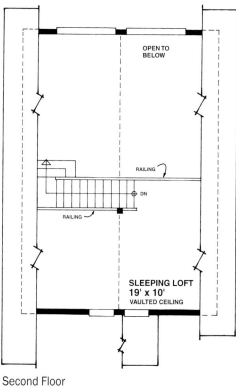

Plan #F07-080D-0002

Dimensions:	20' W x 40' D
Heated Sq. Ft.:	796
Bedrooms: 1	**Bathrooms:** 1
Exterior Walls:	2" x 6"
Foundation:	Crawl space

See index for more information

Features

- This handsome home is perfect for a narrow lot
- The covered front entry is protected from the elements and adds to the curb appeal
- A vaulted ceiling and two sets of sliding glass doors to the rear sun deck can be found in the delightful great room
- The second floor sleeping loft has the ability to be partitioned if additional privacy is warranted

Images provided by designer/architect

© Copyright by designer/architect

SUNDECK

GREAT ROOM
19' X 14'
VAULTED CEILING

UP

KIT
11' x 10'

COVERED PORCH

First Floor
560 sq. ft.

OPEN TO BELOW

RAILING

DN

RAILING

SLEEPING LOFT
19' x 10'
VAULTED CEILING

Second Floor
236 sq. ft.

Plan #F07-069D-0117

Images provided by designer/architect

Dimensions: 38' W x 40' D
Heated Sq. Ft.: 1,094
Bedrooms: 2 **Bathrooms:** 2
Foundation: Crawl space or slab, please specify when ordering

See index for more information

SCR. PORCH 18' x 10'

MASTER BR 14' x 14'

CLOSET

MASTER BATH

DINING 10' x 12'

KIT'N 10' x 9'5"

BATH

HALL

GREAT RM 18' x 12'

UTILITY

BEDRM 2 11' x 11'11"

© Copyright by designer/architect

PORCH

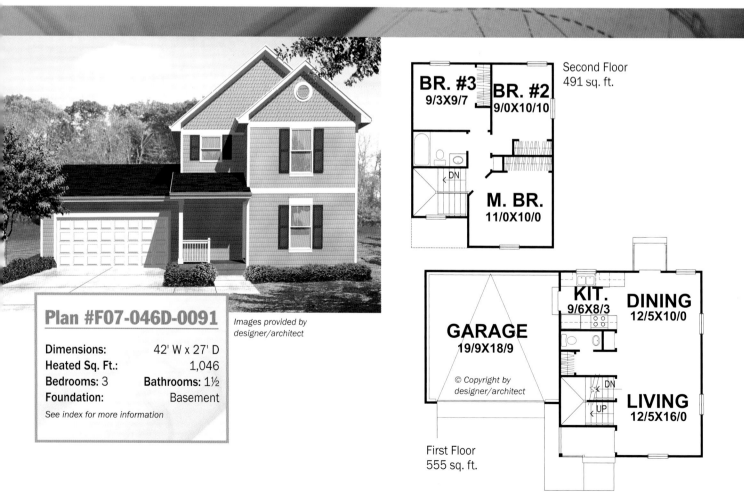

Plan #F07-046D-0091

Images provided by designer/architect

Dimensions: 42' W x 27' D
Heated Sq. Ft.: 1,046
Bedrooms: 3 **Bathrooms:** 1½
Foundation: Basement

See index for more information

Second Floor 491 sq. ft.

BR. #3 9/3X9/7

BR. #2 9/0X10/10

DN

M. BR. 11/0X10/0

GARAGE 19/9X18/9

© Copyright by designer/architect

KIT. 9/6X8/3

DINING 12/5X10/0

DN

UP

LIVING 12/5X16/0

First Floor 555 sq. ft.

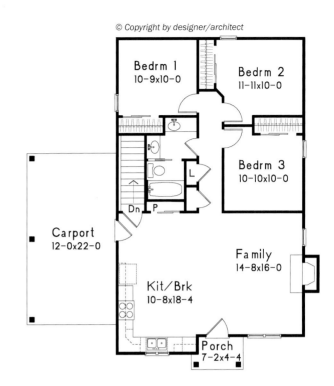

Plan #F07-058D-0236

Images provided by designer/architect

Dimensions:	40'4" W x 44' D
Heated Sq. Ft.:	1,067
Bedrooms: 3	Bathrooms: 1
Foundation:	Basement

See index for more information

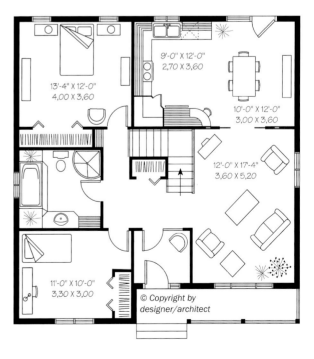

Plan #F07-032D-0542

Images provided by designer/architect

Dimensions:	34' W x 35' D
Heated Sq. Ft.:	1,113
Bedrooms: 2	Bathrooms: 1
Exterior Walls:	2" x 6"

Foundation: Basement standard; crawl space, floating slab or monolithic slab available for an additional fee

See index for more information

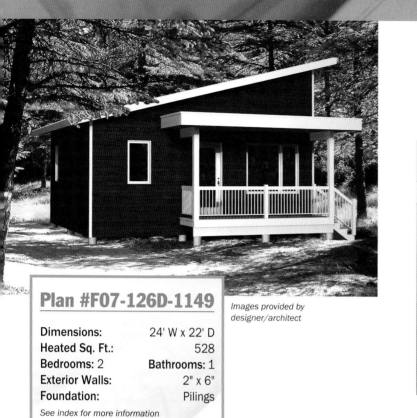

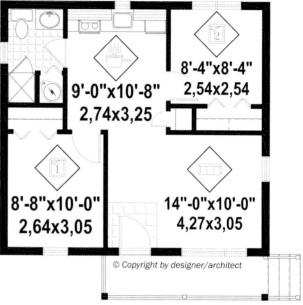

9'-0"x10'-8"
2,74x3,25

8'-4"x8'-4"
2,54x2,54

8'-8"x10'-0"
2,64x3,05

14"-0"x10'-0"
4,27x3,05

© Copyright by designer/architect

Plan #F07-126D-1149

Images provided by designer/architect

Dimensions:	24' W x 22' D
Heated Sq. Ft.:	528
Bedrooms: 2	Bathrooms: 1
Exterior Walls:	2" x 6"
Foundation:	Pilings

See index for more information

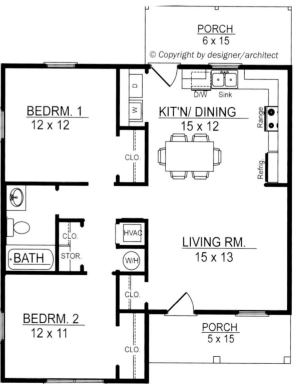

PORCH
6 x 15
© Copyright by designer/architect

BEDRM. 1
12 x 12

KIT'N/ DINING
15 x 12

LIVING RM.
15 x 13

BATH

BEDRM. 2
12 x 11

PORCH
5 x 15

Plan #F07-069D-0107

Images provided by designer/architect

Dimensions:	30' W x 38' D
Heated Sq. Ft.:	856
Bedrooms: 2	Bathrooms: 1
Foundation:	Crawl space or slab, please specify when ordering

See index for more information

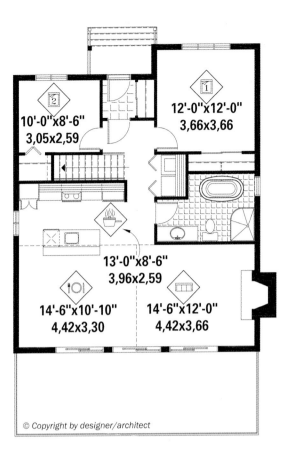

Plan #F07-126D-0998

Images provided by designer/architect

Dimensions:	30' W x 36' D
Heated Sq. Ft.:	1,021
Bedrooms: 2	Bathrooms: 1
Exterior Walls:	2" x 6"
Foundation:	Basement

See index for more information

10'-0"x8'-6"
3,05x2,59

12'-0"x12'-0"
3,66x3,66

13'-0"x8'-6"
3,96x2,59

14'-6"x10'-10"
4,42x3,30

14'-6"x12'-0"
4,42x3,66

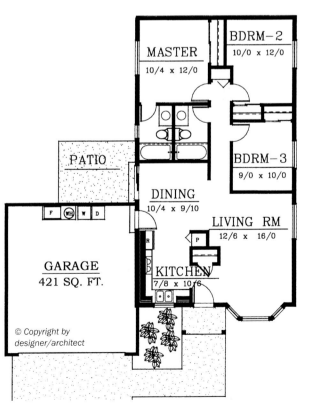

Plan #F07-015D-0019

Images provided by designer/architect

Dimensions:	43'6" W x 49' D
Heated Sq. Ft.:	1,018
Bedrooms: 3	Bathrooms: 2

Foundation: Crawl space, slab or basement, please specify when ordering

See index for more information

MASTER
10/4 x 12/0

BDRM-2
10/0 x 12/0

PATIO

BDRM-3
9/0 x 10/0

DINING
10/4 x 9/10

LIVING RM
12/6 x 16/0

GARAGE
421 SQ. FT.

KITCHEN
7/8 x 10/6

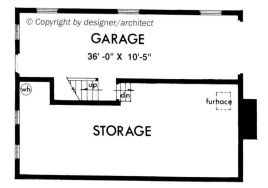

Plan #F07-072D-0036

Dimensions:	38'1" W x 26' D
Heated Sq. Ft.:	1,188
Bedrooms: 3	**Bathrooms: 2**
Foundation:	Walk-out basement

See index for more information

Images provided by designer/architect

Features

- The large living room with fireplace enjoys a ceiling height of 15' and access to the large deck
- The second floor bedroom is a nice escape with its own bath and private deck
- A large eating counter in the kitchen creates casual dining space
- The lower level has a huge amount of storage space, perfect for yard equipment and other necessities
- 2-car tandem drive under side entry garage

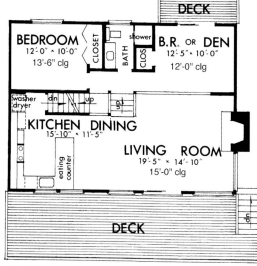

First Floor
936 sq. ft.

Second Floor
252 sq. ft.

© Copyright by designer/architect

Lower Level

Plan #F07-172D-0023

Dimensions:	39'6 W x 49' D
Heated Sq. Ft.:	1,069
Bonus Sq. Ft.:	1,069
Bedrooms: 2	Bathrooms: 2

Foundation: Basement standard; crawl space, monolithic slab, stem wall slab, daylight basement or walk-out basement available for an additional fee

See index for more information

Features

- This terrific cottage is everything today's homeowner is looking for with its simple exterior style and compact, yet open floor plan
- Enter the family from the covered front porch and discover a living space that blends with the kitchen
- The master bedroom has a private bath with a separate toilet area
- The optional lower level has an additional 1,069 square feet of living area and includes space for a living room, an office, two bedrooms, and a full bath
- 2-car front entry garage

© Copyright by designer/architect

First Floor
1,069 sq. ft.

Images provided by designer/architect

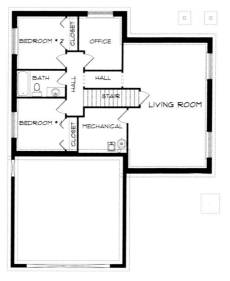

Optional Lower Level
1,069 sq. ft.

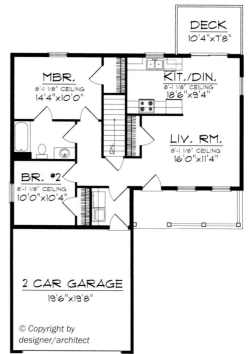

Plan #F07-051D-0888

Dimensions: 38' W x 48' D
Heated Sq. Ft.: 950
Bedrooms: 2 **Bathrooms:** 1
Exterior Walls: 2" x 6"
Foundation: Basement standard; crawl space or slab available for an additional fee

See index for more information

Images provided by designer/architect

© Copyright by designer/architect

Plan #F07-008D-0016

Dimensions: 32' W x 24' D
Heated Sq. Ft.: 768
Bonus Sq. Ft.: 288
Bedrooms: 2 **Bathrooms:** 1
Foundation: Crawl space or slab, please specify when ordering

See index for more information

Images provided by designer/architect

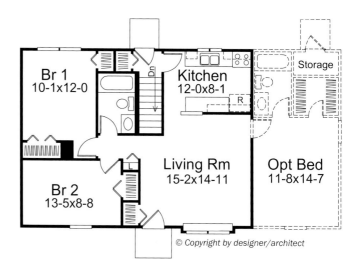

© Copyright by designer/architect

Plan #F07-156D-0008

Dimensions: 25' W x 20'6" D
Heated Sq. Ft.: 400
Bedrooms: 1   **Bathrooms:** 1
Foundation: Slab standard; crawl space available for an additional fee

See index for more information

Images provided by designer/architect

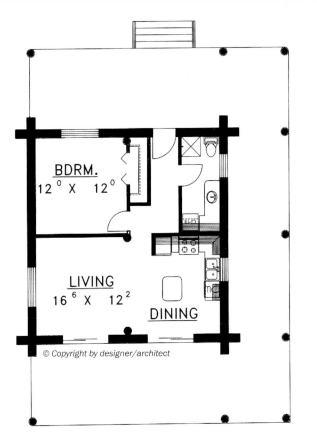

Plan #F07-088D-0326

Images provided by designer/architect

Dimensions: 25' W x 26' D
Heated Sq. Ft.: 689
Bedrooms: 1   **Bathrooms:** 1
Exterior Walls.: Log
Foundation: Crawl space

See index for more information

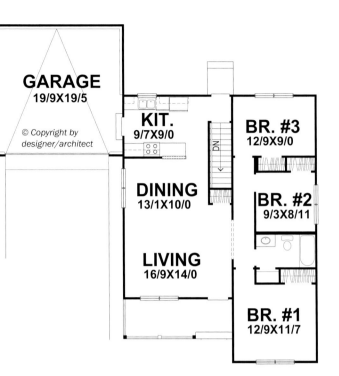

Plan #F07-046D-0093

Dimensions:	50'4" W x 51'4" D
Heated Sq. Ft.:	1,069
Bedrooms: 3	Bathrooms: 1
Foundation:	Basement

See index for more information

Images provided by designer/architect

GARAGE
19/9X19/5

© Copyright by designer/architect

KIT.
9/7X9/0

DINING
13/1X10/0

LIVING
16/9X14/0

BR. #3
12/9X9/0

BR. #2
9/3X8/11

BR. #1
12/9X11/7

DN

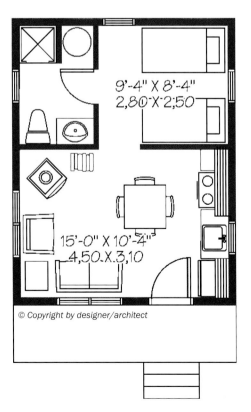

Plan #F07-032D-0706

Dimensions:	16' W x 20' D
Heated Sq. Ft.:	320
Bedrooms: 1	Bathrooms: 1
Exterior Walls:	2" x 6"

Foundation: Screw pile standard; crawl space, floating slab or mono-lithic slab available for an additional fee

See index for more information

Images provided by designer/architect

9'-4" X 8'-4"
2,80 X 2,50

15'-0" X 10'-4"
4,50 X 3,10

© Copyright by designer/architect

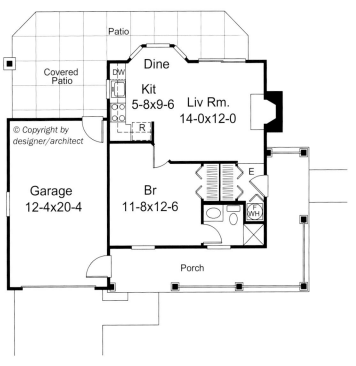

Plan #F07-007D-0142

Dimensions:	38' W x 30' D
Heated Sq. Ft.:	480
Bedrooms: 1	**Bathrooms:** 1
Foundation:	Slab

See index for more information

Images provided by designer/architect

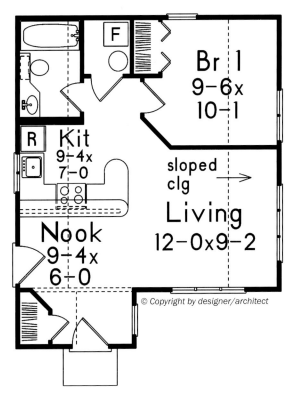

Plan #F07-008D-0154

Dimensions:	22' W x 26'6" D
Heated Sq. Ft.:	527
Bedrooms: 1	**Bathrooms:** 1
Foundation:	Crawl space

See index for more information

Images provided by designer/architect

Second Floor
298 sq. ft.

BR.
11/8 X 11/0
(11' CLG.)

(8' CLG.)

W/D

LINEN

DN

DESK

Images provided by
designer/architect

© Copyright by designer/architect

Plan #F07-011D-0616

Dimensions: 15' W x 24' D
Heated Sq. Ft.: 628
Bedrooms: 1 Bathrooms: 1
Exterior Walls: 2" x 6"
Foundation: Crawl space or slab standard; basement available for an additional fee

See index for more information

LIVING
14/0 X 12/8
(9' CLG.)

6/10 X 7/6

REF

UP

First Floor
330 sq. ft.

Plan #F07-126D-1012

Dimensions: 30' W x 30' D
Heated Sq. Ft.: 815
Bedrooms: 1 Bathrooms: 1
Exterior Walls: 2" x 6"
Foundation: Basement

See index for more information

Images provided by
designer/architect

© Copyright by designer/architect

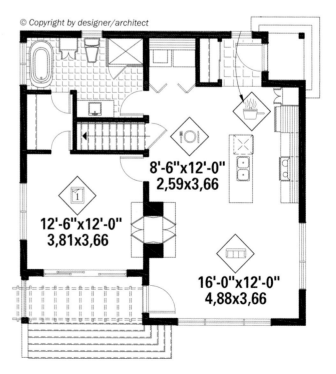

8'-6"x12'-0"
2,59x3,66

12'-6"x12'-0"
3,81x3,66

16'-0"x12'-0"
4,88x3,66

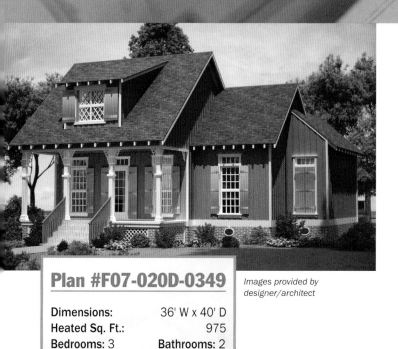

Plan #F07-020D-0349

Images provided by designer/architect

Dimensions: 36' W x 40' D
Heated Sq. Ft.: 975
Bedrooms: 3   Bathrooms: 2
Exterior Walls: 2" x 6"
Foundation: Crawl space standard; slab available for an additional fee

See index for more information

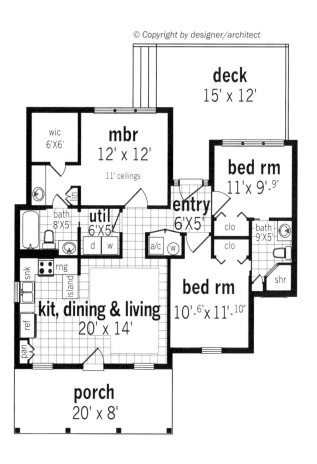

© Copyright by designer/architect

deck
15' x 12'

wic
6'X6'

mbr
12' x 12'

11' ceilings

bed rm
11'x 9'-9"

bath
8'X5'

util
6'X5'

entry
6'X5'

clo

clo

bath
9'X5'

d w

a/c

w

shr

snk

rng

island

kit, dining & living
20' x 14'

ref

pan

bed rm
10'.6"x 11'-10"

porch
20' x 8'

Plan #F07-058D-0010

Images provided by designer/architect

Dimensions: 26' W x 32' D
Heated Sq. Ft.: 676
Bedrooms: 1   Bathrooms: 1
Foundation: Crawl space

See index for more information

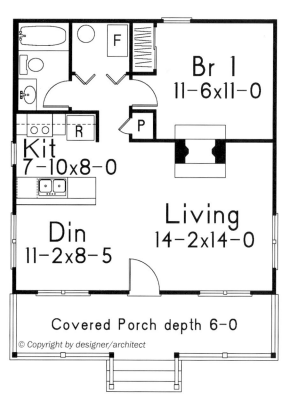

F

Br 1
11-6x11-0

R

P

Kit
7-10x8-0

Din
11-2x8-5

Living
14-2x14-0

Covered Porch depth 6-0

© Copyright by designer/architect

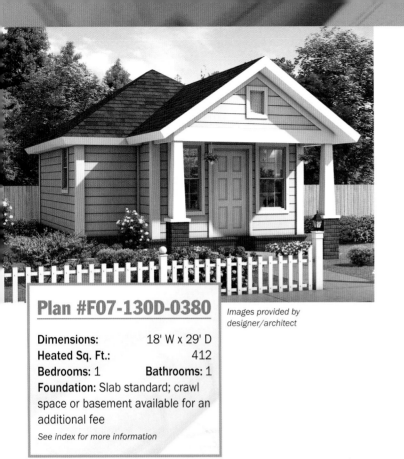

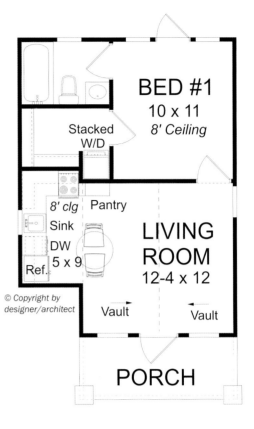

BED #1
10 x 11
8' Ceiling

Stacked W/D

8' clg Pantry

Sink

DW
5 x 9

Ref.

LIVING ROOM
12-4 x 12

Vault   Vault

© Copyright by designer/architect

PORCH

Plan #F07-130D-0380

Images provided by designer/architect

Dimensions: 18' W x 29' D
Heated Sq. Ft.: 412
Bedrooms: 1   **Bathrooms:** 1
Foundation: Slab standard; crawl space or basement available for an additional fee

See index for more information

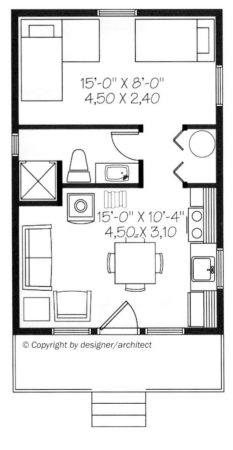

15'-0" X 8'-0"
4,50 X 2,40

15'-0" X 10'-4"
4,50 X 3,10

© Copyright by designer/architect

Plan #F07-032D-0707

Images provided by designer/architect

Dimensions: 16' W x 24' D
Heated Sq. Ft.: 384
Bedrooms: 1   **Bathrooms:** 1
Exterior Walls: 2" x 6"
Foundation: Screw pile standard; crawl space, floating slab or monolithic slab available for an additional fee

See index for more information

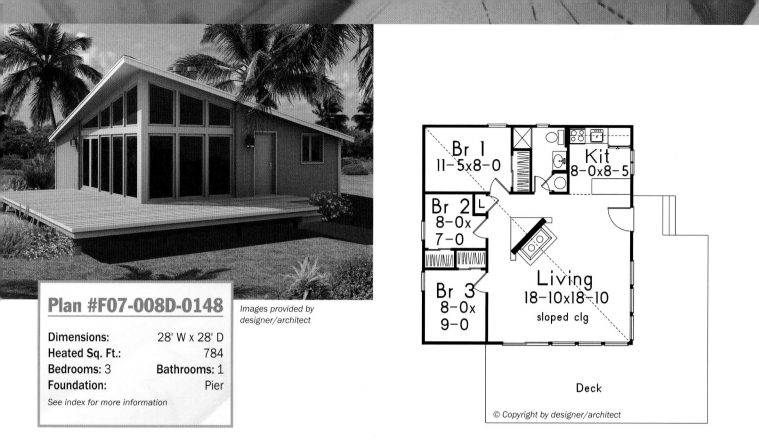

Plan #F07-008D-0148

Images provided by
designer/architect

Dimensions:	28' W x 28' D
Heated Sq. Ft.:	784
Bedrooms: 3	Bathrooms: 1
Foundation:	Pier

See index for more information

© Copyright by designer/architect

Plan #F07-040D-0029

Images provided by
designer/architect

Dimensions:	30' W x 30'6" D
Heated Sq. Ft.:	1,028
Bedrooms: 3	Bathrooms: 1
Foundation:	Crawl space

See index for more information

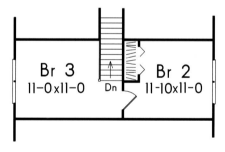

Second Floor
300 sq. ft.

© Copyright by
designer/architect

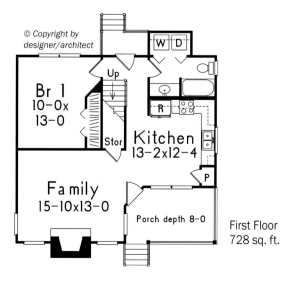

First Floor
728 sq. ft.

Plan #F07-126D-1355

Images provided by designer/architect

Dimensions:	40' W x 32' D
Heated Sq. Ft.:	896
Bedrooms: 2	Bathrooms: 1
Exterior Walls:	2" x 6"
Foundation:	Basement

See index for more information

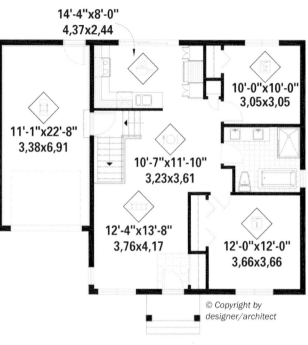

14'-4"x8'-0"
4,37x2,44

10'-0"x10'-0"
3,05x3,05

11'-1"x22'-8"
3,38x6,91

10'-7"x11'-10"
3,23x3,61

12'-4"x13'-8"
3,76x4,17

12'-0"x12'-0"
3,66x3,66

© Copyright by designer/architect

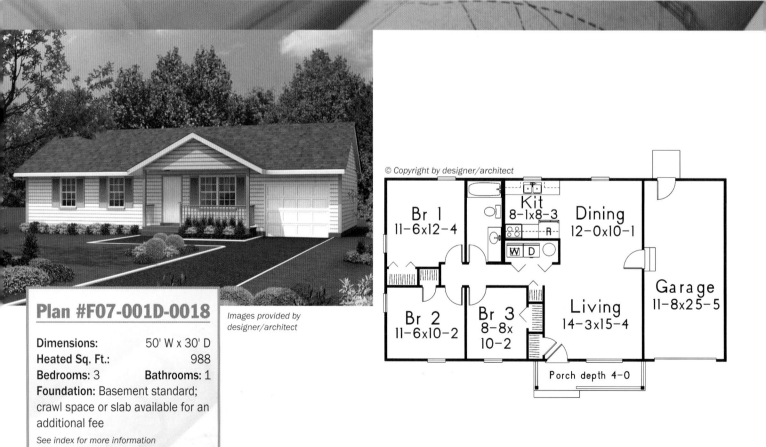

Plan #F07-001D-0018

Images provided by designer/architect

Dimensions:	50' W x 30' D
Heated Sq. Ft.:	988
Bedrooms: 3	Bathrooms: 1

Foundation: Basement standard; crawl space or slab available for an additional fee

See index for more information

© Copyright by designer/architect

Br 1
11-6x12-4

Kit
8-1x8-3

Dining
12-0x10-1

Br 2
11-6x10-2

Br 3
8-8x
10-2

Living
14-3x15-4

Garage
11-8x25-5

Porch depth 4-0

Plan #F07-008D-0026

Images provided by
designer/architect

Dimensions: 52' W x 32' D
Heated Sq. Ft.: 1,120
Bedrooms: 3 **Bathrooms:** 1
Foundation: Basement standard;
crawl space or slab available for an
additional fee

See index for more information

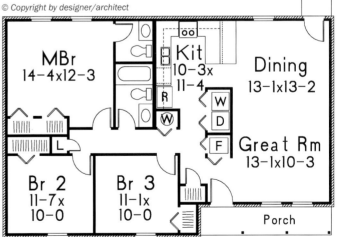

Plan #F07-001D-0082

Images provided by
designer/architect

Dimensions: 44' W x 28' D
Heated Sq. Ft.: 1,160
Bedrooms: 3 **Bathrooms:** 1½
Foundation: Crawl space standard;
basement or slab available for an
additional fee

See index for more information

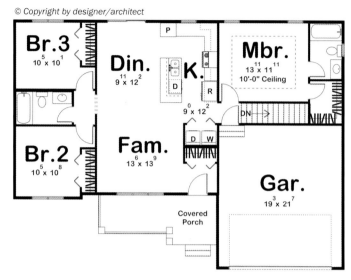

© Copyright by designer/architect

Images provided by designer/architect

Plan #F07-123D-0060

Dimensions:	52' W x 38' D
Heated Sq. Ft.:	1,185
Bedrooms: 3	Bathrooms: 2

Foundation: Basement standard; crawl space, slab or walk-out basement available for an additional fee

See index for more information

Images provided by designer/architect

Plan #F07-126D-0995

Dimensions:	30' W x 20' D
Heated Sq. Ft.:	600
Bedrooms: 2	Bathrooms: 1
Exterior Walls:	2" x 6"
Foundation:	Pier

See index for more information

Plan #F07-141D-0230

Images provided by designer/architect

Dimensions: 26' W x 32' D
Heated Sq. Ft.: 676
Bedrooms: 1 **Bathrooms:** 1
Foundation: Slab or crawl space standard; basement or daylight basement available for an additional fee

See index for more information

STOOP

BATHROOM 11 x 8

SHWR 5 X 3 UTILITY L 5 x 3

CLO CLO

LIN

P

EAT-IN KITCHEN 14 x 11

BEDROOM 11 x 16

LIVING ROOM 14 x 14

© Copyright by designer/architect

COVERED PORCH 26 X 6

Plan #F07-022D-0024

Images provided by designer/architect

Dimensions: 34'8" W x 52' D
Heated Sq. Ft.: 1,127
Bedrooms: 2 **Bathrooms:** 2
Foundation: Basement

See index for more information

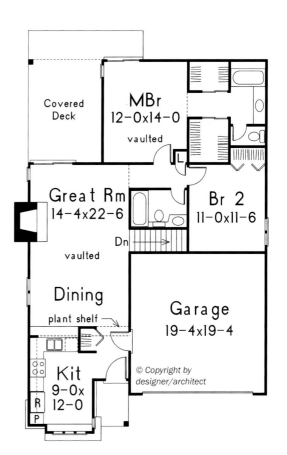

Covered Deck

MBr 12-0x14-0 vaulted

Great Rm 14-4x22-6 vaulted

Br 2 11-0x11-6

Dn

Dining

plant shelf

Kit 9-0x 12-0

Garage 19-4x19-4

© Copyright by designer/architect

Plan #F07-123D-0263

Dimensions:	36' W x 23' D
Heated Sq. Ft.:	756
Bedrooms: 1	**Bathrooms:** 1

Foundation: Slab standard; crawl space, basement or walk-out available for an additional fee

See index for more information

Features

- This terrific cottage has a Modern Farmhouse bungalow feel and a covered metal awning overhang above the front porch creating excellent curb appeal
- Enter through the double French doors and discover a mud room style entry so popular today with a coat closet on the left, and a built-in bench with hooks above on the right
- The kitchen has a great little island offering additional prep space or even a easy spot for a quick meal on-the-go
- The great room, dining space and kitchen are designed to enjoy plenty of sunshine from multiple windows
- The bedroom is directly across the hall from a full bath, which is adjacent to a washer and dryer closet

Images provided by designer/architect

© Copyright by designer/architect

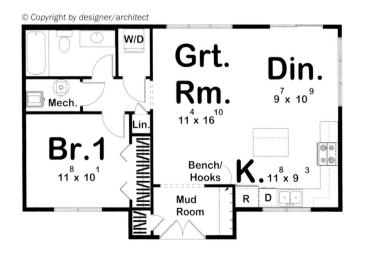

Plan #F07-126D-1039

Dimensions:	24' W x 28' D
Heated Sq. Ft.:	1,015
Bedrooms: 2	**Bathrooms:** 2
Exterior Walls:	2" x 6"
Foundation:	Basement

See index for more information

Images provided by designer/architect

Features

- This country cottage boasts great outdoor living spaces that include a covered deck as well as a screened porch, perfect for pest-free dining

- The living area is open to the kitchen and has an enormous fireplace keeping the space cozy

- The second floor includes a bedroom and a space that overlooks to the living room below, perfect for a home office

- The kitchen enjoys a roomy wrap-around countertop and double doors leading to the covered deck

© Copyright by designer/architect

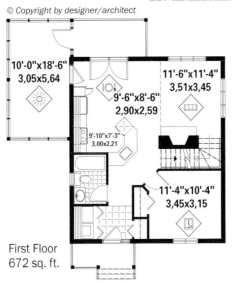

First Floor
672 sq. ft.

Second Floor
343 sq. ft.

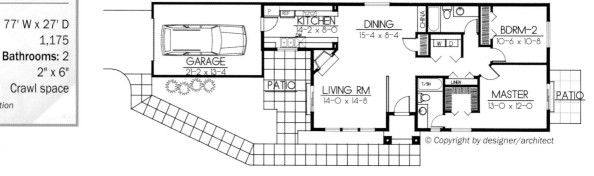

Images provided by designer/architect

Plan #F07-015D-0087

Dimensions:	77' W x 27' D
Heated Sq. Ft.:	1,175
Bedrooms: 2	Bathrooms: 2
Exterior Walls:	2" x 6"
Foundation:	Crawl space

See index for more information

© Copyright by designer/architect

Plan #F07-126D-0162

Images provided by designer/architect

Dimensions:	24' W x 37' D
Heated Sq. Ft.:	888
Bedrooms: 2	Bathrooms: 1
Exterior Walls:	2" x 6"
Foundation:	Basement

See index for more information

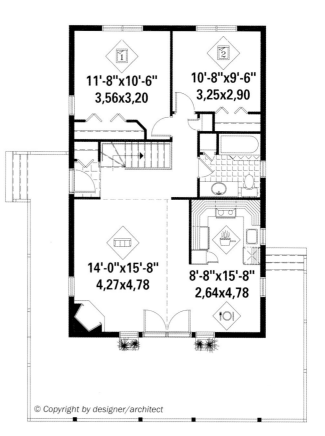

© Copyright by designer/architect

Plan #F07-007D-0199

Dimensions:	39' W x 33' D
Heated Sq. Ft.:	496
Bedrooms: 1	**Bathrooms:** 1
Foundation:	Slab

See index for more information

Images provided by designer/architect

© Copyright by designer/architect

Bedroom
11-3x10-6

Porch

WH Fur.

Kit.

P

R

Garage
19-3x22-4

Dine

Liv. Rm
16-9x12-0

Entry

Porch

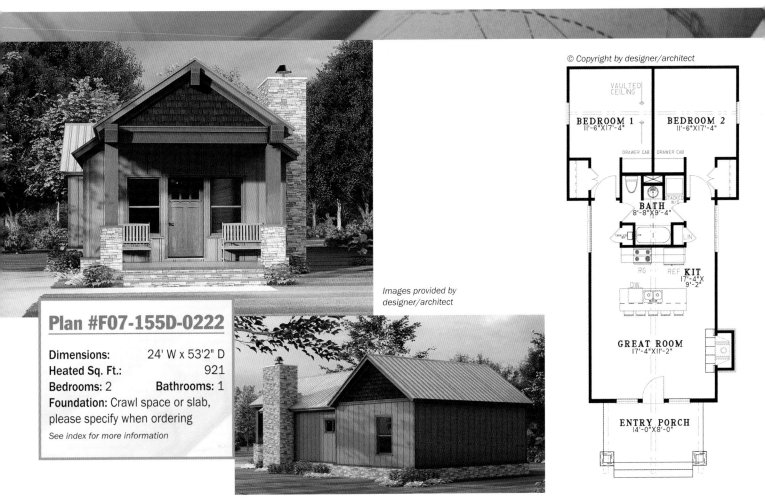

Plan #F07-155D-0222

Dimensions:	24' W x 53'2" D
Heated Sq. Ft.:	921
Bedrooms: 2	**Bathrooms:** 1
Foundation: Crawl space or slab, please specify when ordering	

See index for more information

Images provided by designer/architect

© Copyright by designer/architect

VAULTED CEILING

BEDROOM 1
11'-6"X17'-4"

BEDROOM 2
11'-6"X17'-4"

DRAWER CAB DRAWER CAB

BATH
8'-8"X9'-4"

STACKED W/D

RG   REF KIT
17'-4"X
9'-2"

DW

GREAT ROOM
17'-4"X11'-2"

ENTRY PORCH
14'-0"X8'-0"

Plan #F07-060D-0606

Dimensions:	28' W x 21'2" D
Heated Sq. Ft.:	592
Bedrooms: 1	**Bathrooms:** 1
Foundation:	Slab

See index for more information

Features

- Don't be fooled by this tiny looking exterior, this small home has so much style and function you won't miss the square footage
- Enter from the covered porch and find an open kitchen with a built-in eating bar
- The living area is steps away and opens onto a spacious deck, perfect for summertime entertaining or dining alfresco
- The bath features an oversized walk-in shower that's large enough for a wheelchair making it very accessible for people of ages
- A huge walk-in closet completes the bedroom and adds noteworthy storage space

Images provided by designer/architect

© Copyright by designer/architect

Plan #F07-155D-0215

Dimensions:	40' W x 39'8" D
Heated Sq. Ft.:	1,174
Bedrooms: 3	Bathrooms: 2

Foundation: Crawl space or slab, please specify when ordering

See index for more information

Images provided by designer/architect

Plan #F07-020D-0015

Images provided by designer/architect

Dimensions:	44'6" W x 59' D
Heated Sq. Ft.:	1,191
Bedrooms: 3	Bathrooms: 2
Exterior Walls:	2" x 6"

Foundation: Slab standard; crawl space or basement available for an additional fee

See index for more information

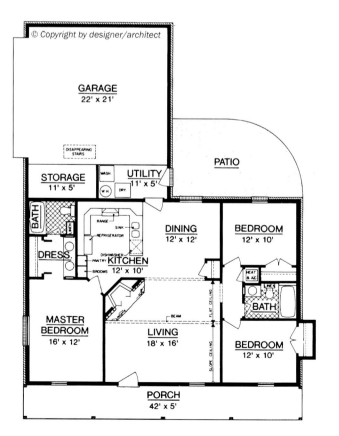

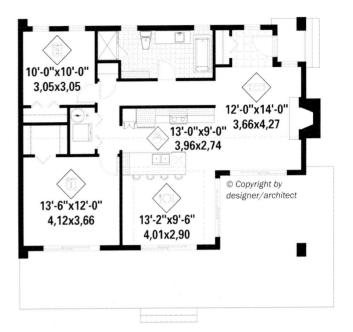

Images provided by
designer/architect

© Copyright by
designer/architect

Plan #F07-126D-1151

Dimensions:	40' W x 30' D
Heated Sq. Ft.:	1,060
Bedrooms: 2	Bathrooms: 1
Exterior Walls:	2" x 6"
Foundation:	Crawl space

See index for more information

10'-0"x10'-0"
3,05x3,05

12'-0"x14'-0"
3,66x4,27

13'-0"x9'-0"
3,96x2,74

13'-6"x12'-0"
4,12x3,66

13'-2"x9'-6"
4,01x2,90

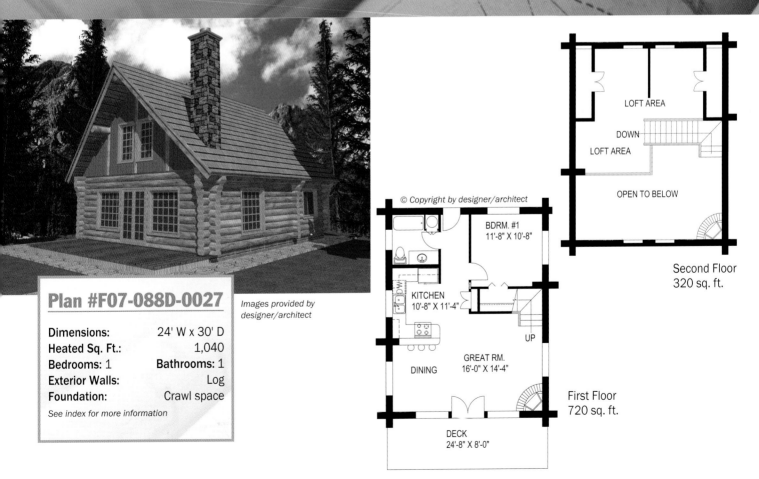

Images provided by
designer/architect

Plan #F07-088D-0027

Dimensions:	24' W x 30' D
Heated Sq. Ft.:	1,040
Bedrooms: 1	Bathrooms: 1
Exterior Walls:	Log
Foundation:	Crawl space

See index for more information

LOFT AREA

DOWN

LOFT AREA

OPEN TO BELOW

Second Floor
320 sq. ft.

© Copyright by designer/architect

BDRM. #1
11'-8" X 10'-8"

KITCHEN
10'-8" X 11'-4"

UP

DINING

GREAT RM.
16'-0" X 14'-4"

First Floor
720 sq. ft.

DECK
24'-8" X 8'-0"

Plan #F07-028D-0090

Dimensions:	31' W x 40' D
Heated Sq. Ft.:	992
Bedrooms: 2	Bathrooms: 1
Exterior Walls:	2" x 6"

Foundation: Crawl space or slab, please specify when ordering

See index for more information

Features

- Charming country living is easily achieved in this smaller one-story with a deep covered front porch
- The great room enjoys built-ins on one wall and space designated for a ventless fireplace for added coziness
- The kitchen enjoys plenty of counterspace and includes great extras like a center prep island, a corner walk-in pantry and a snack bar that overlooks the great room
- A small dining space extends off the kitchen and has sliding glass doors leading to the outdoors
- Two bedrooms are in a private location and both feature walk-in closets and a full bath nearby
- A convenient laundry room is steps from the bedrooms

BEDROOM 1
13' x 12'

LAUNDRY

BEDROOM 2
12' x 10'

BATH

WH

LINEN

DINING AREA
10' x 6'

VENTLESS GAS FIREPLACE

GREAT ROOM
18' x 14'

SNACK BAR

KITCHEN
13' x 13'

PANTRY

8' WIDE COVERED PORCH

© Copyright by designer/architect

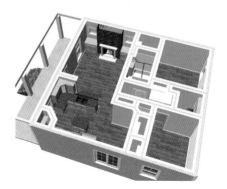

Images provided by designer/architect

Plan #F07-077D-0286

Dimensions: 30' W x 36' D
Heated Sq. Ft.: 1,016
Bedrooms: 2   **Bathrooms:** 1
Foundation: Crawl space standard; slab available for an additional fee

See index for more information

Features

- The Country style exterior of this home brings back the memories of days gone by

- The open floor plan makes this little home feel much larger than its true size thanks to the open loft space above

- The kitchen features a vaulted ceiling and direct access to the screened porch

- Enjoy the screened-in back porch and the luxury of a loft space above make this a most inviting home

- A charming home that will fulfill many families' getaway home needs

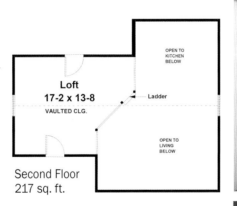

Second Floor
217 sq. ft.

First Floor
799 sq. ft.

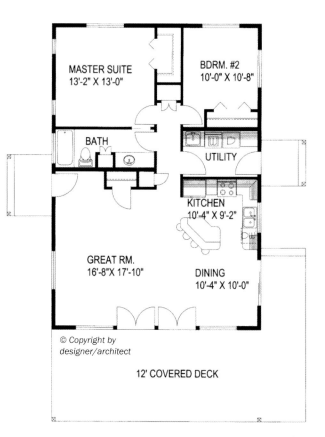

MASTER SUITE
13'-2" X 13'-0"

BDRM. #2
10'-0" X 10'-8"

BATH

UTILITY

KITCHEN
10'-4" X 9'-2"

GREAT RM.
16'-8"X 17'-10"

DINING
10'-4" X 10'-0"

© Copyright by
designer/architect

12' COVERED DECK

*Images provided by
designer/architect*

Plan #F07-088D-0216

Dimensions:	40' W x 52' D
Heated Sq. Ft.:	1,120
Bedrooms: 2	Bathrooms: 1
Exterior Walls:	2" x 6"
Foundation:	Crawl space

See index for more information

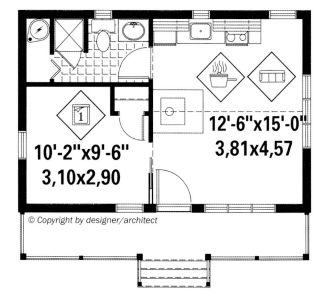

10'-2"x9'-6"
3,10x2,90

12'-6"x15'-0"
3,81x4,57

© Copyright by designer/architect

*Images provided by
designer/architect*

Plan #F07-126D-0987

Dimensions:	24' W x 16' D
Heated Sq. Ft.:	384
Bedrooms: 1	Bathrooms: 1
Exterior Walls:	2" x 6"
Foundation:	Pier

See index for more information

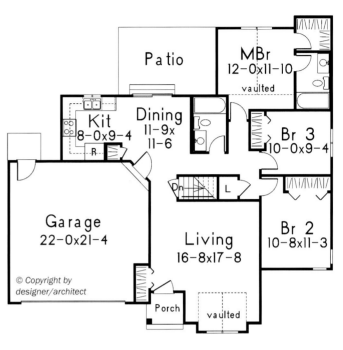

Plan #F07-041D-0004

Images provided by designer/architect

Dimensions:	50' W x 47' D
Heated Sq. Ft.:	1,195
Bedrooms: 3	**Bathrooms:** 2
Foundation:	Basement

See index for more information

Plan #F07-032D-0811

Images provided by designer/architect

Dimensions:	20' W x 38' D
Heated Sq. Ft.:	700
Bedrooms: 2	**Bathrooms:** 1
Exterior Walls:	2" x 6"

Foundation: Crawl space standard; floating slab or monolithic slab available for an additional fee

See index for more information

© Copyright by designer/architect

Br 1
13-0x12-0

Hall

Dn

Br 2
11-10x10-8

Attic

Second Floor
519 sq. ft.

Entry

Shop / Studio or Great Rm
17-4x26-6

Porch

First Floor
612 sq. ft.

Plan #F07-007D-0179

Images provided by designer/architect

Dimensions:	20' W x 39' D
Heated Sq. Ft.:	1,131
Bedrooms: 2	**Bathrooms:** 1½
Foundation:	Slab

See index for more information

© Copyright by designer/architect

Atrium

Kit
9-4x
11-8

Garage
21-0x11-8

Dine

Great Rm
20-0x15-4
vaulted

Hall

Porch

Br 2
11-6x13-0

MBr
11-6x15-3

vaulted

First Floor
1,114 sq. ft.

Patio

Optional Game Rm
9-4x11-8

Atrium open to above

Optional Family Rm
15-0x20-6

Basement

Optional Lower Level
364 sq. ft.

Plan #F07-007D-0169

Images provided by designer/architect

Dimensions:	53'8" W x 38'8" D
Heated Sq. Ft.:	1,114
Bonus Sq. Ft.:	364
Bedrooms: 2	**Bathrooms:** 1
Foundation:	Walk-out basement

See index for more information

Plan #F07-008D-0144

Dimensions: 42' W x 28' D
Heated Sq. Ft.: 1,176
Bedrooms: 4   **Bathrooms:** 2
Foundation: Crawl space standard; slab available for an additional fee

See index for more information

Images provided by designer/architect

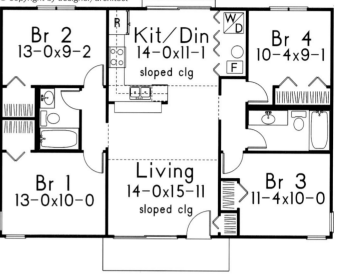

© Copyright by designer/architect

Br 2
13-0x9-2

Kit/Din
14-0x11-1
sloped clg

Br 4
10-4x9-1

Br 1
13-0x10-0

Living
14-0x15-11
sloped clg

Br 3
11-4x10-0

Plan #F07-141D-0003

Dimensions: 32' W x 48' D
Heated Sq. Ft.: 765
Bonus Sq. Ft.: 792
Bedrooms: 1   **Bathrooms:** 1
Foundation: Slab standard; crawl space, basement or walk-out basement available for an additional fee

See index for more information

Images provided by designer/architect

BATH #2
10 x 5

UTILITY
6 x 6

WET BAR
10 x 10

BEDROOM
10 x 12

MECH
5 x 8

CLO
5 x 6

CLO

DEN
20 x 13

UP

PORCH
DECK
ABOVE

COVERED PATIO AREA
21 x 8

Optional
Lower Level
792 sq. ft.

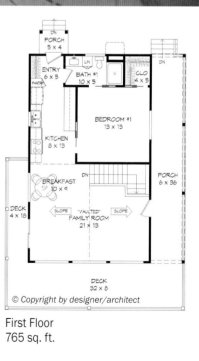

PORCH
5 x 4

ENTRY
6 x 5

BATH #1
10 x 5

CLO
4 x 5

BEDROOM #1
13 x 13

KITCHEN
8 x 13

BREAKFAST
10 x 9

PORCH
6 x 36

DECK
4 x 18

SLOPE   "VAULTED"   SLOPE
FAMILY ROOM
21 x 13

DECK
32 x 8

© Copyright by designer/architect

First Floor
765 sq. ft.

Plan #F07-032D-0828

Images provided by designer/architect

Dimensions: 40' W x 50' D
Heated Sq. Ft.: 1,040
Bedrooms: 2   **Bathrooms:** 2
Exterior Walls: 2" x 6"
Foundation: Basement standard; crawl space, floating slab or monolithic slab available for an additional fee

See index for more information

© Copyright by designer/architect

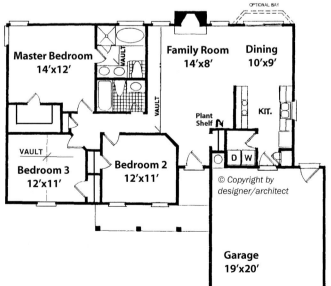

Plan #F07-013D-0002

Images provided by designer/architect

Dimensions: 52' W x 42' D
Heated Sq. Ft.: 1,197
Bedrooms: 3   **Bathrooms:** 2
Foundation: Crawl space or slab standard; basement available for an additional fee

See index for more information

© Copyright by designer/architect

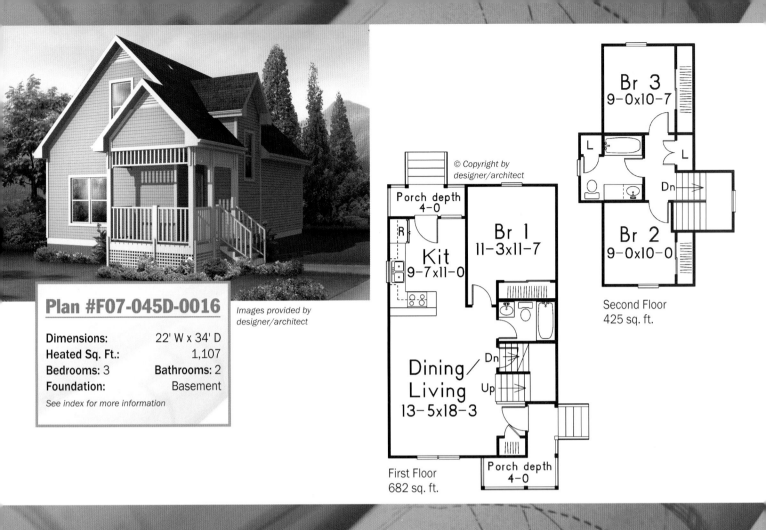

Plan #F07-045D-0016

Dimensions: 22' W x 34' D
Heated Sq. Ft.: 1,107
Bedrooms: 3 **Bathrooms:** 2
Foundation: Basement

See index for more information

Images provided by designer/architect

© Copyright by designer/architect

Second Floor 425 sq. ft.

First Floor 682 sq. ft.

Br 3 9-0x10-7
Br 2 9-0x10-0
Dn
L L

Porch depth 4-0
R
Kit 9-7x11-0
Br 1 11-3x11-7
Dining Living 13-5x18-3
Dn
Up
Porch depth 4-0

Plan #F07-007D-0175

Dimensions: 26' W x 40' D
Heated Sq. Ft.: 882
Bedrooms: 2 **Bathrooms:** 1
Foundation: Crawl space standard; slab or basement available for an additional fee

See index for more information

Images provided by designer/architect

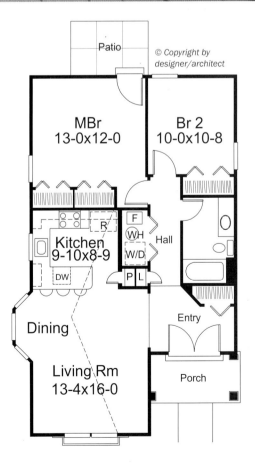

© Copyright by designer/architect

Patio
MBr 13-0x12-0
Br 2 10-0x10-8
F
WH
W/D
Hall
Kitchen 9-10x8-9
R
DW
P L
Dining
Entry
Living Rm 13-4x16-0
Porch

Dn

8-5x7-0
Bath

W/D

Kit./Brk.
12-8x10-1

R

P

L

Sitting
13-8x13-3

Bedroom
11-4x11-2

Covered
Porch
8-0x4-4

Plan #F07-058D-0211

Images provided by designer/architect

Dimensions:	28' W x 28'4" D
Heated Sq. Ft.:	658
Bedrooms: 1	Bathrooms: 1
Foundation:	Basement

See index for more information

Plan #F07-060D-0014

Images provided by designer/architect

Dimensions:	38' W x 32' D
Heated Sq. Ft.:	1,021
Bedrooms: 3	Bathrooms: 2

Foundation: Slab or crawl space, please specify when ordering

See index for more information

COFFERED
CEILING
MASTER
SUITE
12-5 x 11-0

B.1

WALK-IN
CLOSET

WASH/DRY

BRK.
11-0 x 14-11

KIT.

CLOSET

KN
SP

B.2

SHV

DW. SINK RANGE REF

2 CAR
GARAGE
(OPTIONAL)

PULL-DN
STAIRS

HALL

B.R. 2
9-0 x 10-0

B.R. 3
10-0 x 9-0

LIN
CTS

ENT

GREAT
ROOM
13-0 x 16-0

© Copyright by designer/architect

PORCH

SLOPE   11' CEILING   SLOPE

Plan #F07-007D-0154

Images provided by designer/architect

Dimensions: 40' W x 42' D
Heated Sq. Ft.: 1,196
Bedrooms: 3   **Bathrooms:** 2
Foundation: Crawl space standard; slab available for an additional fee

See index for more information

Plan #F07-087D-0009

Images provided by designer/architect

Dimensions: 22' W x 58' D
Heated Sq. Ft.: 1,148
Bedrooms: 3   **Bathrooms:** 2
Foundation: Slab

See index for more information

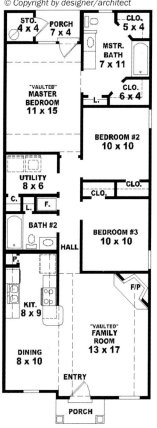

Plan #F07-028D-0084

Dimensions:	33' W x 42' D
Heated Sq. Ft.:	1,122
Bedrooms: 2	**Bathrooms:** 2

Foundation: Crawl space or slab, please specify when ordering

See index for more information

Images provided by designer/architect

Features

- The charming front porch is the perfect spot for enjoying the outdoors
- The efficient kitchen includes an optional center island and convenient snack bar
- An ample amount of closet space thanks to roomy walk-in closets in both bedrooms makes organizing a breeze

Porch no. 2

BEDROOM 1
13-0 x 14-4

KITCHEN DINING
12-0 x 16-6

LINEN   PANTRY

COUNTER HIGH SNACK BAR

HVAC

BEDROOM 2
13-0 x 12-0

GREAT ROOM
20-0 x 14-0

Porch no. 1

© Copyright by designer/architect

Plan #F07-007D-0193

Dimensions:	26'4" W x 28' D
Heated Sq. Ft.:	771
Bedrooms: 1	**Bathrooms:** 1½
Foundation:	Walk-out basement

See index for more information

Images provided by designer/architect

Features

- The living room includes a vaulted ceiling, a separate entry with a guest closet, and sliding glass doors to the rear deck
- A vaulted ceiling and overhead plant shelf are two attractive features of the L-shaped kitchen that open up to the living room
- The lower level is comprised of a spacious bedroom complete with a private bath, a walk-in closet, and sliding glass doors to the rear patio
- 1-car side entry garage

Lower Level
358 sq. ft.

© Copyright by designer/architect

First Floor
413 sq. ft.

Plan #F07-011D-0471

Dimensions:	24' W x 14' D
Heated Sq. Ft.:	728
Bedrooms: 1	**Bathrooms:** 1
Exterior Walls:	2" x 6"

Foundation: Crawl space or slab standard; basement available for an additional fee

See index for more information

Images provided by designer/architect

Features

- Build this striking Contemporary home as a vacation home, or as the efficiently designed micro-home you've always wanted

- The first floor features a combined kitchen and living room

- Although this home has a compact design, you'll still have plenty of space in the kitchen to prepare meals

- The second floor features the main bedroom, a full bath, and a washer and dryer closet

- On the third floor, there is room for a built-in guest bed with optional drawers underneath if you'd like to host a friend or, instead utilize this space as a small office

Rear View

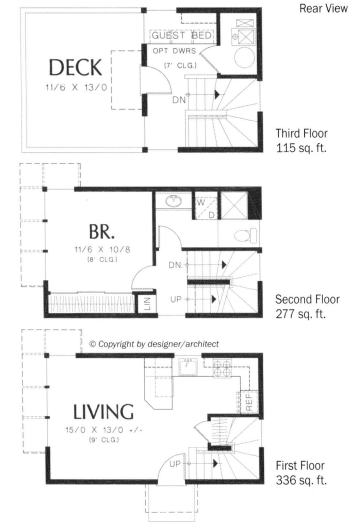

DECK 11/6 X 13/0

GUEST BED
OPT DWRS
(7' CLG.)
DN

Third Floor
115 sq. ft.

BR. 11/6 X 10/8
(8' CLG.)
DN.
UP
LIN

Second Floor
277 sq. ft.

© *Copyright by designer/architect*

LIVING 15/0 X 13/0 +/-
(9' CLG.)
UP

First Floor
336 sq. ft.

Alternate Exterior Colors

Images provided by designer/architect

Plan #F07-032D-0812

Dimensions:	20' W x 30' D
Heated Sq. Ft.:	943
Bedrooms: 3	**Bathrooms:** 2
Exterior Walls:	2" x 6"

Foundation: Basement standard; crawl space, floating slab or monolithic slab available for an additional fee

See index for more information

Features

- Perfect for a rural or city setting with its narrow footprint and charming curb appeal, this home offers a very livable floor plan that includes an open living and dining space that is also incorporated into the kitchen
- The master suite has direct outdoor access onto a private patio and a double door entry
- The two second floor bedrooms have large windows for plenty of light and share a bath

© Copyright by designer/architect

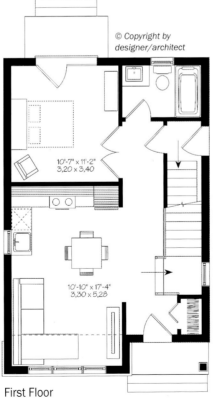

First Floor
576 sq. ft.

10'-7" x 11'-2"
3,20 x 3,40

10'-10" x 17'-4"
3,30 x 5,28

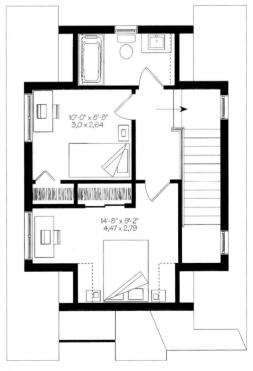

Second Floor
367 sq. ft.

10'-0" x 8'-8"
3,0 x 2,64

14'-8" x 9'-2"
4,47 x 2,79

Left Side Elevation

Plan #F07-057D-0034

Dimensions: 34'8" W x 40' D
Heated Sq. Ft.: 1,020
Bedrooms: 2   Bathrooms: 1
Exterior Walls: 2" x 6"
Foundation: Basement

See index for more information

© Copyright by designer/architect

Images provided by designer/architect

MBr
11-8x14-9

Br 2
10-11x10-9

L

Dn

Front of House

Living/Dining
22-0x13-7

Kit
9-0x13-7

R

Porch
32-0x8-0

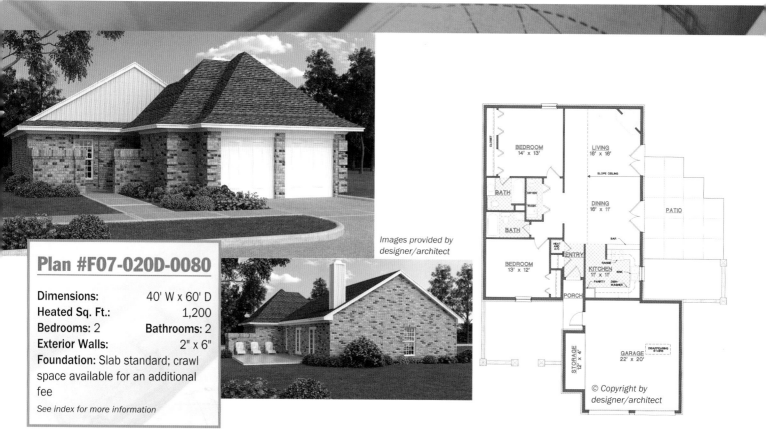

Images provided by designer/architect

Plan #F07-020D-0080

Dimensions: 40' W x 60' D
Heated Sq. Ft.: 1,200
Bedrooms: 2   Bathrooms: 2
Exterior Walls: 2" x 6"
Foundation: Slab standard; crawl space available for an additional fee

See index for more information

BEDROOM
14' x 13'

LIVING
18' x 16'

SLOPE CEILING

BATH

DRYER

WASH

DINING
16' x 11'

PATIO

BATH

BEDROOM
13' x 12'

HEAT
AND
A/C

ENTRY

KITCHEN
11' x 11'

BAR

PANTRY

RANGE

DISH
WASHER

PORCH

STORAGE
12' x 4'

GARAGE
22' x 20'

DISAPPEARING
STAIRS

© Copyright by designer/architect

Plan #F07-088D-0077

Images provided by designer/architect

Dimensions:	44' W x 31'9" D
Heated Sq. Ft.:	1,192
Bedrooms: 3	Bathrooms: 1
Exterior Walls:	ICF
Foundation:	Slab

See index for more information

© Copyright by designer/architect

BDRM. #2
10⁰ X 10¹

KITCHEN
10⁰ X 9⁹

DINING
13⁶ X 8⁰

W.H.
REF.
DW

BDRM. #1
12⁴ X 10¹

BDRM. #3
10⁰ X 9⁹

LIVING
13⁶ X 16⁰

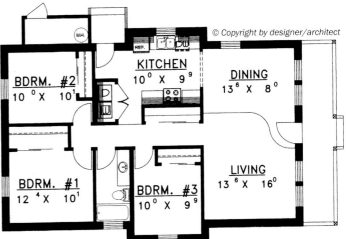

Plan #F07-028D-0076

Images provided by designer/architect

Dimensions:	33' W x 36' D
Heated Sq. Ft.:	1,073
Bedrooms: 2	Bathrooms: 2
Foundation: Crawl space or slab, please specify when ordering	

See index for more information

© Copyright by designer/architect

BEDROOM 2
13-0 X 12-0

KITCHEN/
DINING
12-0 X 16-6

SNACK BAR

BEDROOM 1
12-0 X 13-0

GREAT ROOM
18-8 X 14-0

PORCH
5-6 DEEP

economize your home & save more money by BUILDING GREEN

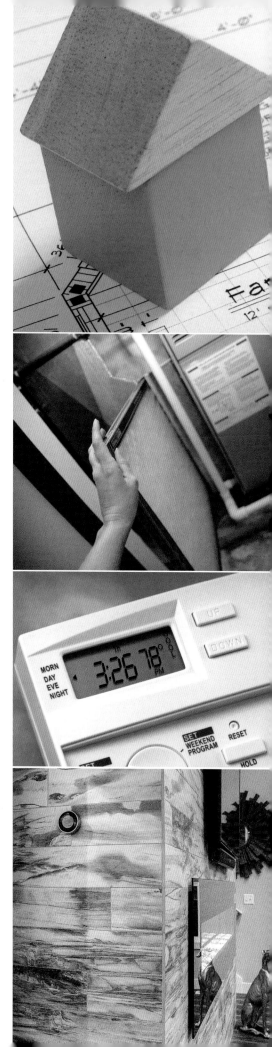

The cost of running a home day-to-day hasn't gotten any cheaper. From daily maintenance to gas, water, and electric usage, families are paying closer attention than ever on how their home spends their income. As people try to live a life that is more efficient, there are ways to better economize your home so that it doesn't drain you of every last penny. The top three culprits are utilities. So, it's easy to see why there is a lot of buzz about green building and it's for good reason. These ideas below will have you being more mindful of your actions within your home and offer some better solutions for saving money, resources and the environment.

COOL CHANGE

No one likes to feel chilled in their own home, but some small changes with your gas usage can make a big difference when you get your monthly bill. Set your thermostat as low as you can in the winter. For every degree you raise your thermostat setting, your gas bill rises 3%. So maybe wearing a cozy sweatshirt indoors to stay warm doesn't sound so bad after all.

CLEAR THE AIR

Clean or replace your air filter every three months, or as needed to improve your system's efficiency by as much as 10%. You can also consider adding extra caulking and weather stripping to exterior seams, cracks, or openings around your home. Pay special attention to points where two different materials meet as well as around the window frames. Closing these drafty spots will keep your home noticeably warmer all winter.

Another idea is to close off rooms in your home that aren't in use. Shut the vents so the air can be directed into the parts of your home that you do use daily.

Page 234, top to bottom: green home with blueprints, istockphoto.com; Changing your furnace filter keeps energy costs down, istockphoto.com; a digital thermostat can be programmed for even more savings, istock-photo.com; Sleek digital thermostat, Matthew Ralphs, photographer, miralphsphotography.com; Page 235, top: energy efficient light bulb, istockphoto.com, Eric Delmar, photographer, bottom: Dripping water faucet, © David Acosta Allely, photographer.

GO DIGITAL

Installing a digital thermostat is an inexpensive way to reduce the cost of your heating and air-conditioning bills. According to the Department of Energy you can save 10-15% on your heating and cooling bills annually by reducing the temperature by 10% for eight hours a day. That means while you're at work drop your home's temperature to 63 degrees and then have it programmed to increase to 70 degrees right before you get home. You will save money without any sacrifice in comfort.

FAN CLUB

Using fans all throughout your home will make your home feel cooler than it is. So, turn up a fan and let a brisk breeze blow through the rooms. Be sure to keep all of your blinds or draperies closed to keep spaces cooler, too. Rooms warm up when direct sunlight filters into them, so to keep it cooler, shut the blinds especially on windows facing the west and south.

BRIGHT IDEA

Other quick and easy electricity saving ideas include: using compact fluorescent light bulbs, plugging appliances into a power strip that can be turned off and buying Energy Star® appliances.

Building green will take your savings to whole other level. Buildings, including homes, account for almost half of the total U.S. energy consumption. Relatively simple changes in a home's design including its solar orientation, air sealing technique, use of high performance windows, installation of an efficient HVAC, and increased insulation can cut costs in half, or by even more.

START SAVING $$$ NOW

There are many ways to stop wasting water and minimizing water usage throughout your home. Being aware of your actions and making simple changes can make a big difference in savings. Use the tips to the right to get started!

Minimize Your Water Usage

- Check faucets and pipes and make sure there are no leaks. Even the smallest drip can waste 20 gallons of water per day.

- Don't use the toilet for a waste can or ashtray. Each time you flush a conventional toilet 5 to 7 gallons of water is wasted. Be aware of how you dispose of items and learn to reuse or recycle first, then toss in the trash instead of flushing.

- Take shorter showers, turn off the sink when brushing your teeth, clean vegetables without the sink running, rinse dishes without running your dishwasher, and only run the washing machine when full. These easy adjustments cut costs and save water without even noticing.

- When building or renovating a home, cut water usage in half by using the following items: Low flow faucets and shower heads, low flow or dual-flush toilets, Energy Star® or water sense dishwashers and washing machines, plant native and drought resistant landscaping, and install a water sensing irrigation system. Every gallon of water conserved means less energy to purify, deliver to a home, and then treat and return to the environment.

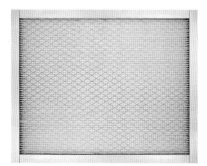

It's Easy To Be Green

Besides conserving water and energy, consider these other important reasons for building green:

GREEN BUILDING IS HEALTHIER

Indoor pollutant levels may be 2-5 times higher than outdoor levels, and on average, Americans spend about 90% of their time indoors. Green building improves indoor air quality by air sealing, proper ventilation, air filtration, moisture management, and avoiding potential sources of pollutants such as VOCs and formaldehyde, which will result in far less illness.

GREEN BUILDING IS A BETTER INVESTMENT

The demand for green homes is growing greater every year. Green certified homes increase in value over time and save you money each and every month because of lower water, electric, and gas bills. All green certified homes have what is called a Home Energy Rating (HERS rating). Homes with Green Certifications, or HERS ratings, maintain better indoor air quality and will continue to enjoy higher resale values.

GREEN BUILDING PROTECTS FROM FURTHER POLLUTION

The pavement poured in subdivisions around homes for driveways and sidewalks in neighborhoods replaces natural surfaces with impermeable surfaces, creating runoff that washes sediments and pollution into waterways. This runoff is the fourth leading source of pollution in rivers, third in lakes, and second in estuaries. Green building prevents this runoff by reducing impermeable surfaces, minimizing soil disturbance and erosion, and managing storm water by using low-impact development.

GREEN BUILDING REDUCES WASTE

By offering efficient floor plans, utilizing advanced framing techniques, using materials that require fewer resources, incorporating renewable resources, reclaimed or recycled materials, green building reduces waste from start to finish.

GREEN BUILDING REDUCES OUR CARBON FOOTPRINT

By reducing energy requirements, and the amount of materials and resources needed for construction green building reduces our carbon footprint. Green development also works to site homes and businesses near essential services and sources of mass transit. In 1969, 48% of students walked or biked to and from school compared to less than 15% in 2001. By changing the focus of our developments from automobiles to humans, we can impact the CO^2 emissions that come from autos.

Understanding the reasons for green building and implementing them in your home will add money back into your pocket, while providing a safer, more comfortable environment for everyone in your home, and the world around you.

the big advantages of living in a small home

more money
Whether you want to shrink your mortgage, or you use the proceeds of selling your current home to pay entirely for a new smaller home, you will end up with more money in your pocket for saving, or spending another way. Not only does a small home cost less, but the utilities and on-going maintenance will also be less. Cutting costs is an instant way to increase your savings. So, whether you retire in 5 years, or you're just starting out, think about the added financial security a smaller home will bring to your future and your financial situation. Smaller homes don't have wasted space, so you will also be living more efficiently. Using less energy means lower utility bills, a more responsible take on homeownership, and a smaller ecological footprint.

more time
Less rooms and smaller ones will cut the time it takes to keep your home clean and maintained. Use the extra free time for something you actually enjoy doing.

less waste
From furniture to home decor, if there is no place to put it, you will think twice before buying it. That means you will automatically spend less on food, clothing, and other consumer goods probably without really noticing it.

less stress
A smaller home means less responsibility and time with chores, less hefty maintenance bills, unforeseen repairs, and other expensive monthly homeowner obligations. Those who successfully downsize appear happier when they are no longer overwhelmed by the high demand of a larger home.

237

saving money for your
HOME & LIFE

SO YOU THINK YOU CAN'T AFFORD YOUR OWN HOME?

If you're a current homeowner, before you put up a FOR SALE sign on your front lawn, or before you decide to build a new home for the first time, it is always wise to understand how you spend your money. Even if you're scaling down, or choosing to build something small to start, you don't want to find yourself financially strapped. Perhaps you and your family spend way too much money going out to eat. A smaller home will help alleviate your expenses, but it won't change you eating and spending habits. If freeing up some money for your savings or other reasons is your goal, examine your lifestyle and identify your spending habits to see if any changes in how you live are in order. This may be the perfect time to decide what you want to spend your money on, and then cut out the things that aren't important to you.

Consumer spending is alive and well contrary to many beliefs, but that does not mean that people are out of debt. Studies show that Americans spend an extra 15% of their income on unnecessary purchases. The top items Americans tend to waste their money on include dining out, gifts, electronics, fees, alcohol and tobacco.

OPEN THE WINDOW OF OPPORTUNITY

To figure out how to cut your spending, or begin saving to build a new home, track your spending to see where your money is actually going. Then, you can figure out where your budget "fat" is and how to reduce it. After you cut all of the fat out, you will be able to redirect your money to pay off debt, or to another area of spending that's more productive financially. Remember, rule #1 when trying to budget your money is to figure out what you "want" verses what you can't live without.

Besides determining what you can save as you make money, changing some of your spending habits, or making lifestyle changes is another way to keep extra cash in your pocket. Years ago, when people would save and reuse items daily in their home and life, they may have been considered "stingy or thrifty," which sounds a bit old-fashioned. Today, people "enjoy" finding ways to cut corners, reuse, re-purpose, and recycle just about everything. There is great satisfaction in getting more for your money and being less wasteful. As recycling has become a way of life for everyone, identifying ways to save money and reuse everyday products has become even more important in the challenge of creating a healthier environment and world.

Guilty?
Americans spend an extra 15% of their income on unnecessary purchases.

Tips for Saving Money

People are becoming more mindful of how they spend money, but bad habits never go out of style. Incorporate all, or some of these tips into your everyday life, and soon you will have extra money available for building the new home you've always wanted, all while living more responsibly.

- Swap, trade, or borrow clothes with friends.
- Use one of many apps to sell items you no longer use, or take to a consignment shop.
- Have a yard or estate sale. Advertise online and post photos of your best items.
- Follow Buy, Sell, Trade pages on social media.
- Post notices for items you no longer want at schools, churches and other public places.
- Sell items on Craigslist® and Ebay®. Craigslist is great for selling larger items such as furniture, appliances, and home décor. Ebay is ideal for selling record albums, books, and other collectibles.
- Take your lunch to work instead of going out. Not only is brown bagging healthier, it saves you tons of money.
- Reuse paper bags, or buy reusable bags.
- Use cloth towels instead of paper towels that are expensive and wasteful.

- Make homemade gifts like baked goods instead of buying presents. The personal touch will be long remembered.
- Use plastic bread wrappers and produce bags for freezer use.
- Do home repairs yourself or swap services and skills with friends and family who can do home projects that you don't know how to do.
- Search your community for free attractions like picnic areas, libraries, public tennis courts, swimming pools, parks, or zoos. Most communities have websites spotlighting these attractions.
- Buy things from discount stores, and before buying anything, ask yourself if you need it.
- Learn to sew and knit to avoid alteration fees.
- Put money away "for a rainy day."
- Grow your own food and cook at home instead of going out. It's healthy, organic, and trying new recipes is a fun hobby.
- Use real china, utensils and glasses instead of disposable plastic.
- Frequent garage sales for reasonably priced items often in good condition.
- Rent or borrow sporting and camping equipment instead of buying it.
- Rent movies from Redbox®, or subscribe to a streaming service like Netflix™.
- Swap vacation homes with a friend.
- Pay for only cable channels you watch.
- Cook in large quantities so you have leftovers for other meals.
- Avoid high price coffee and brew your own at home. Even buying a high-end coffeemaker pays for itself if you use it daily instead of picking up a coffee on your way to work every morning.

Use these ideas as a guide and make it a game among family members to see who can save the most money in a month. Before long you'll see even more ways to save in your daily routine!

Page 238, top to bottom: Open window, Tea Potocnik, photographer, istockphoto.com; Family with For Sale sign, istockphoto.com; Sold sign on land, istockphoto.com, Page 239, top to bottom: Garage sale sign, istockphoto.com; Garage sale items, istockphoto.com; Spools of thread, istockphoto.com.

Plan #F07-126D-1045

Images provided by designer/architect

Dimensions:	24' W x 36' D
Heated Sq. Ft.:	808
Bedrooms: 1	Bathrooms: 1
Exterior Walls:	2" x 6"
Foundation:	Basement

See index for more information

Features

- This is the perfect two-story home if you have pleasant views thanks to the large two-story windows in the open living and dining areas

- Two sets of sliding glass doors flank the fireplace in the living and dining areas making deck access easy

- The bedroom is located on the first floor for convenience with a full bath nearby

- The second floor has another space that would be ideal as a home office, or even additional sleeping space for guests

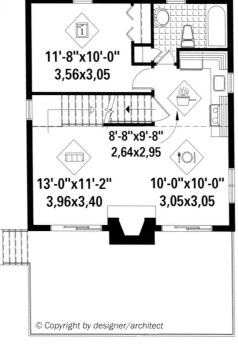

11'-8"x10'-0"
3,56x3,05

8'-8"x9'-8"
2,64x2,95

13'-0"x11'-2"
3,96x3,40

10'-0"x10'-0"
3,05x3,05

© Copyright by designer/architect

First Floor
624 sq. ft.

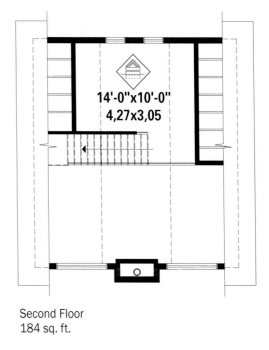

14'-0"x10'-0"
4,27x3,05

Second Floor
184 sq. ft.

Plan #F07-045D-0018

Images provided by designer/architect

Dimensions:	20' W x 21' D
Heated Sq. Ft.:	858
Bedrooms: 2	**Bathrooms:** 1
Foundation:	Crawl space

See index for more information

Features

- This quaint Country style two-story home with a large covered front porch gracing the exterior is perfect as a starter home and for a small lot space
- The friendly living room has a handy coat closet for added convenience
- A stackable washer/dryer unit is conveniently located in the delightful U-shaped kitchen
- Both of the bedrooms have walk-in closets and share the full bath on the second floor

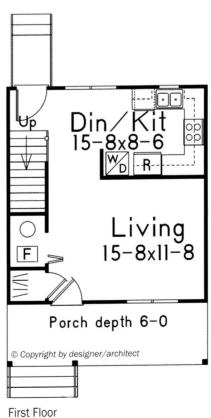

Up

Din/Kit
15-8x8-6

W/D   R

F

Living
15-8x11-8

Porch depth 6-0

© Copyright by designer/architect

First Floor
420 sq. ft.

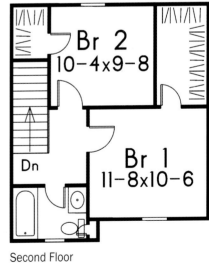

Br 2
10-4x9-8

Dn

Br 1
11-8x10-6

Second Floor
438 sq. ft.

Plan #F07-008D-0161

Images provided by designer/architect

Dimensions:	20' W x 30' D
Heated Sq. Ft.:	618
Bedrooms: 1	Bathrooms: 1
Foundation:	Pier

See index for more information

Features

- Memorable family events are certain to be enjoyed on this fabulous partially covered deck
- Equally impressive is the living area with its cathedral ceiling and exposed rafters above for a rustic, alpine feel
- A kitchenette, a bedroom and a bath conclude the first floor with a delightful vaulted sleeping loft on the second floor

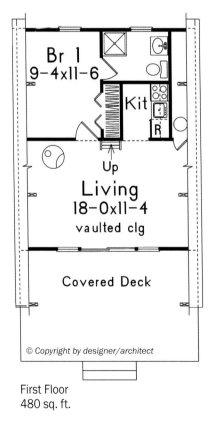

Br 1
9-4x11-6

Kit

Up

Living
18-0x11-4
vaulted clg

Covered Deck

© Copyright by designer/architect

First Floor
480 sq. ft.

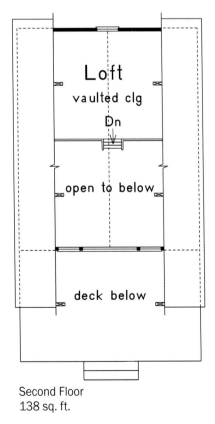

Loft
vaulted clg

Dn

open to below

deck below

Second Floor
138 sq. ft.

Rear View

Images provided by designer/architect

Plan #F07-011D-0446

Dimensions: 25'6" W x 41'6" D
Heated Sq. Ft.: 1,076
Bedrooms: 2   **Bathrooms:** 2½
Exterior Walls: 2" x 6"
Foundation: Crawl space or slab standard; basement available for an additional fee

See index for more information

Features

- Unique details, luxurious finishes, and a discerning use of space bestow this home with unrivaled style and affordability

- A sharply triangular, gabled roof line impresses along the exterior, where compact construction makes the most of contemporary design

- A wrap-around, covered porch adds additional character and year-round outdoor space

- Two vaulted bedroom suites include their own individual attached baths

- An updated kitchen, plenty of second floor storage and built-ins point to the caliber of this home's artistry, which far exceeds its modest size

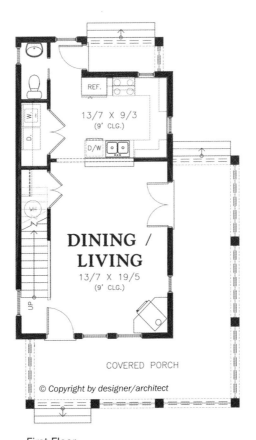

REF.

13/7 X 9/3
(9' CLG.)

D/W

DINING /
LIVING
13/7 X 19/5
(9' CLG.)

UP

COVERED PORCH

© Copyright by designer/architect

First Floor
572 sq. ft.

VAULTED
BR. 2
10/7 X 10/3

LINEN

LINEN   STOR.

DN.

VAULTED
BR. 1
13/7 X 10/9

Second Floor
504 sq. ft.

Plan #F07-007D-0030

Images provided by designer/architect

Dimensions: 46' W x 32' D
Heated Sq. Ft.: 1,140
Bedrooms: 3 **Bathrooms:** 2
Foundation: Basement standard; crawl space or slab available for an additional fee

See index for more information

© Copyright by designer/architect

Garage Below

Deck

MBr
13-4x10-8

Kit
11-0x9-6

Din
10-4x11-0

Hall

Br 2
10-0x8-9

Br 3
9-1x10-0

Living
19-0x13-4

Entry

Porch

Plan #F07-144D-0018

Images provided by designer/architect

Dimensions: 24' W x 24' D
Heated Sq. Ft.: 576
Bedrooms: 2 **Bathrooms:** 1
Exterior Walls: 2" x 6"
Foundation: Crawl space

See index for more information

© Copyright by designer/architect

QUEEN

BED - 1
11'2 X 11'2

QUEEN

BED - 2
11'2 X 11'2

WARDROBE

WARDROBE

W/D

WOOD STOVE

BATH
6'0 X 11'2

FR

LIVING AREA
16'6 X 11'2

OPEN PATIO
8 X 12

ON DEMAND
HOT WATER
UNDER SINK

OPEN PATIO
12 X 8

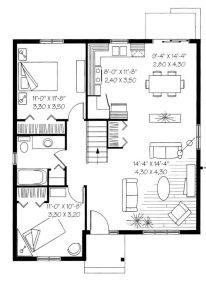

Plan #F07-032D-0111

Images provided by
designer/architect

Dimensions: 30' W x 34' D
Heated Sq. Ft.: 948
Bedrooms: 2   **Bathrooms:** 1
Exterior Walls: 2" x 6"
Foundation: Basement standard;
crawl space, floating slab or
monolithic slab available for an
additional fee

See index for more information

Plan #F07-087D-0012

Images provided by
designer/architect

Dimensions: 45' W x 43' D
Heated Sq. Ft.: 1,175
Bedrooms: 3   **Bathrooms:** 2
Foundation: Slab

See index for more information

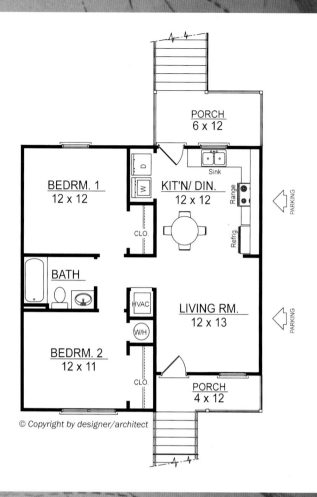

Plan #F07-069D-0106

Dimensions:	27' W x 33' D
Heated Sq. Ft.:	736
Bedrooms: 2	Bathrooms: 1
Foundation:	Pier

See index for more information

Images provided by designer/architect

© Copyright by designer/architect

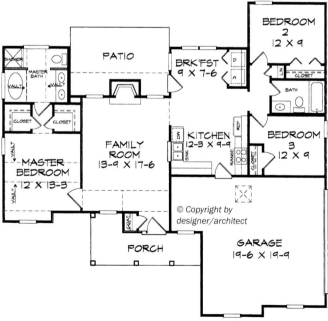

Plan #F07-076D-0013

Dimensions:	51'6" W x 48'3" D
Heated Sq. Ft.:	1,177
Bedrooms: 3	Bathrooms: 2
Foundation:	Slab

See index for more information

Images provided by designer/architect

© Copyright by designer/architect

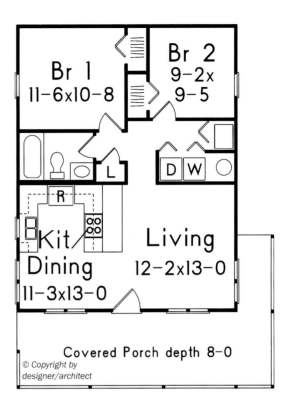

Plan #F07-002D-7531

Images provided by designer/architect

Dimensions:	24' W x 30' D
Heated Sq. Ft.:	720
Bedrooms: 2	Bathrooms: 1

Foundation: Crawl space or slab, please specify when ordering

See index for more information

Plan #F07-032D-0096

Images provided by designer/architect

Dimensions:	38' W x 28' D
Heated Sq. Ft.:	1,064
Bedrooms: 2	Bathrooms: 1
Exterior Walls:	2" x 6"

Foundation: Basement standard; crawl space, floating slab or monolithic slab available for an additional fee

See index for more information

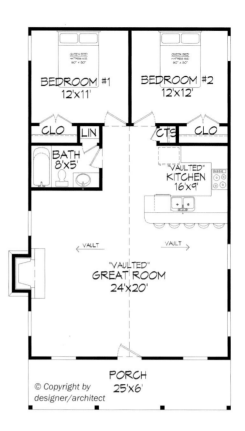

Images provided by designer/architect

Plan #F07-141D-0077

Dimensions:	27' W x 46' D
Heated Sq. Ft.:	1,000
Bedrooms: 2	**Bathrooms:** 1

Foundation: Slab standard; crawl space, basement or walk-out basement available for an additional fee

See index for more information

© Copyright by designer/architect

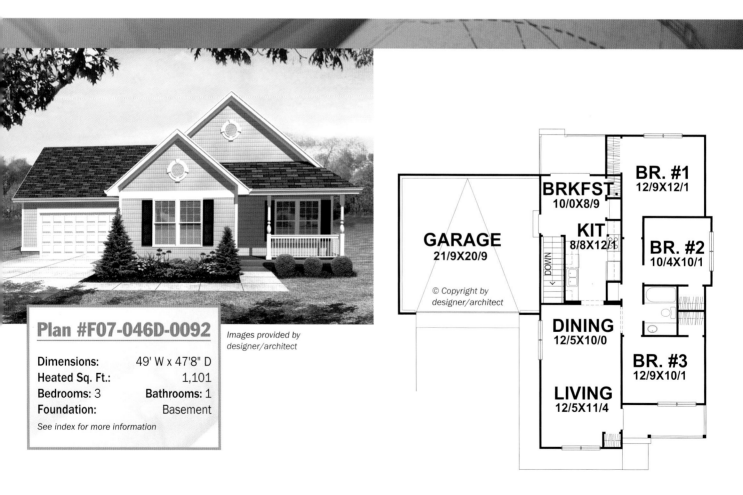

Images provided by designer/architect

© Copyright by designer/architect

Plan #F07-046D-0092

Dimensions:	49' W x 47'8" D
Heated Sq. Ft.:	1,101
Bedrooms: 3	**Bathrooms:** 1
Foundation:	Basement

See index for more information

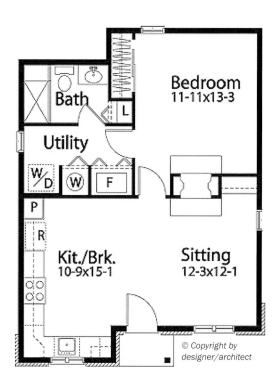

Plan #F07-058D-0226

Images provided by designer/architect

Dimensions: 24'8" W x 32' D
Heated Sq. Ft.: 691
Bedrooms: 1   Bathrooms: 1
Exterior Walls: 2" x 6"
Foundation: Slab

See index for more information

© Copyright by designer/architect

Plan #F07-025D-0001

Images provided by designer/architect

Dimensions: 38' W x 37'6" D
Heated Sq. Ft.: 1,123
Bedrooms: 3   Bathrooms: 2
Foundation: Crawl space or slab, please specify when ordering

See index for more information

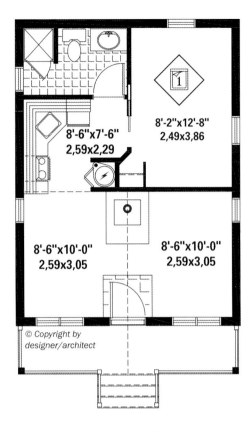

Images provided by
designer/architect

8'-6"x7'-6"
2,59x2,29

8'-2"x12'-8"
2,49x3,86

8'-6"x10'-0"
2,59x3,05

8'-6"x10'-0"
2,59x3,05

© Copyright by
designer/architect

Plan #F07-126D-0991

Dimensions:	18' W x 24' D
Heated Sq. Ft.:	432
Bedrooms: 1	Bathrooms: 1
Exterior Walls:	2" x 6"
Foundation:	Pilings

See index for more information

Images provided by
designer/architect

STOR.
6 x 4

EAT-IN
KITCHEN
14 x 10

BEDROOM #2
11 x 10

BEDROOM #3
11 x 10

P. CLO. C.

L. CLO.

HALL

BATH
#2

"VAULTED"
FAMILY ROOM
17 x 15

F.

UTIL.

E.

"VAULTED"
MASTER
BEDROOM
14 x 12

MSTR.
BATH

PORCH
18 x 4

CLO.
5 x 5

© Copyright by designer/architect

Plan #F07-087D-0008

Dimensions:	38' W x 37' D
Heated Sq. Ft.:	1,146
Bedrooms: 3	Bathrooms: 2

Foundation: Crawl space or slab,
please specify when ordering

See index for more information

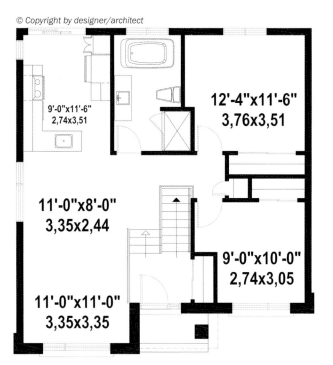

9'-0"x11'-6"
2,74x3,51

12'-4"x11'-6"
3,76x3,51

11'-0"x8'-0"
3,35x2,44

9'-0"x10'-0"
2,74x3,05

11'-0"x11'-0"
3,35x3,35

Plan #F07-126D-0544

Images provided by designer/architect

Dimensions:	30'10" W x 32' D
Heated Sq. Ft.:	892
Bedrooms: 2	Bathrooms: 1
Exterior Walls:	2" x 6"
Foundation:	Basement

See index for more information

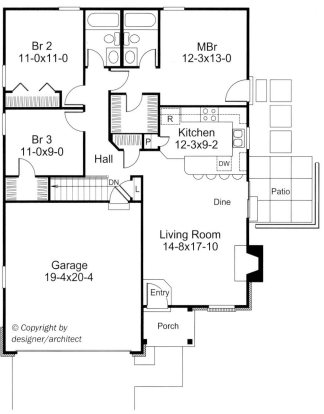

Br 2
11-0x11-0

MBr
12-3x13-0

Br 3
11-0x9-0

Hall

Kitchen
12-3x9-2

R

P

DW

DN

L

Dine

Patio

Living Room
14-8x17-10

Garage
19-4x20-4

Entry

Porch

Plan #F07-007D-0201

Images provided by designer/architect

Dimensions:	37'4" W x 47'8" D
Heated Sq. Ft.:	1,153
Bedrooms: 3	Bathrooms: 2
Foundation:	Basement

See index for more information

First Floor
1,020 sq. ft.

Optional Lower Level
1,020 sq. ft.

© Copyright by designer/architect

Plan #F07-032D-1077

Images provided by designer/architect

Dimensions:	34' W x 30' D
Heated Sq. Ft.:	1,020
Bonus Sq. Ft.:	1,020
Bedrooms: 2	Bathrooms: 1
Exterior Walls:	2" x 6"

Foundation: Basement standard; crawl space, floating slab or monolithic slab available for an additional fee

See index for more information

© Copyright by designer/architect

Plan #F07-058D-0216

Images provided by designer/architect

Dimensions:	24' W x 36'8" D
Heated Sq. Ft.:	664
Bedrooms: 1	Bathrooms: 1
Foundation:	Crawl space

See index for more information

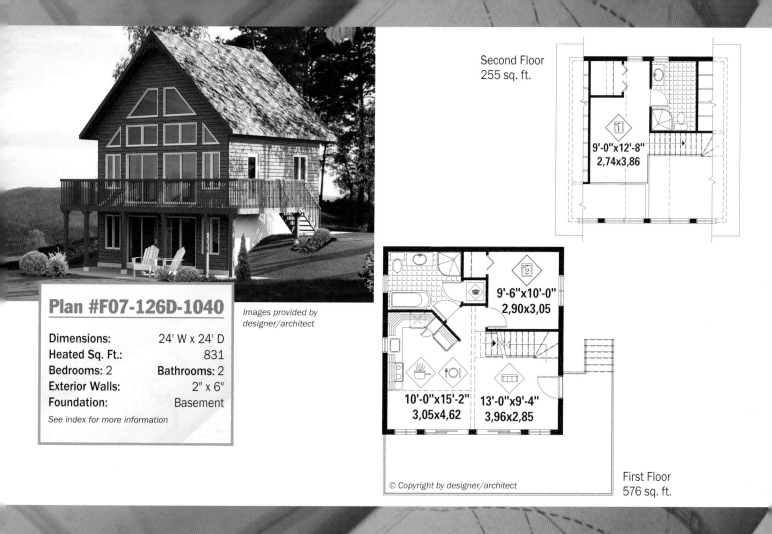

1   9'-0"x12'-8"
2,74x3,86

2   9'-6"x10'-0"
2,90x3,05

10'-0"x15'-2"
3,05x4,62

13'-0"x9'-4"
3,96x2,85

© Copyright by designer/architect

First Floor
576 sq. ft.

Plan #F07-126D-1040

Images provided by
designer/architect

Dimensions:	24' W x 24' D
Heated Sq. Ft.:	831
Bedrooms: 2	Bathrooms: 2
Exterior Walls:	2" x 6"
Foundation:	Basement

See index for more information

Plan #F07-045D-0014

Images provided by
designer/architect

Dimensions:	27' W x 43' D
Heated Sq. Ft.:	987
Bedrooms: 3	Bathrooms: 1
Foundation:	Basement

See index for more information

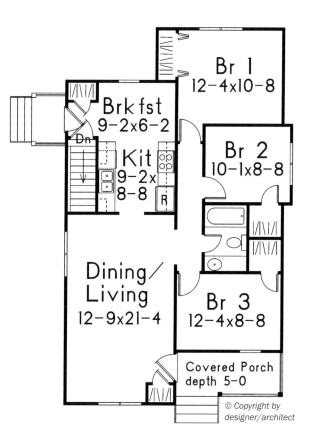

Br 1
12-4x10-8

Brk fst
9-2x6-2

Dn

Kit
9-2x
8-8

Br 2
10-1x8-8

Dining/
Living
12-9x21-4

Br 3
12-4x8-8

Covered Porch
depth 5-0

© Copyright by
designer/architect

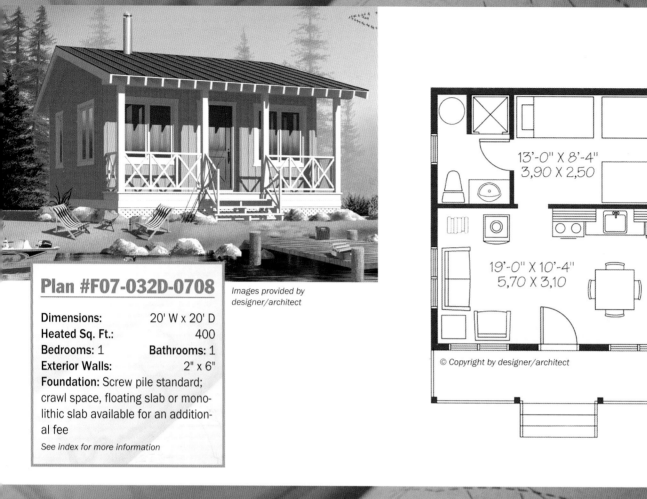

Plan #F07-032D-0708

Images provided by designer/architect

Dimensions: 20' W x 20' D
Heated Sq. Ft.: 400
Bedrooms: 1   **Bathrooms:** 1
Exterior Walls: 2" x 6"
Foundation: Screw pile standard; crawl space, floating slab or monolithic slab available for an additional fee

See index for more information

13'-0" X 8'-4"
3,90 X 2,50

19'-0" X 10'-4"
5,70 X 3,10

© Copyright by designer/architect

Plan #F07-126D-1037

Images provided by designer/architect

Dimensions: 26' W x 28' D
Heated Sq. Ft.: 1,165
Bedrooms: 2   **Bathrooms:** 2
Exterior Walls: 2" x 6"
Foundation: Basement

See index for more information

© Copyright by designer/architect

12'-0"x11'-4"
3,66x3,45

12'-0"x15'-4"
3,66x4,67

Second Floor
477 sq. ft.

8'-6"x11'-4"
2,59x3,45

8'-4"x11'-8"
2,54x3,56

23'-0"x12'-0"
7,01x3,66

First Floor
688 sq. ft.

PATIO
16/0 x 10/0

BDRM-2
10/6 x 10/4

MASTER
14/6 x 12/8

TUB

W.I.C.

TUB

DN

HALF WALL

DINING
12/10 x 10/0

LIVING
16/2 x 16/10

PASS THRU

KIT.
12/6 x 9/6

PANT.

REF.

RANGE

COVERED PORCH
22/0 x 6/0

© Copyright by designer/architect

Plan #F07-096D-0050

Images provided by designer/architect

Dimensions:	30' W x 46' D
Heated Sq. Ft.:	1,200
Bedrooms: 2	Bathrooms: 2
Exterior Walls:	2" x 6"
Foundation:	Basement

See index for more information

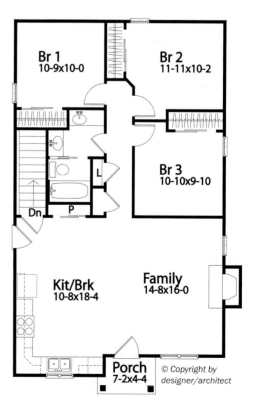

Br 1
10-9x10-0

Br 2
11-11x10-2

Br 3
10-10x9-10

L

P

Dn

Kit/Brk
10-8x18-4

Family
14-8x16-0

Porch
7-2x4-4

© Copyright by designer/architect

Plan #F07-058D-0220

Images provided by designer/architect

Dimensions:	28' W x 44' D
Heated Sq. Ft.:	1,067
Bedrooms: 3	Bathrooms: 1
Foundation:	Basement

See index for more information

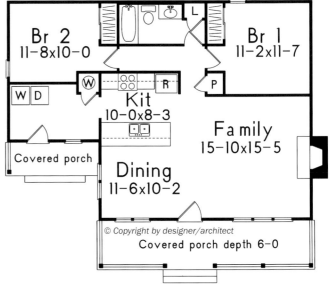

Br 2
11-8x10-0

Br 1
11-2x11-7

W D

Kit
10-0x8-3

Family
15-10x15-5

Covered porch

Dining
11-6x10-2

© Copyright by designer/architect

Covered porch depth 6-0

Plan #F07-058D-0029

Dimensions: 42' W x 34' D
Heated Sq. Ft.:   1,000
Bedrooms: 2   Bathrooms: 1
Foundation: Crawl space

See index for more information

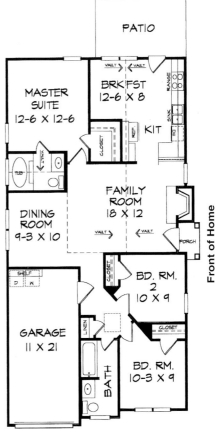

PATIO

MASTER
SUITE
12-6 X 12-6

BRK'FST
12-6 X 8

KIT

DINING
ROOM
9-3 X 10

FAMILY
ROOM
18 X 12

PORCH

Front of Home

BD. RM.
2
10 X 9

GARAGE
11 X 21

BD. RM.
10-3 X 9

BATH

© Copyright by designer/architect

Plan #F07-076D-0017

Dimensions: 30' W x 50' D
Heated Sq. Ft.:   1,123
Bedrooms: 3   Bathrooms: 2
Foundation: Crawl space or slab, please specify when ordering

See index for more information

Plan #F07-126D-1019

Images provided by
designer/architect

Dimensions:	24' W x 40' D
Heated Sq. Ft.:	924
Bedrooms: 2	Bathrooms: 1
Exterior Walls:	2" x 6"
Foundation:	Basement

See index for more information

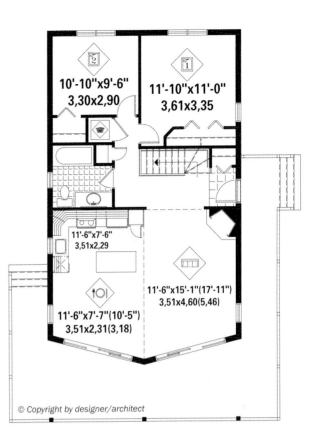

10'-10"x9'-6"
3,30x2,90

11'-10"x11'-0"
3,61x3,35

11'-6"x7'-6"
3,51x2,29

11'-6"x15'-1"(17'-11")
3,51x4,60(5,46)

11'-6"x7'-7"(10'-5")
3,51x2,31(3,18)

© Copyright by designer/architect

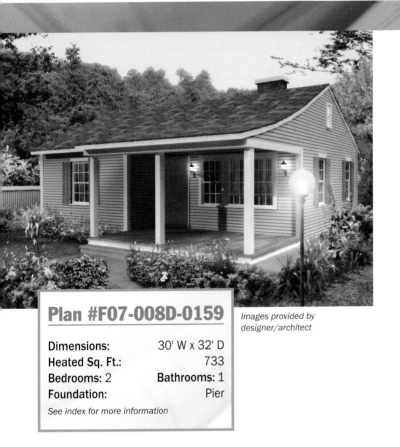

Plan #F07-008D-0159

Images provided by
designer/architect

Dimensions:	30' W x 32' D
Heated Sq. Ft.:	733
Bedrooms: 2	Bathrooms: 1
Foundation:	Pier

See index for more information

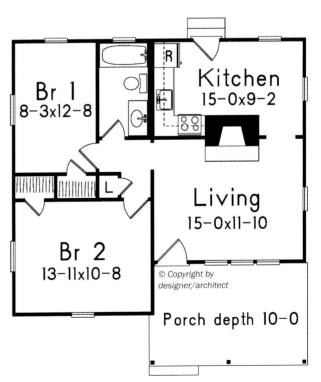

Br 1
8-3x12-8

Kitchen
15-0x9-2

Br 2
13-11x10-8

Living
15-0x11-10

© Copyright by
designer/architect

Porch depth 10-0

Plan #F07-141D-0072

Images provided by designer/architect

Dimensions: 20' W x 32'9" D
Heated Sq. Ft.: 1,140
Bedrooms: 2   **Bathrooms:** 2½
Exterior Walls: 2" x 6"
Foundation: Slab standard; crawl space, basement or walk-out basement available for an additional fee

See index for more information

© Copyright by designer/architect

First Floor
575 sq. ft.

Second Floor
565 sq. ft.

Plan #F07-123D-0085

Images provided by designer/architect

Dimensions: 29' W x 37' D
Heated Sq. Ft.: 999
Bedrooms: 1   **Bathrooms:** 1
Foundation: Slab standard; crawl space, basement or walk-out basement available for an additional fee

See index for more information

© Copyright by designer/architect

Second Floor
312 sq. ft.

First Floor
687 sq. ft.

Plan #F07-010D-0006

Images provided by designer/architect

Dimensions:	47'4" W x 52' D
Heated Sq. Ft.:	1,170
Bedrooms: 3	Bathrooms: 2
Foundation:	Slab

See index for more information

© Copyright by designer/architect

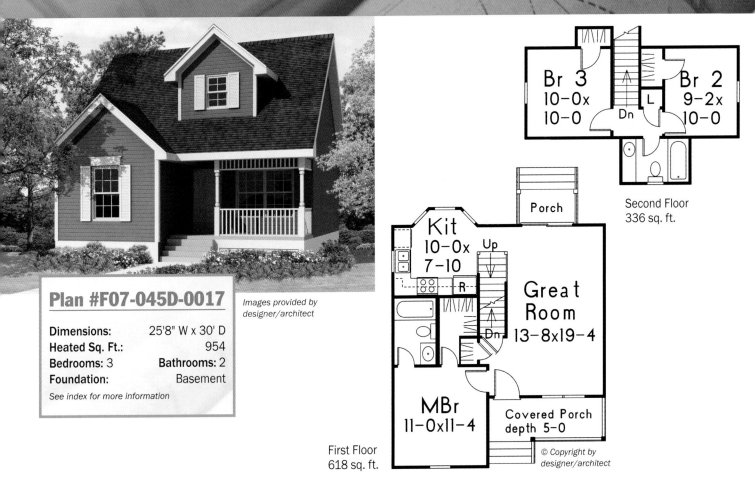

Plan #F07-045D-0017

Images provided by designer/architect

Dimensions:	25'8" W x 30' D
Heated Sq. Ft.:	954
Bedrooms: 3	Bathrooms: 2
Foundation:	Basement

See index for more information

Second Floor
336 sq. ft.

First Floor
618 sq. ft.

© Copyright by designer/architect

Images provided by designer/architect

Plan #F07-013D-0054

Dimensions:	40' W x 23' D
Heated Sq. Ft.:	999
Bonus Sq. Ft.:	300
Bedrooms: 2	**Bathrooms:** 2

Foundation: Slab standard; crawl space available for an additional fee

See index for more information

Features

- The dramatic entry is brightened by a glass front door and an arched transom window
- Vaulted ceilings adorn the kitchen, family and dining rooms providing a feeling of spaciousness
- A future studio on the lower level has an additional 300 square feet of living area and features a bath and a kitchenette making it ideal for a college student or in-law
- 2-car drive under front entry garage

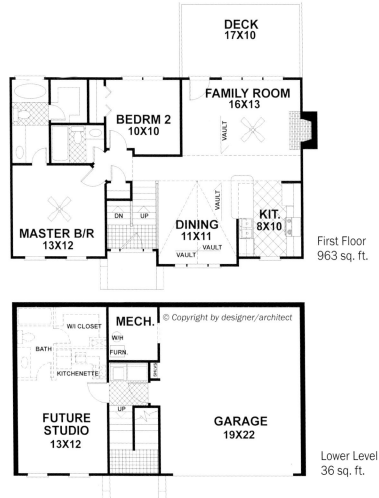

DECK 17X10

FAMILY ROOM 16X13

BEDRM 2 10X10

MASTER B/R 13X12

DINING 11X11

KIT. 8X10

DN UP

VAULT

First Floor 963 sq. ft.

© Copyright by designer/architect

MECH.

W/I CLOSET

W/H

FURN.

BATH

KITCHENETTE

UP

FUTURE STUDIO 13X12

GARAGE 19X22

Lower Level 36 sq. ft.

Plan #F07-011D-0612

Dimensions:	29' W x 29' D
Heated Sq. Ft.:	803
Bedrooms: 2	Bathrooms: 1½
Exterior Walls:	2" x 6"

Foundation: Crawl space or slab standard; basement available for an additional fee

See index for more information

Features

- Craftsman details and a covered front porch provide the utmost style and charming curb appeal
- The open living/dining area enjoys a cozy fireplace and a nearby U-shaped kitchen with a laundry closet near the garage
- Upstairs, there are two vaulted bedrooms, a built-in desk and a well-designed shared bath
- 1-car front entry garage

Second Floor
371 sq. ft.

First Floor
432 sq. ft.

© Copyright by designer/architect

Images provided by designer/architect

Plan #F07-026D-0218

Dimensions: 40' W x 48'8" D
Heated Sq. Ft.: 1,195
Bedrooms: 3   **Bathrooms:** 2
Foundation: Basement standard; slab, crawl space or walk-out basement available for an additional fee

See index for more information

Images provided by designer/architect

© Copyright by designer/architect

COVERED PORCH

Kit. 11⁰ x 9³

Mbr. 12⁰ x 13⁰

Br.2 10⁰ x 10⁶

DINING AREA

Br.3 10⁰ x 10⁶

Fam. Room 13⁸ x 20⁰

DN

Gar. 19⁴ x 21⁴

COVERED PORCH

Plan #F07-032D-1121

Dimensions: 52' W x 36' D
Heated Sq. Ft.: 1,178
Bonus Sq. Ft.: 1,178
Bedrooms: 2   **Bathrooms:** 1
Exterior Walls: 2" x 6"
Foundation: Basement standard; crawl space available for an additional fee

See index for more information

Images provided by designer/architect

DECK 11-0 X 6-0

MAIN LIVING 20-8 X 12-2

1-CAR GARAGE 16-4 X 22-4

MASTER BED. 12-8 X 11-2

KITCHEN 15-0 X 8-4

BATHROOM

PANTRY 6-8 X 4-0

MUD ROOM 7-10 X 4-0

ENTRANCE 7-2 X 8-2

BEDROOM 2 12-8 X 9-0

FRONT PORCH 19-2 X 4-2

First Floor 1,178 sq. ft.

MECH.

LAUNDRY ROOM 6-8 X 9-0

Optional Lower Level 1,178 sq. ft.

© Copyright by designer/architect

Plan #F07-058D-0237

Dimensions:	42'4" W x 48' D
Heated Sq. Ft.:	1,181
Bedrooms: 3	Bathrooms: 2
Foundation:	Basement

See index for more information

Images provided by designer/architect

© Copyright by designer/architect

Plan #F07-058D-0231

Dimensions:	60' W x 36' D
Heated Sq. Ft.:	1,158
Bedrooms: 3	Bathrooms: 2
Foundation:	Basement

See index for more information

Images provided by designer/architect

© Copyright by designer/architect

Plan #F07-020D-0050

Dimensions:	40' W x 34' D
Heated Sq. Ft.:	848
Bedrooms: 1	Bathrooms: 1
Exterior Walls:	2" x 6"
Foundation:	Crawl space

See index for more information

Images provided by designer/architect

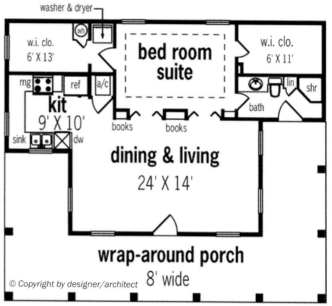

washer & dryer

w.i. clo.
6' X 13'

bed room
suite

w.i. clo.
6' X 11'

rng | ref | a/c

kit
9' X 10'

books

books

bath

lin

shr

sink | dw

dining & living
24' X 14'

wrap-around porch
8' wide

© Copyright by designer/architect

Plan #F07-011D-0305

Dimensions:	20' W x 30' D
Heated Sq. Ft.:	600
Bedrooms: 1	Bathrooms: 1
Exterior Walls:	2" x 6"
Foundation: Crawl space or slab standard; basement available for an additional fee	

See index for more information

Images provided by designer/architect

© Copyright by designer/architect

BR.
12/0 X 10/10
(9' CLG.)

MECH

LIVING
16/8 X 15/0
(9' CLG.)

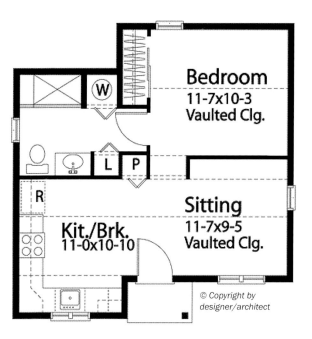

Plan #F07-058D-0225

Dimensions:	23'8" W x 24'4" D
Heated Sq. Ft.:	494
Bedrooms: 1	Bathrooms: 1
Exterior Walls:	2" x 6"
Foundation:	Slab

See index for more information

Images provided by designer/architect

© Copyright by designer/architect

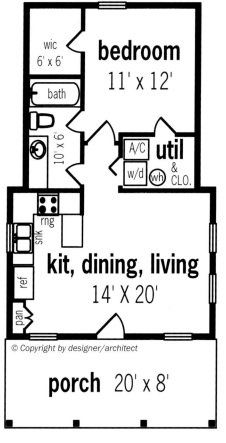

Plan #F07-020D-0330

Dimensions:	20' W x 39' D
Heated Sq. Ft.:	569
Bedrooms: 1	Bathrooms: 1
Exterior Walls:	2" x 6"
Foundation:	Crawl space or slab, please specify when ordering

See index for more information

Images provided by designer/architect

© Copyright by designer/architect

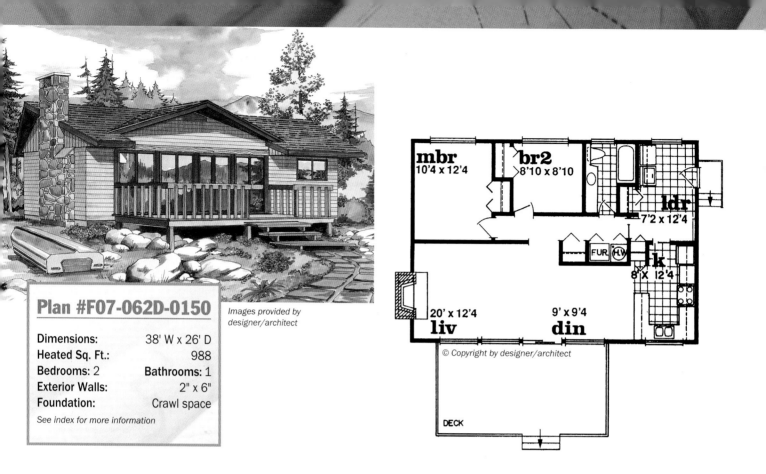

Plan #F07-062D-0150

Images provided by designer/architect

Dimensions:	38' W x 26' D
Heated Sq. Ft.:	988
Bedrooms: 2	Bathrooms: 1
Exterior Walls:	2" x 6"
Foundation:	Crawl space

See index for more information

mbr 10'4 x 12'4

br2 8'10 x 8'10

ldr 7'2 x 12'4

FUR HW

k 8' X 12'4

liv 20' x 12'4

din 9' x 9'4

© Copyright by designer/architect

DECK

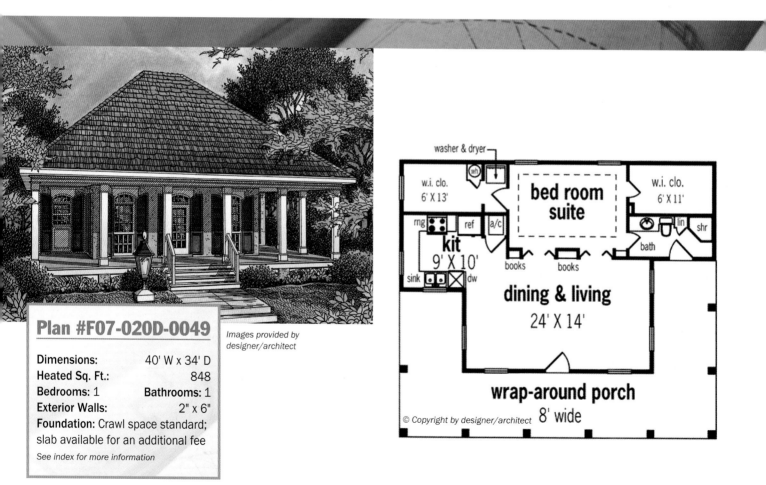

Plan #F07-020D-0049

Images provided by designer/architect

Dimensions:	40' W x 34' D
Heated Sq. Ft.:	848
Bedrooms: 1	Bathrooms: 1
Exterior Walls:	2" x 6"
Foundation: Crawl space standard; slab available for an additional fee	

See index for more information

washer & dryer

w.i. clo. 6' X 13'

bed room suite

w.i. clo. 6' 11'

rng ref a/c

kit 9' X 10'

sink dw

books

books

bath

lin shr

dining & living 24' X 14'

wrap-around porch 8' wide

© Copyright by designer/architect

Plan #F07-034D-0037

Images provided by
designer/architect

Dimensions:	47'6" W x 39' D
Heated Sq. Ft.:	1,145
Bedrooms: 2	**Bathrooms:** 2
Foundation:	Basement

See index for more information

Plan #F07-034D-0066

Images provided by
designer/architect

Dimensions:	50' W x 36' D
Heated Sq. Ft.:	1,129
Bedrooms: 2	**Bathrooms:** 2
Foundation:	Basement

See index for more information

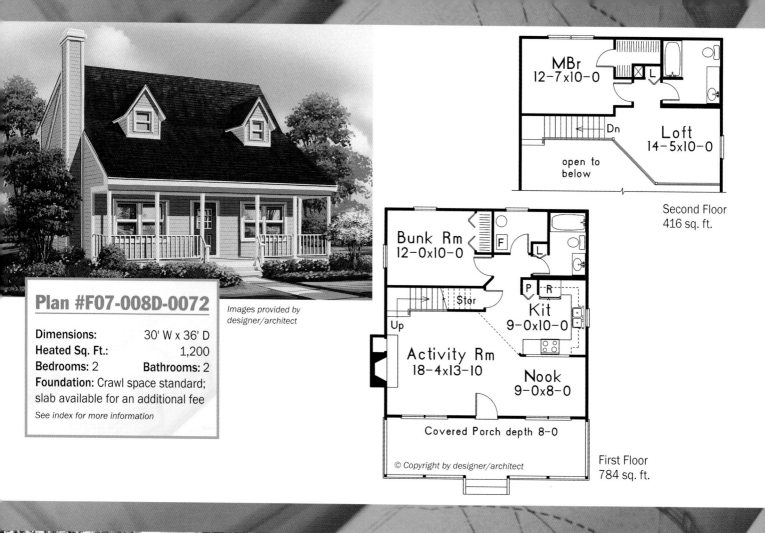

Second Floor
416 sq. ft.

MBr
12-7x10-0

Loft
14-5x10-0

open to below

Dn

Bunk Rm
12-0x10-0

Kit
9-0x10-0

Stor

Up

Activity Rm
18-4x13-10

Nook
9-0x8-0

Covered Porch depth 8-0

© Copyright by designer/architect

First Floor
784 sq. ft.

Plan #F07-008D-0072

Images provided by designer/architect

Dimensions:	30' W x 36' D
Heated Sq. Ft.:	1,200
Bedrooms: 2	**Bathrooms:** 2

Foundation: Crawl space standard; slab available for an additional fee

See index for more information

Plan #F07-055D-0944

Images provided by designer/architect

Dimensions:	55'5" W x 34'3" D
Heated Sq. Ft.:	1,128
Bedrooms: 2	**Bathrooms:** 1

Foundation: Crawl space or slab, please specify when ordering

See index for more information

BEDROOM 1
12'-0"X11'-6"

BEDROOM 2
12'-0"X11'-6"

BATH
5'-10"
9'-4"

LIN

LAU
5'-6"
9'-2"

W.
D.

KIT
11'-4"X12'-8"

DW
RG
REF
PAN
HIGH BAR

STONE FIREPLACE

DINING
10'-10"X15'-8"

VAULTED CEILING

GREAT ROOM
12'-10"X23'-4"

VAULTED CEILING

GRILLING PORCH
10'-10"X24'-0"

VAULTED CEILING

ENTRY PORCH

© Copyright by designer/architect

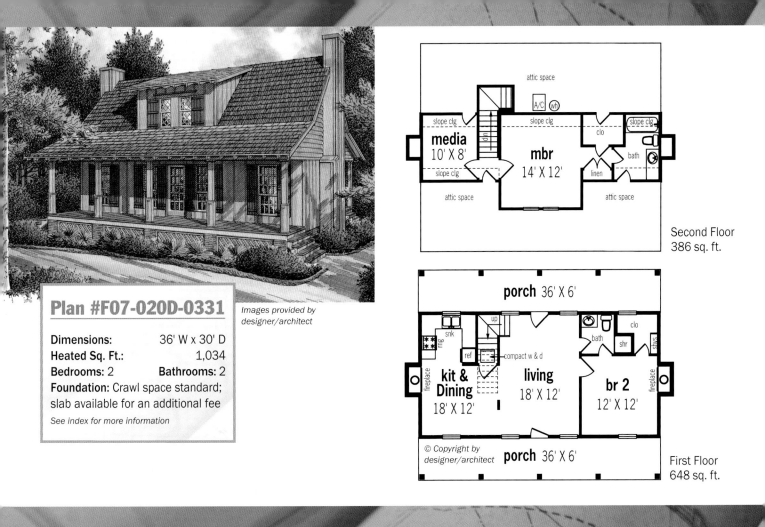

Second Floor
386 sq. ft.

media
10' X 8'

mbr
14' X 12'

bath

clo

linen

attic space

attic space

slope clg

slope clg

slope clg

A/C WH

porch 36' X 6'

kit &
Dining
18' X 12'

living
18' X 12'

br 2
12' X 12'

bath

clo

shr

fireplace

fireplace

compact w & d

ref

snk

frig

up

© Copyright by
designer/architect

porch 36' X 6'

First Floor
648 sq. ft.

Plan #F07-020D-0331

*Images provided by
designer/architect*

Dimensions:	36' W x 30' D
Heated Sq. Ft.:	1,034
Bedrooms: 2	**Bathrooms:** 2

Foundation: Crawl space standard;
slab available for an additional fee

See index for more information

*Images provided by
designer/architect*

Plan #F07-055D-0943

Dimensions:	58' W x 18' D
Heated Sq. Ft.:	828
Bedrooms: 1	**Bathrooms:** 1

Foundation: Crawl space or slab,
please specify when ordering

See index for more information

TRANSOM
WINDOWS

BEDROOM
11'-0" X 17'-4"

BATH
8'-0" X 7'-4"

KITCHEN
13'-0" X 8'-0"

LIVING
11'-0" X 17'-4"

SCREENED
PORCH
12'-0" X 18'-0"

DINING
12'-4" X 9'-4"

VAULTED
CEILING

WH

© Copyright by designer/architect

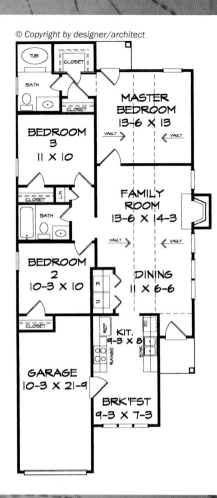

© Copyright by designer/architect

Plan #F07-076D-0018

Images provided by designer/architect

Dimensions:	28' W x 61' D
Heated Sq. Ft.:	1,116
Bedrooms: 3	Bathrooms: 2

Foundation: Crawl space or slab, please specify when ordering

See index for more information

© Copyright by designer/architect

Plan #F07-055D-0115

Images provided by designer/architect

Dimensions:	28' W x 69'6" D
Heated Sq. Ft.:	1,120
Bedrooms: 2	Bathrooms: 2
Exterior Walls:	2" x 6"

Foundation: Crawl space or slab, please specify when ordering

See index for more information

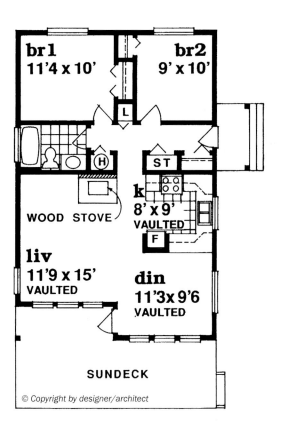

br1
11'4 x 10'

br2
9' x 10'

L

ST

WOOD STOVE

k
8' x 9'
VAULTED

F

liv
11'9 x 15'
VAULTED

din
11'3 x 9'6
VAULTED

SUNDECK

Plan #F07-062D-0326

Images provided by designer/architect

Dimensions:	24' W x 36' D
Heated Sq. Ft.:	817
Bedrooms: 2	Bathrooms: 1
Exterior Walls:	2" x 6"
Foundation:	Crawl space

See index for more information

BATH
5'-8" X
12'-0"

BEDROOM 1
9'-2"X11'-0"

KIT
11'-8"X13'-4"

GREAT ROOM
13'-10"X18'-0"

GRILLING PORCH
12'-0"X10'-0"

BEDROOM 2
9'-2"X11'-0"

COVERED PORCH
15'-0"X8'-0"

Plan #F07-055D-0945

Images provided by designer/architect

Dimensions:	36' W x 39' D
Heated Sq. Ft.:	859
Bedrooms: 2	Bathrooms: 1

Foundation: Crawl space or slab, please specify when ordering

See index for more information

Plan #F07-032D-1150

Dimensions:	41'8" W x 28' D
Heated Sq. Ft.:	998
Bonus Sq. Ft.:	998
Bedrooms: 2	**Bathrooms:** 1
Exterior Walls:	2" x 6"

Foundation: Basement standard; crawl space, monolithic slab or floating slab available for an additional fee

See index for more information

Features

- This compact ranch home has an open floor plan that merges dining, living, and cooking into one main gathering space

- Two bedrooms share a centrally located full bath with ease, and the bath features a laundry room wall

- A coat closet is found by the front entry and a walk-in pantry is located in the kitchen behind a barn style door to maximize space

- Sliding glass doors off the dining area add light and outdoor access to a patio

- Straightforward and functional, this small home promises to make life easy and comfortable

- And, if the need arises, there's plenty of space to expand in the lower level

- The optional lower level has an additional 998 square feet off living area

First Floor
998 sq. ft.

Images provided by designer/architect

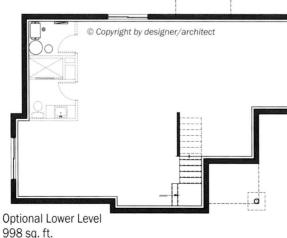

© Copyright by designer/architect

Optional Lower Level
998 sq. ft.

Plan #F07-088D-0347

Dimensions:	26'4" W x 46' D
Heated Sq. Ft.:	1,140
Bedrooms: 1	Bathrooms: 1
Exterior Walls:	2" x 6"
Foundation:	Crawl space

See index for more information

Features

- Cozy vacation cottage offers a covered deck area, ideal for relaxing in all types of weather
- This cottage offers all of the comforts of home in a small and compact space perfect for today's lot sizes
- The large living room is warmed by a center fireplace making it the ideal focal point
- There is a huge bathroom on the first floor with a claw-footed free-standing tub as well as a closet for the washer and dryer
- The second floor has a private bedroom and loft space

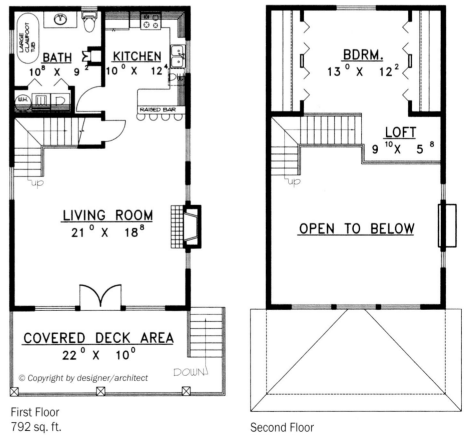

First Floor
792 sq. ft.

Second Floor
348 sq. ft.

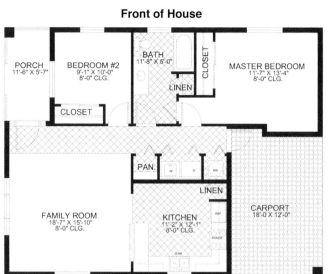

Front of House

PORCH
11'-6" X 5'-7"

BEDROOM #2
9'-1" X 10'-0"
8'-0" CLG.

BATH
11'-8" X 5'-0"

CLOSET

LINEN

MASTER BEDROOM
11'-7" X 13'-4"
8'-0" CLG.

CLOSET

PAN.

LINEN

FAMILY ROOM
18'-7" X 15'-10"
8'-0" CLG.

KITCHEN
11'-2" X 12'-1"
8'-0" CLG.

CARPORT
18'-0 X 12'-0"

Plan #F07-106D-0001

Dimensions:	42' W x 32' D
Heated Sq. Ft.:	1,052
Bedrooms: 2	**Bathrooms:** 1
Exterior Walls:	Concrete block
Foundation:	Monolithic slab

See index for more information

Images provided by designer/architect

STORAGE
15'-8" X 3'-0"

GARAGE
21'-0" X 19'-0"

BREAKFAST
14'-8" X 7'-10"

KITCHEN
10'-10" X 8'-0"

LAU.
6'-2" X 5'-8"

BATH

W.I.C.

MASTER
SUITE
OPT. 9' BOXED
CEILING
11'-8" X 11'-0"

GREAT
ROOM
14'-8" X 16'-10"
OPT. 9' CEILING

BATH

COVERED
PORCH
15'-5" X 8'-0"

BEDROOM 2
11'-8" X 11'-6"

Plan #F07-055D-0478

Dimensions:	48'8" W x 45'10" D
Heated Sq. Ft.:	1,067
Bedrooms: 2	**Bathrooms:** 2

Foundation: Slab or crawl space, please specify when ordering

See index for more information

Images provided by designer/architect

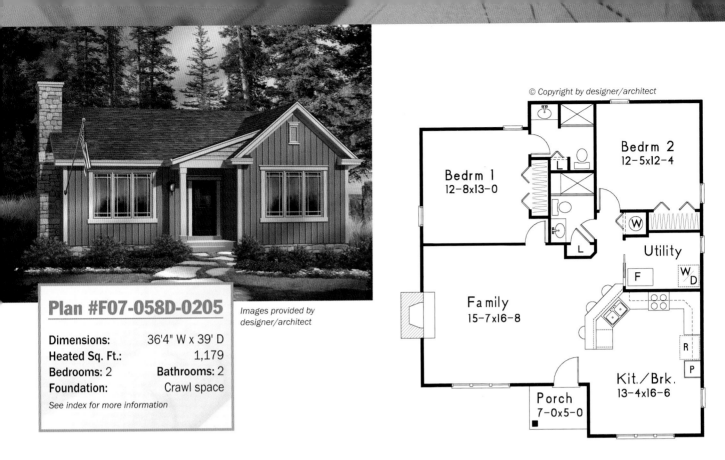

Plan #F07-058D-0205

Images provided by designer/architect

Dimensions:	36'4" W x 39' D
Heated Sq. Ft.:	1,179
Bedrooms: 2	Bathrooms: 2
Foundation:	Crawl space

See index for more information

Plan #F07-077D-0011

Images provided by designer/architect

Dimensions:	30' W x 38'4" D
Heated Sq. Ft.:	1,000
Bedrooms: 2	Bathrooms: 2
Foundation: Crawl space or slab, please specify when ordering	

See index for more information

Home Plans Index

Plan Number	Square Feet	PDF File	5-Sets	CAD File	Material List	Page	Plan Number	Square Feet	PDF File	5-Sets	CAD File	Material List	Page
F07-001D-0018	988	$789	$789	$1,239	$125	206	F07-008D-0159	733	$589	$589	-	$125	257
F07-001D-0040	864	$789	$789	$1,239	$125	115	F07-008D-0161	618	$589	$589	-	$125	242
F07-001D-0041	1,000	$789	$789	$1,239	$125	142	F07-008D-0162	865	$789	$789	-	$125	123
F07-001D-0043	1,104	$889	$889	$1,389	$125	160	F07-010D-0006	1,170	$889	$889	$1,389	$125	259
F07-001D-0045	1,197	$889	$889	$1,389	$125	173	F07-011D-0291	972	$992	$1,192	$1,984	$275	64
F07-001D-0081	1,160	$889	$889	$1,389	$125	73	F07-011D-0305	600	$880	$1,080	$1,760	$275	264
F07-001D-0082	1,160	$889	$889	$1,389	$125	207	F07-011D-0306	899	$995	$1,195	$1,990	$275	101
F07-001D-0085	720	$589	$589	$989	$125	141	F07-011D-0312	544	$863	$1,063	$1,726	$275	82
F07-001D-0086	1,154	$889	$889	$1,389	$125	176	F07-011D-0313	782	$935	$1,135	$1,870	$275	8
F07-001D-0088	800	$589	$589	$989	$125	137	F07-011D-0314	780	$989	$1,189	$1,978	$275	78
F07-002D-7531	720	$650	$700	-	Included	247	F07-011D-0315	960	$963	$1,163	$1,926	$275	121
F07-007D-0029	1,576	$589	$589	$989	$125	140	F07-011D-0316	960	$963	$1,163	$1,926	$275	100
F07-007D-0030	1,140	$889	$889	$1,389	$125	244	F07-011D-0358	981	$994	$1,194	$1,988	$275	132
F07-007D-0031	1,092	$789	$789	$1,239	$125	119	F07-011D-0359	950	$1,010	$1,210	$2,020	$275	65
F07-007D-0040	632	$575	$625	$1,025	$125	146	F07-011D-0430	1,105	$1,127	$1,327	$2,254	$275	127
F07-007D-0042	914	$789	$789	-	$125	79	F07-011D-0431	300	$815	$1,015	$1,630	$275	10
F07-007D-0043	647	$589	$589	$989	$125	138	F07-011D-0446	1,076	$1,048	$1,248	$2,096	$275	243
F07-007D-0105	1,084	$789	$789	$1,239	$125	136	F07-011D-0447	1,076	$1,048	$1,248	$2,096	$275	85
F07-007D-0108	983	$789	$789	$1,239	$125	135	F07-011D-0471	728	$968	$1,168	$1,938	$275	230
F07-007D-0109	888	$789	$789	$1,239	$125	49	F07-011D-0591	960	$988	$1,188	$1,976	$275	166
F07-007D-0110	1,169	$889	$889	$1,389	$125	97	F07-011D-0603	312	$769	$969	$1,538	$275	68
F07-007D-0112	1,062	$789	$789	-	$125	177	F07-011D-0612	803	$1,013	$1,213	$2,026	$275	261
F07-007D-0128	1,072	$789	$789	$1,239	$125	139	F07-011D-0616	628	$913	$1,113	$1,826	$275	202
F07-007D-0135	801	$789	$789	$1,239	$125	131	F07-011D-0676	1,196	$1,074	$1,274	$2,148	$275	37
F07-007D-0142	480	$349	$349	$699	$125	201	F07-012D-7507	322	$772	$972	$1,544	$275	92
F07-007D-0148	1,167	$889	$889	-	$125	74	F07-012D-7510	276	$758	$958	$1,516	$275	76
F07-007D-0154	1,196	$889	$889	$1,389	$125	227	F07-013D-0002	1,197	$1,045	$1,145	$1,495	$195	224
F07-007D-0169	1,114	$889	$889	$1,389	$125	222	F07-013D-0054	999	$945	$995	$1,350	$195	260
F07-007D-0175	882	$789	$789	$1,239	$125	225	F07-013D-0133	953	$945	$995	$1,350	$195	144
F07-007D-0177	1,102	$889	$889	$1,389	$125	171	F07-013D-0243	514	$945	$995	$1,350	$195	99
F07-007D-0179	1,131	$889	$889	-	$125	222	F07-013D-0248	1,137	$1,045	$1,145	$1,495	$195	93
F07-007D-0181	1,140	$889	$889	$1,389	$125	83	F07-013D-0257	1,059	$1,045	$1,145	$1,495	$195	97
F07-007D-0193	771	$589	$589	-	$125	229	F07-015D-0019	1,018	$750	$800	$1,200	-	195
F07-007D-0196	421	$349	$349	$699	$125	151	F07-015D-0087	1,175	$750	$800	$1,200	-	212
F07-007D-0199	496	$349	$349	$699	$125	213	F07-020D-0015	1,191	$800	$950	$1,500	$90	216
F07-007D-0201	1,153	$889	$889	$1,389	$125	251	F07-020D-0030	1,168	$800	$950	-	$90	79
F07-008D-0016	768	$589	$589	$989	$125	198	F07-020D-0049	848	$670	$800	$1,240	-	266
F07-008D-0026	1,120	$889	$889	$1,389	$125	207	F07-020D-0050	848	$670	$800	$1,240	-	264
F07-008D-0072	1,200	$889	$889	$1,389	$125	268	F07-020D-0056	963	$670	$800	$1,240	$70	16
F07-008D-0121	960	$789	$789	$1,239	$125	173	F07-020D-0080	1,200	$800	$950	-	$90	232
F07-008D-0133	624	$589	$589	-	$125	101	F07-020D-0330	569	$670	$800	$1,240	-	265
F07-008D-0136	1,106	$889	$889	-	$125	180	F07-020D-0331	1,034	$800	$950	$1,500	-	269
F07-008D-0144	1,176	$889	$889	-	$125	223	F07-020D-0349	975	$670	$800	$1,240	-	203
F07-008D-0148	784	$589	$589	$989	$125	205	F07-020D-0394	902	$670	$800	$1,240	-	18
F07-008D-0153	792	$589	$589	$989	$125	145	F07-022D-0001	1,039	$789	$789	-	$125	178
F07-008D-0154	527	$589	$589	-	$125	201	F07-022D-0024	1,127	$889	$889	-	$125	209
F07-008D-0155	1,200	$889	$889	$1,389	$125	71	F07-025D-0001	1,123	$800	$700	-	-	249
							F07-026D-0218	1,195	$1,005	-	$1,650	$175	262

Home Plans Index

Plan Number	Square Feet	PDF File	5-Sets	CAD File	Material List	Page	Plan Number	Square Feet	PDF File	5-Sets	CAD File	Material List	Page
F07-026D-0219	1,195	$1,005	-	$1,650	$175	36	F07-032D-0810	631	$890	$1,015	$1,490	-	91
F07-026D-0972	1,142	$1,005	-	$1,650	$175	72	F07-032D-0811	700	$890	$1,015	$1,490	-	221
F07-026D-1667	1,091	$1,005	-	$1,650	$175	110	F07-032D-0812	943	$915	$1,040	$1,515	-	231
F07-026D-1833	1,195	$1,005	-	$1,650	$175	27	F07-032D-0813	686	$890	$1,015	$1,490	-	102
F07-026D-1861	1,136	$1,005	-	$1,650	$175	42	F07-032D-0815	643	$890	$1,015	$1,490	-	149
F07-026D-2053	682	$955	-	$1,580	-	129	F07-032D-0828	1,040	$1,020	$1,145	$1,620	-	224
F07-026D-2054	800	$955	-	$1,580	$175	213	F07-032D-0833	1,007	$1,020	$1,145	$1,620	-	96
F07-028D-0001	864	$745	$810	-	$100	31	F07-032D-0835	1,146	$1,020	$1,145	$1,620	-	109
F07-028D-0023	1,097	$795	$910	-	-	46	F07-032D-0863	1,200	$1,110	$1,235	$1,710	-	169
F07-028D-0032	864	$745	$810	-	$100	76	F07-032D-0872	629	$890	$1,015	$1,490	-	68
F07-028D-0057	1,007	$795	$910	-	-	70	F07-032D-0887	1,212	$1,110	$1,235	$1,710	-	50
F07-028D-0058	1,152	$795	$910	-	-	150	F07-032D-0902	835	$915	$1,040	$1,515	-	24
F07-028D-0076	1,073	$795	$910	-	$100	233	F07-032D-0903	880	$915	$1,040	$1,515	-	21
F07-028D-0084	1,122	$795	$910	-	-	228	F07-032D-0904	975	$915	$1,040	$1,515	-	20
F07-028D-0090	992	$745	$810	-	$100	218	F07-032D-0905	1,146	$1,020	$1,145	$1,620	-	13
F07-028D-0108	890	$745	$810	-	-	98	F07-032D-0928	1,028	$1,020	$1,145	$1,620	-	30
F07-028D-0109	890	$745	$810	-	-	29	F07-032D-0932	1,102	$1,020	$1,145	$1,620	-	61
F07-028D-0115	1,035	$795	$910	-	-	19	F07-032D-0935	1,050	$1,020	$1,145	$1,620	-	106
F07-028D-0116	1,120	$795	$910	-	-	12	F07-032D-0963	1,178	$1,020	$1,145	$1,620	-	116
F07-032D-0001	1,092	$1,020	$1,145	$1,620	-	175	F07-032D-0965	1,024	$1,020	$1,145	$1,620	-	15
F07-032D-0013	1,124	$1,020	$1,145	$1,620	-	25	F07-032D-0985	988	$915	$1,040	$1,515	-	131
F07-032D-0050	840	$915	$1,040	$1,515	-	162	F07-032D-1077	1,020	$1,020	$1,145	$1,620	-	252
F07-032D-0091	1,102	$1,020	$1,145	$1,620	-	34	F07-032D-1107	,1050	$1,020	$1,145	$1,620	-	60
F07-032D-0096	1,064	$1,020	$1,145	$1,620	-	247	F07-032D-1108	1,188	$1,020	$1,145	$1,620	-	147
F07-032D-0108	1,094	$1,020	$1,145	$1,620	-	35	F07-032D-1113	1,167	$1,020	$1,145	$1,620	-	129
F07-032D-0111	948	$915	$1,040	$1,515	-	245	F07-032D-1121	1,178	$1,020	$1,145	$1,620	-	262
F07-032D-0116	946	$915	$1,040	$1,515	-	26	F07-032D-1150	998	$915	$1,040	$1,515	-	272
F07-032D-0357	874	$915	$1,040	$1,515	-	111	F07-034D-0037	1,145	$905	$625	-	-	267
F07-032D-0358	1,148	$1,020	$1,145	$1,620	-	51	F07-034D-0066	1,129	$905	$625	-	-	267
F07-032D-0403	1,073	$1,020	$1,145	$1,620	-	112	F07-040D-0028	828	$789	$789	-	$125	66
F07-032D-0414	1,163	$1,020	$1,145	$1,620	-	31	F07-040D-0029	1,028	$789	$789	-	$125	205
F07-032D-0542	1,113	$1,020	$1,145	$1,620	-	193	F07-041D-0004	1,195	$889	$889	$1,389	$125	221
F07-032D-0561	1,181	$1,020	$1,145	$1,620	-	124	F07-041D-0006	1,189	$889	$889	-	$125	108
F07-032D-0588	1,077	$1,020	$1,145	$1,620	-	113	F07-045D-0014	987	$789	$789	$1,239	$125	253
F07-032D-0656	1,184	$1,020	$1,145	$1,620	-	24	F07-045D-0015	977	$789	$789	-	$125	177
F07-032D-0706	320	$890	$1,015	$1,490	-	200	F07-045D-0016	1,107	$889	$889	$1,389	$125	225
F07-032D-0707	384	$890	$1,015	$1,490	-	204	F07-045D-0017	954	$789	$789	$1,239	$125	259
F07-032D-0708	400	$890	$1,015	$1,490	-	254	F07-045D-0018	858	$789	$789	$1,239	$125	241
F07-032D-0709	480	$890	$1,015	$1,490	-	32	F07-046D-0091	1,046	$789	$789	$1,239	-	192
F07-032D-0710	540	$890	$1,015	$1,490	-	72	F07-046D-0092	1,101	$889	$889	$1,389	-	248
F07-032D-0725	896	$915	$1,040	$1,515	-	77	F07-046D-0093	1,069	$789	$789	$1,239	-	200
F07-032D-0730	1,017	$1,020	$1,145	$1,620	-	27	F07-046D-0095	1,077	$789	$789	$1,239	-	150
F07-032D-0732	1,160	$1,020	$1,145	$1,620	-	16	F07-049D-0007	1,118	$700	$800	$1,400	$85	83
F07-032D-0754	1,054	$1,020	$1,145	$1,620	-	118	F07-051D-0847	1,047	$1,066	$852	$1,683	-	87
F07-032D-0806	976	$915	$1,040	$1,515	-	190	F07-051D-0848	1,069	$1,066	$852	$1,683	-	148
F07-032D-0807	1,015	$1,020	$1,145	$1,620	-	126	F07-051D-0849	1,170	$1,066	$852	$1,683	-	121
F07-032D-0808	900	$1,020	$1,145	$1,620	-	143	F07-051D-0888	950	$1,066	$852	$1,683	-	198
F07-032D-0809	924	$915	$1,040	$1,515	-	95							

Home Plans Index

Plan Number	Square Feet	PDF File	5-Sets	CAD File	Material List	Page	Plan Number	Square Feet	PDF File	5-Sets	CAD File	Material List	Page
F07-051D-0889	967	$1,066	$852	$1,683	-	73	F07-069D-0107	856	$789	$789	-	$125	194
F07-051D-0890	1,183	$1,107	$882	$1,744	-	111	F07-069D-0108	856	$789	$789	-	$125	165
F07-051D-0891	1,139	$1,107	$882	$1,744	-	119	F07-069D-0109	1,013	$789	$789	-	$125	118
F07-055D-0115	1,120	$700	$800	$1,400	-	270	F07-069D-0110	1,013	$789	$789	-	$125	172
F07-055D-0478	1,067	$700	$800	$1,400	-	274	F07-069D-0117	1,094	$789	$789	-	$125	192
F07-055D-0941	691	$700	$800	$1,400	-	39	F07-071D-0013	1,000	$1,350	-	$2,500	-	33
F07-055D-0943	828	$700	$800	$1,400	-	269	F07-071D-0014	1,000	$1,350	-	$2,500	-	20
F07-055D-0944	1,128	$700	$800	$1,400	-	268	F07-072D-0036	1,188	$889	$889	$1,389	$125	196
F07-055D-0945	859	$700	$800	$1,400	-	271	F07-076D-0013	1,177	$1,200	$795	$1,400	-	246
F07-057D-0012	1,112	$889	$889	-	$125	162	F07-076D-0017	1,123	$1,200	$795	$1,400	-	256
F07-057D-0013	1,117	$889	$889	$1,389	$125	170	F07-076D-0018	1,116	$1,200	$795	$1,400	-	270
F07-057D-0033	1,056	$789	$789	-	$125	164	F07-077D-0008	600	$1,175	$1,075	$1,575	$125	49
F07-057D-0034	1,020	$789	$789	$1,239	$125	232	F07-077D-0009	800	$1,175	$1,075	$1,575	$125	65
F07-058D-0007	1,013	$550	$535	$650	$80	148	F07-077D-0011	1,000	$1,300	$1,200	$1,725	$150	275
F07-058D-0009	448	$550	$535	$650	$80	67	F07-077D-0085	400	$1,175	$1,075	$1,575	$125	163
F07-058D-0010	676	$550	$535	$650	$80	203	F07-077D-0088	800	$1,175	$1,075	$1,575	$125	69
F07-058D-0014	416	$550	$535	$650	$80	174	F07-077D-0105	1,100	$1,300	$1,200	$1,725	$150	106
F07-058D-0029	1,000	$550	$535	$650	$80	256	F07-077D-0106	1,200	$1,300	$1,200	$1,725	$150	179
F07-058D-0030	990	$550	$535	$650	$80	171	F07-077D-0208	1,200	$1,300	$1,200	$1,725	$150	63
F07-058D-0194	1,112	$500	$450	$600	$70	176	F07-077D-0286	1,016	$1,300	$1,200	$1,725	$150	219
F07-058D-0205	1,179	$550	$535	$650	$80	275	F07-080D-0001	583	$695	$575	-	$95	80
F07-058D-0211	658	$550	$535	$650	$80	226	F07-080D-0002	796	$695	$575	-	$95	191
F07-058D-0212	692	$550	$535	$650	$80	128	F07-080D-0004	1,154	$895	$675	-	$95	22
F07-058D-0213	644	$550	$535	$650	$80	43	F07-084D-0051	815	$995	$1,095	$1,895	$65	93
F07-058D-0214	866	$550	$535	$650	$80	82	F07-084D-0052	1,170	$995	$1,095	$1,895	-	44
F07-058D-0216	664	$550	$535	$650	$80	252	F07-087D-0002	1,057	$1,010	$830	$1,090	-	107
F07-058D-0220	1,067	$625	$560	$725	$80	255	F07-087D-0008	1,146	$1,010	$830	$1,090	-	250
F07-058D-0221	1,181	$625	$560	$725	$80	107	F07-087D-0009	1,148	$1,010	$830	$1,090	-	227
F07-058D-0223	1,149	$625	$560	$725	$80	124	F07-087D-0011	1,163	$1,010	$830	$1,090	-	78
F07-058D-0224	1,054	$500	$450	$600	$70	172	F07-087D-0012	1,175	$1,010	$830	$1,090	-	245
F07-058D-0225	494	$550	$535	$650	$80	265	F07-087D-0016	1,199	$1,010	$830	$1,090	-	114
F07-058D-0226	691	$550	$535	$650	$80	249	F07-087D-1682	740	$1,010	$830	$1,090	-	17
F07-058D-0227	610	$550	$535	$650	$80	178	F07-088D-0027	1,040	$990	$935	$990	-	217
F07-058D-0228	403	$550	$535	$650	$80	92	F07-088D-0077	1,192	$990	$935	$990	-	233
F07-058D-0231	1,158	$625	$560	$725	$80	263	F07-088D-0216	1,120	$990	$935	$990	-	220
F07-058D-0236	1,067	$625	$560	$725	$80	193	F07-088D-0326	689	$990	$935	$990	-	199
F07-058D-0237	1,181	$625	$560	$725	$80	263	F07-088D-0347	1,140	$990	$935	$990	-	273
F07-058D-0239	1,040	$625	$560	$725	$80	110	F07-096D-0050	1,200	$900	$850	$1,400	-	255
F07-058D-0256	1,088	$625	$560	$725	$80	130	F07-101D-0155	952	$1,350	-	$2,650	-	11
F07-060D-0013	1,053	$789	$789	-	-	125	F07-101D-0161	744	$1,350	-	$2,650	-	38
F07-060D-0014	1,021	$789	$789	-	-	226	F07-106D-0001	1,052	$1,100	-	$1,600	-	274
F07-060D-0606	592	$589	$589	-	-	214	F07-109D-7500	576	$805	$625	-	$75	164
F07-062D-0150	988	$650	$750	-	$85	266	F07-111D-0032	1,094	$995	-	$1,995	-	13
F07-062D-0326	817	$650	$750	-	$85	271	F07-111D-0033	1,157	$995	-	$1,995	-	15
F07-065D-0397	1,136	$895	$950	$1,350	-	48	F07-111D-0034	1,200	$995	$1,095	$1,995	-	71
F07-069D-0105	736	$589	$589	-	$125	174	F07-111D-0042	1,074	$995	-	$1,995	-	46
F07-069D-0106	736	$589	$589	-	$125	246	F07-121D-0033	944	$789	$789	$1,239	$125	67

Home Plans Index

Plan Number	Square Feet	PDF File	5-Sets	CAD File	Material List	Page	Plan Number	Square Feet	PDF File	5-Sets	CAD File	Material List	Page
F07-122D-0001	1,105	$889	$889	$1,389	$125	84	F07-130D-0363	597	$925	-	$1,220	-	75
F07-123D-0060	1,185	$1,100	-	$1,600	$150	208	F07-130D-0380	412	$925	-	$1,220	-	204
F07-123D-0068	576	$600	-	$1,100	$150	30	F07-137D-0271	1,094	$789	$789	-	-	28
F07-123D-0084	831	$1,000	-	$1,500	$150	167	F07-139D-0001	1,068	$1,495	$1,620	$2,995	-	39
F07-123D-0085	999	$1,000	-	$1,500	$150	258	F07-141D-0001	561	$1,113	$1,344	$1,533	-	70
F07-123D-0096	1,096	$1,000	-	$1,500	$150	14	F07-141D-0003	765	$1,113	$1,344	$1,533	-	223
F07-123D-0097	1,106	$1,100	-	$1,600	$150	21	F07-141D-0013	1,200	$1,253	$1,484	$1,883	-	149
F07-123D-0119	932	$1,000	-	$1,500	$150	47	F07-141D-0066	1,050	$1,253	$1,484	$1,883	-	63
F07-123D-0172	1,192	$1,100	-	$1,600	$150	35	F07-141D-0072	1,140	$1,253	$1,484	$1,883	-	258
F07-123D-0173	1,192	$1,100	-	$1,600	$150	88	F07-141D-0077	1,000	$1,113	$1,344	$1,533	-	248
F07-123D-0263	756	$800	-	$1,300	$150	210	F07-141D-0207	1,000	$1,253	$1,484	$1,883	-	43
F07-123D-0264	733	$800	-	$1,300	$150	104	F07-141D-0230	676	$1,113	$1,344	$1,533	-	209
F07-126D-0162	888	$742	$567	$1,378	$95	212	F07-141D-0232	1,185	$1,253	$1,484	$1,883	-	115
F07-126D-0174	1,044	$875	$716	$1,463	$105	161	F07-141D-0250	999	$1,113	$1,344	$1,533	-	62
F07-126D-0356	845	$742	$567	$1,378	$95	161	F07-141D-0315	750	$1,113	$1,344	$1,533	-	77
F07-126D-0544	892	$742	$567	$1,378	$95	251	F07-141D-0327	1,050	$1,253	$1,484	$1,883	-	37
F07-126D-0545	992	$875	$716	$1,463	$105	47	F07-144D-0013	624	$1,040	$1,165	$1,535	$85	122
F07-126D-0562	894	$742	$567	$1,378	$95	125	F07-144D-0015	967	$1,040	$1,165	$1,535	-	69
F07-126D-0563	821	$742	$567	$1,378	$95	114	F07-144D-0016	967	$1,040	$1,165	$1,535	-	87
F07-126D-0984	992	$875	$716	$1,463	$105	105	F07-144D-0018	576	$1,040	$1,165	$1,535	-	244
F07-126D-0987	384	$742	$567	$1,378	$95	220	F07-144D-0019	1,112	$1,090	$1,215	$1,585	$95	38
F07-126D-0988	850	$742	$567	$1,378	$95	86	F07-144D-0022	896	$1,040	$1,165	$1,535	$85	168
F07-126D-0991	432	$742	$567	$1,378	$95	250	F07-144D-0023	928	$1,040	$1,165	$1,535	$85	40
F07-126D-0993	572	$742	$567	$1,378	$95	170	F07-144D-0024	1,024	$1,090	$1,215	$1,585	$95	94
F07-126D-0995	600	$742	$567	$1,378	$95	208	F07-148D-0008	1,072	$1,273	$892	$1,897	-	36
F07-126D-0998	1,021	$875	$716	$1,463	$105	195	F07-148D-0017	1,180	$1,273	$892	$1,897	-	179
F07-126D-0999	613	$742	$567	$1,378	$95	151	F07-148D-0047	720	$1,273	$892	$1,897	-	120
F07-126D-1003	624	$742	$567	$1,378	$95	91	F07-148D-0405	1,168	$1,273	$892	$1,897	-	25
F07-126D-1004	813	$742	$567	$1,378	$95	160	F07-155D-0100	970	$1,100	$1,200	$2,200	-	90
F07-126D-1012	815	$742	$567	$1,378	$95	202	F07-155D-0171	1,131	$1,000	$1,100	$2,000	-	64
F07-126D-1016	756	$742	$567	$1,378	$95	48	F07-155D-0215	1,174	$700	$800	$1,500	-	216
F07-126D-1018	900	$742	$567	$1,378	$95	96	F07-155D-0217	1,025	$800	$900	$1,600	-	34
F07-126D-1019	924	$875	$716	$1,463	$105	257	F07-155D-0220	696	$700	$800	$1,500	-	26
F07-126D-1037	1,165	$1,007	$769	$1,564	$115	254	F07-155D-0222	921	$700	$800	$1,500	-	213
F07-126D-1039	1,015	$875	$716	$1,463	$105	211	F07-156D-0001	400	$675	$775	$1,475	-	175
F07-126D-1040	831	$742	$567	$1,378	$95	253	F07-156D-0003	664	$675	$775	$1,475	-	90
F07-126D-1045	808	$742	$567	$1,378	$95	240	F07-156D-0004	600	$675	$775	$1,475	-	120
F07-126D-1076	896	$742	$567	$1,378	$95	42	F07-156D-0006	550	$675	$775	$1,475	-	163
F07-126D-1149	528	$742	$567	$1,378	$95	194	F07-156D-0008	400	$675	$775	$1,475	-	199
F07-126D-1151	1,060	$875	$716	$1,463	$105	217	F07-156D-0012	621	$675	$775	$1,475	-	165
F07-126D-1152	599	$742	$567	$1,378	$95	86	F07-156D-0014	551	$675	$775	$1,475	-	89
F07-126D-1153	776	$742	$567	$1,378	$95	62	F07-159D-0017	1,200	$800	$700	$1,600	-	100
F07-126D-1354	1,051	$875	$716	$1,463	$105	17	F07-163D-0004	681	$1,150	-	$1,650	-	12
F07-126D-1355	896	$742	$567	$1,378	$95	206	F07-172D-0002	1,190	$850	$800	$1,500	-	14
F07-130D-0360	664	$925	-	$1,220	-	181	F07-172D-0020	943	$750	$650	$1,350	-	66
F07-130D-0361	550	$925	-	$1,220	-	130	F07-172D-0023	1,069	$850	$800	$1,500	-	197
F07-130D-0362	395	$925	-	$1,220	-	128							

why buy
stock plans?

Building a home yourself presents many opportunities to showcase your creativity, individuality, and dreams turned into reality. With these opportunities, many challenges and questions will crop up. Location, size, and budget are all important to consider, as well as special features and amenities. When you begin to examine everything, it can become overwhelming to search for your dream home. But, before you get too anxious, start the search process an easier way and choose a home design that's a stock home plan.

Custom home plans, as well as stock home plans, offer positives and negatives; what is "best" can only be determined by your lifestyle, budget, and time. A customized home plan is one that a homeowner and designer or architect work together to develop from scratch, taking ideas and putting them down on paper. These plans require extra patience, as it may be months before the architect has them drawn and ready. A stock plan is a pre-developed plan that fits the needs and desires of a group of people, or the general population. These are often available within days of purchasing and typically cost up to one-tenth of the price of customized home plans. They still have all of the amenities you were looking for in a home, and usually at a much more affordable price than having custom plans drawn for you.

When compared to a customized plan, some homeowners fear that a stock home will be a carbon copy home, taking away the opportunity for individualism and creating a unique design. This is a common misconception that can waste a lot of money and time!

As you can see from the home designs throughout this book, the variety of stock plans available is truly impressive, encompassing the most up-to-date features and amenities. With a little patience, browse the numerous available stock plans available throughout this book, and easily purchase a plan and be ready to build almost immediately.

Plus, stock plans can be customized. For example, perhaps you see a stock plan that is just about perfect, but you wish the mud room was a tad larger. Rather than go through the cost and time of having a custom home design drawn, you could have our customizing service modify the stock home plan and have your new dream plan ready to go in no time. Also, stock home plans often have a material list available, helping to eliminate unknown costs from developing during construction.

It's often a good idea to speak with someone who has recently built. Did they use stock or custom plans? What would they recommend you do, or do not undertake? Can they recommend professionals that will help you narrow down your options? As you take a look at plans throughout this publication, don't hesitate to take notes, or write down questions. Also, take advantage of our website, houseplansandmore.com. This website is very user-friendly, allowing you to search for the perfect house design by style, size, budget, and a home's features. With all of these tools readily available to you, you'll find the home design of your dreams in no time at all, thanks to the innovative stock plans readily available today that take into account your wishes in a floor plan as well as your wallet.

how can I find out if I can **afford** to build a home?

GET AN ACCURATE ESTIMATED COST-TO-BUILD REPORT

The most important question for someone wanting to build a new home is, "How much is it going to cost?" Obviously, you must have an accurate budget set before ordering house plans and beginning construction, or your dream home will quickly turn into a nightmare. We make building your dream home a much simpler reality thanks to the estimated cost-to-build report available for all of the home plans in this book and on our website, houseplansandmore.com.

Price is always the number one factor when choosing a new home. Price dictates the size and the quality of materials you will use. So, it comes as no surprise that having an accurate building estimate prior to making your final decision on a home plan quite possibly is the most important step.

If you feel you've found "the" home, then before buying the plans, order a cost-to-build report for the zip code where you want to build. This report is created specifically for you when ordered, and it will educate you on all costs associated with building the home. Simply order the cost-to-build report on houseplansandmore.com for the home design you want to build and gain knowledge of the material and labor cost. Not only does the report allow you to choose the quality of the materials, you can also select from various options from lot condition to contractor fees. Successfully manage your construction budget in all areas, clearly see where the majority of the costs lie, and save money from start to finish.

Listed to the right are the categories included in a cost-to-build report. Each category breaks down labor cost, material cost, funds needed, and the report offers the ability to manipulate over/under adjustments if necessary.

BASIC INFORMATION includes your contact information, the state and zip code where you intend to build and material class. This section also includes: square footage, number of windows, fireplaces, balconies, baths, garage location and size, decks, foundation type, and bonus room square footage.

GENERAL SOFT COSTS include cost for plans, customizing (if applicable), building permits, pre-construction services, and planning expenses.

SITE WORK & UTILITIES include water, sewer, electric, and gas. Choose the type of site work and if you'll need a driveway.

FOUNDATION includes a menu that lists the most common types.

FRAMING ROUGH SHELL calculates rough framing costs including framing for fireplaces, balconies, decks, porches, basements and bonus rooms.

ROOFING includes several common options.

DRY OUT SHELL allows you to select doors, windows, and siding.

ELECTRICAL includes wiring and the quality of the light fixtures.

PLUMBING includes labor costs, plumbing materials, plumbing fixtures, and fire proofing materials.

HVAC includes costs for both labor and materials.

INSULATION includes costs for both labor and materials.

FINISH SHELL includes drywall, interior doors and trim, stairs, shower doors, mirrors, bath accessories, and labor costs.

CABINETS & VANITIES select the grade of your cabinets, vanities, kitchen countertops, and bathroom vanity materials, as well as appliances.

PAINTING includes all painting materials, paint quality, and labor.

FLOORING includes over a dozen flooring material options.

SPECIAL EQUIPMENT NEEDS calculate cost for unforeseen expenses.

CONTRACTOR FEE / PROJECT MANAGER includes the cost of your cost-to-build report, project manager and/or general contractor fees. If you're doing the managing yourself, your costs will be tremendously lower in this section.

LAND PAYOFF includes the cost of your land.

RESERVES / CLOSING COSTS includes interest, contingency reserves, and closing costs.

We've taken the guesswork out of figuring out what your new home is going to cost. Take control of construction, determine the major expenses, and save money. Supervise all costs, from labor to materials and manage construction with confidence, which allows you to avoid costly mistakes and unforeseen expenses. To order a Cost-To-Build Report, visit houseplansandmore.com and search for the specific plan. Then, look for the button that says, "Request Your Report" and get started.

what kind of plan package do I need?

SELECT AND ORDER THE TYPES OF BLUEPRINTS THAT BEST FIT YOUR SITUATION

PLEASE NOTE: *Not all plan packages listed below are available for every plan. There may be additional plan options available. Please visit houseplansandmore.com for a plan's options and pricing, or call 1-800-373-2646 for all current options. The plan pricing shown in this book is subject to change without notice.*

5-SET PLAN PACKAGE includes five complete sets of construction drawings. Besides one set for yourself, additional sets of blueprints will be required for your lender, your local building department, your contractor, and any other tradespeople working on your project. Please note: These 5 sets of plans are copyrighted, so they can't be altered or copied.

8-SET PLAN PACKAGE includes eight complete sets of construction drawings. Besides one set for yourself, additional sets of blueprints will be required for your lender, your local building department, your contractor, and any other tradespeople working on your project. Please note: These 8 sets of plans are copyrighted, so they can't be altered or copied.

REPRODUCIBLE MASTERS is one complete paper set of construction drawings that can be modified. They include a one-time build copyright release that allows you to draw changes on the plans. This allows you, your builder, or local design professional to make the necessary drawing changes without the major expense of entirely redrawing the plans. Easily make minor drawing changes by using correction fluid to cover up small areas of the existing drawing, then draw in your modifications. Once the plan has been altered to fit your needs, you have the right to copy, or reproduce the modified plans as needed for building your home. Please note: The right of building only one home from these plans is li-

censed exclusively to the buyer. You may not use this design to build a second or multiple dwelling(s) without purchasing a multi-build license (see page 287 for more information).

PDF FILE FORMAT is our most popular plan package option because of how fast you can receive them your blueprints (usually within 24 to 48 hours Monday through Friday), and their ability to be easily shared via email with your contractor, subcontractors, and local building officials. The PDF file format is a complete set of construction drawings in an electronic file format. It includes a one-time build copyright release that allows you to make changes and copies of the plans. Typically you will receive a PDF file via email within 24-48 hours (Mon-Fri, 7:30am-4:30pm CST) allowing you to save money on shipping. Upon receiving, visit a local copy or print shop and print the number of plans you need to build your home, or print one and alter the plan by using correction fluid and drawing in your modifications. Please note: These are flat image files and cannot be altered electronically. PDF files are non-refundable and not returnable.

CAD FILE FORMAT is the actual computer files for a plan directly from Auto-CAD, or another computer aided design program. CAD files are the best option if you have a significant amount of changes to make to the plan, or if you need to make the plan fit your local codes. If

you purchase a CAD File, it allows you, or a local design professional the ability to modify the plans electronically in a CAD program, so making changes to the plan is easier and less expensive than using a paper set of plans when modifying. A CAD package also includes a one-time build copyright release that allows you to legally make your changes, and print multiple copies of the plan. See the specific plan page for availability and pricing. Please note: CAD files are non-refundable and not returnable.

MIRROR REVERSE SETS Sometimes a home fits a site better if it is flipped left to right. A mirror reverse set of plans is simply a mirror image of the original drawings causing the lettering and dimensions to read backwards. Therefore, when ordering a mirror reverse set of plans, you must purchase at least one set of the original plans to read from, and use the mirror reverse set for construction. Some plans offer right reading reverse for an additional fee. This means the plan has been redrawn by the designer as the mirrored version and can easily be read.

ADDITIONAL SETS You can order extra plan sets of a plan for an additional fee. A 5-set, 8-set, or reproducible master must have been previously purchased. Please note: Only available within 90 days after purchase of a plan package.

2" X 6" EXTERIOR WALLS 2" x 6" exterior walls can be purchased for some plans for an additional fee (see houseplansandmore. com for availability and pricing).

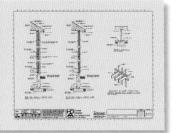

our
plan packages include...

Quality plans for building your future, with extras that provide unsurpassed value, ensure good construction and long-term enjoyment. A quality home - one that looks good, functions well, and provides years of enjoyment - is a product of many things - design, materials, and craftsmanship. But it's also the result of outstanding blueprints - the actual plans and specifications that tell the builder exactly how to build your home.

And with our BLUEPRINT PACKAGES you get the absolute best. A complete set of blueprints is available for every design in this book. These "working drawings" are highly detailed, resulting in two key benefits:

- **BETTER UNDERSTANDING BY THE CONTRACTOR OF HOW TO BUILD YOUR HOME AND...**
- **MORE ACCURATE CONSTRUCTION ESTIMATES THAT WILL SAVE YOU TIME AND MONEY.**

Below is a sample of the plan information included for most of the designs in this book. Specific details may vary with each designer's plan. While this information is typical for most plans, we cannot assure the inclusion of all the following referenced items. Please contact us at 1-800-373-2646 for a plan's specific information, including which of the following items are included.

1 cover sheet
is included with many of the plans, the cover sheet is the artist's rendering of the exterior of the home. It will give you an idea of how your home will look when completed and landscaped.

2 foundation
plan shows the layout of the basement, walk-out basement, crawl space, slab or pier foundation. All necessary notations and dimensions are included. See plan page for the foundation types included. If the home plan you choose does not have your desired foundation type, our Customer Service Representatives can advise you on how to customize your foundation to suit your specific needs or site conditions.

3 floor plans
show the placement of walls, doors, closets, plumbing fixtures, electrical outlets, columns, and beams for each level of the home.

4 interior elevations
provide views of special interior elements such as fireplaces, kitchen cabinets, built-in units and other features of the home.

5 exterior elevations
illustrate the front, rear and both sides of the house, with all details of exterior materials and the required dimensions.

6 sections
show detail views of the home or portions of the home as if it were sliced from the roof to the foundation. This sheet shows important areas such as load-bearing walls, stairs, joists, trusses and other structural elements, which are critical for proper construction.

7 details
show how to construct certain components of your home, such as the roof system, stairs, deck, etc.

do you want to make **changes** to your plan?

We understand that sometimes it is difficult to find blueprints that meet all of your specific needs. That is why we offer home plan modification services so you can build a home exactly the way you want it!

ARE YOU THINKING ABOUT CUSTOMIZING A PLAN?

If you're like many customers, you may want to make changes to your home plan to make it the dream home you've always wanted. That's where our expert design and modification partners come in. You won't find a more efficient and economic way to get your changes done than by using our home plan customizing services.

Whether it's enlarging a kitchen, adding a porch, or converting a crawl space to a basement, we can customize any plan and make it perfect for your needs. Simply create your wish list and let us go to work. Soon you'll have the blueprints for your new home, and at a fraction of the cost of hiring a local architect!

IT'S EASY!

- We can customize any of the plans in this book, or on houseplansandmore.com.
- We provide a FREE cost estimate for your home plan modifications within 24-48 hours (Monday-Friday, 7:30am-4:30pm CST).
- Average turn-around time to complete the modifications is typically 4-5 weeks.
- You will receive one-on-one design consultations.

CUSTOMIZING FACTS

- The average cost to have a house plan customized is typically less than 1 percent of the building costs — compare that to the national average of 7 percent of building costs.
- The average modification cost for a home is typically $800 to $1,500. This does not include the cost of purchasing the PDF file format of the blueprints, which is required to legally make plan changes.

OTHER HELPFUL INFORMATION

- Sketch, or make a specific list of changes you'd like to make on the Home Plan Modification Request Form.
- A home plan modification specialist will contact you within 24-48 hours with your free estimate.
- Upon accepting the estimate, you will need to purchase the PDF or CAD file format.
- A contract, which includes a specific list of changes and fees will be sent to you prior for your approval.
- Upon approving the contract, our design partners will keep you up to date by emailing sketches throughout the project.
- Plans can be converted to metric, or to a Barrier-free layout (also referred to as a universal home design, which allows easy mobility for an individual with limitations of any kind).

2 Easy Steps

1 visit

houseplansandmore.com and click on the Resources tab at the top of the home page, then click "How to Customize Your House Plan," or scan the QR code here to download the Home Plan Modification Request Form.

2 email

your completed form to: customizehpm@designamerica.com, or fax it to: 651-602-5050.

If you are not able to access the Internet, please call 1-800-373-2646 (Monday - Friday, 7:30am - 4:30 pm CST).

285

helpful **building aids**

Your Blueprint Package will contain all of the necessary construction information you need to build your home. But, we also offer the following products and services to save you time and money during the building process.

MATERIAL LIST Many of the home plans in this book have a material list available for purchase that gives you the quantity, dimensions, and description of the building materials needed to construct the home (see the index for availability and pricing). Keep in mind, due to variations in local building code requirements, exact material quantities cannot be guaranteed. Note: Material lists are created with the standard foundation type only. Please review the material list and the construction drawings with your material supplier to verify measurements and quantities of the materials listed before ordering supplies.

THE LEGAL KIT Avoid many legal pitfalls and build your home with confidence using the forms and contracts featured in this kit. Included are request for proposal documents, various fixed price and cost plus contracts, instructions on how and when to use each form, warranty statements and more. Save time and money before you break ground on your new home or start a remodeling project. All forms are reproducible. This kit is ideal for homebuilders and contractors. Cost: $35

DETAIL PLAN PACKAGES - ELECTRICAL, FRAMING & PLUMBING Three separate packages offer homebuilders details for constructing various foundations; numerous floor, wall and roof framing techniques; simple to complex residential wiring; sump and water softener hookups; plumbing connection methods; installation of septic systems, and more. Each package includes three dimensional illustrations and a glossary of terms. Purchase one or all three. Please note: These drawings do not pertain to a specific home plan, but they include general guidelines and tips for construction in all 3 of these trades. Cost: $30 each or all three for $60

EXPRESS DELIVERY Most orders are processed within 24 hours of receipt. Please allow 7-10 business days for standard delivery. If you need to place a rush order, please call us by 11:00 am Monday through Friday CST and ask for express service (allow 1-2 business days). Please see page 287 for all shipping and handling charges.

TECHNICAL ASSISTANCE If you have questions about your blueprints, we offer technical assistance by calling 1-314-770-2228 between 7:30 am and 4:30 pm Monday through Friday CST. Whether it involves design modifications or field assistance, our home plans team is extremely familiar with all of our home designs and will be happy to help. We want your home to be everything you expect it to be.

before you **order**

Please note: Plan pricing is subject to change without notice.
For current pricing, visit houseplansandmore.com, or call us at 1-800-373-2646.

BUILDING CODE REQUIREMENTS

At the time the construction drawings were prepared, every effort was made to ensure that these plans and specifications met nationally recognized codes. These plans conform to most national building codes. Because building codes vary from area to area, some drawing modifications and/or the assistance of a professional designer or architect may be necessary to comply with your local codes, or to accommodate your specific building site conditions. We advise you to consult with your local building official, or a local builder for information regarding codes governing your area prior to ordering blueprints.

COPYRIGHT

Plans are protected under Copyright Law. Reproduction by any means is strictly prohibited. The right of building only one structure from all plan packages is licensed exclusively to the buyer and the plans may not be resold unless by express written authorization from the home designer, or architect. You may not use this plan to build a second or multiple structure(s) without purchasing a multi-build license. Each violation of the Copyright Law is punishable in a fine.

LICENSE TO BUILD

When you purchase a "full set of construction drawings" from Design America, Inc., you are purchasing an exclusive one-time "License to Build," not the rights to the design. Design America, Inc. is granting you permission on behalf of the plan's designer or architect to use the construction drawings one-time for the building of the home. The construction drawings (also referred to as blueprints/plans and any derivative of that plan whether extensive or minor) are still owned and protected under copyright laws by the original designer. The blueprints/plans cannot be resold, transferred, rented, loaned or used by anyone other than the original purchaser of the "License to Build" without written consent from Design America, Inc., or the plan designer. If you are interested in building the plan more than once, please call 1-800-373-2646 and inquire about purchasing a Multi-Build License that will allow you to build a home design more than one time. Please note: A multi-build license can only be purchased if a CAD file or PDF file were initially purchased.

EXCHANGE POLICY

Since blueprints are printed in response to your order, we cannot honor requests for refunds.

SHIPPING & HANDLING CHARGES

U.S. SHIPPING -
(AK and HI express only)
Regular (allow 7-10 business days)	$30.00
Priority (allow 3-5 business days)	$50.00
Express* (allow 1-2 business days)	$75.00

CANADA SHIPPING**
Regular (allow 8-12 business days)	$50.00
Express* (allow 3-5 business days)	$100.00

OVERSEAS SHIPPING/INTERNATIONAL
Call, fax, or e-mail (customerservice@designamerica.com) for shipping costs.

*   For express delivery please call us by 11:00 am Monday-Friday CST

**   Orders may be subject to custom's fees and or duties/taxes.

Note: Shipping and handling does not apply on PDF and CAD File orders. PDF and CAD File orders will be emailed within 24-48 hours (Monday - Friday, 7:30 am - 4:30 pm CST) of purchase.

Order Form

Please note: Plan pricing is subject to change without notice.
For current pricing, visit houseplansandmore.com, or call us at 1-800-373-2646

Please send me the following:

Plan Number: F07-_____

Select Foundation Type: (Select ONE- see plan page for available options).

❏ Slab   ❏ Crawl space   ❏ Basement

❏ Walk-out basement   ❏ Pier

❏ Optional Foundation for an additional fee

    Enter foundation cost here $ _____

Plan Package	Cost
❏ CAD File	$ _____
❏ PDF File Format (recommended)	$ _____
❏ Reproducible Masters	$ _____
❏ 8-Set Plan Package	$ _____
❏ 5-Set Plan Package	$ _____

See the index on pages 276-279 for the most commonly ordered plan packages, or visit houseplansandmore.com to see current pricing and all plan package options available.

Important Extras

For pricing and Material List availability, see the index on pages 512-519. For the other plan options listed below, visit houseplansandmore.com, or call 1-800-373-2646.

❏ Additional plan sets*:

    _____ set(s) at $_____ per set $ _____

❏ Print in right-reading reverse:

    one-time additional fee of $_____ $ _____

❏ Print in mirror reverse:

    _____ set(s) at $_____ per set $ _____
    (where right reading reverse is not available)

❏ Material list (see the index on pages 276-279) $ _____

❏ Legal Kit (001D-9991, see page 286) $ _____

Detail Plan Packages: (see page 286)

    ❏ Framing   ❏ Electrical   ❏ Plumbing $ _____
    (001D-9992)   (001D-9993)   (001D-9994)

Shipping (see page 287) $ _____

SUBTOTAL $ _____

Sales Tax (MO residents only, add 8.24%) $ _____

TOTAL $ _____

*Available only within 90 days after purchase of plan.

HELPFUL TIPS

- You can upgrade to a different plan package within 90 days of your original plan purchase.
- Additional sets cannot be ordered without the initial purchase of a 5-Set, 8-Set, or Reproducible Masters.

Name _____
          (Please print or type)

Street _____
          (Please do not use a P.O. Box)

City _____ State _____

Country _____ Zip _____

Daytime telephone   (_____) _____

E-Mail _____
          (For invoice and tracking information)

<u>Payment</u>   ❏ Bank check/money order. No personal checks.
     Make checks payable to Design America, Inc.

❏ MasterCard   ❏ VISA   ❏ DISCOVER   ❏ AMERICAN EXPRESS Cards

Credit card number _____

Expiration date (mm/yy) _____ CID _____

Signature _____

❏ I hereby authorize Design America, Inc. to charge this purchase to my credit card.

Please check the appropriate box:
❏ I'm building the home for myself
❏ I'm building the home for someone else

ORDER ONLINE

houseplansandmore.com

Use Coupon Code **F07OFFER** for $50 OFF your home plan order!

ORDER TOLL-FREE BY PHONE

1-800-373-2646
Fax: 314-770-2226

EXPRESS DELIVERY

Most orders are processed within 24 hours of receipt. If you need to place a rush order, please call us by 11:00 am CST and ask for express service.
Business Hours: Monday - Friday (7:30 am - 4:30 pm CST)

MAIL YOUR ORDER

Design America, Inc.
734 West Port Plaza, Suite #208
St. Louis, MO 63146

The Big Book of Small Home Plans

SOURCE CODE **F07**